*The Formation
of a Society
on Virginia's
Eastern Shore,
1615–1655*

The Formation
of a Society
on Virginia's
Eastern Shore,
1615–1655

James R. Perry

Published for the Institute of
Early American History and Culture,
Williamsburg, Virginia,
by the University of North Carolina Press,
Chapel Hill and London

Publication of this book has been supported, in part, by a
donation from FIGGIE INTERNATIONAL, INC.,
in memory of the former Governor of Virginia,
JOHN N. DALTON.

The Institute of Early American History and Culture is
sponsored jointly by the College of William and Mary and
the Colonial Williamsburg Foundation.

Library of Congress Cataloging-in-Publication Data

Perry, James R., 1950–
    The formation of a society on Virginia's Eastern
Shore, 1615–1655 / James R. Perry.
        p. cm.
    ISBN 0-8078-1927-1 (alk. paper)
    1. Virginia—History—Colonial period, ca. 1600–
1775. 2. Eastern Shore (Md. and Va.)—History.
I. Institute of Early American History and
Culture (Williamsburg, Va.) II. Title.
F229.P47 1990
975.5′02—dc20   90-11980
                                                         CIP

The paper in this book meets the guidelines for permanence
and durability of the Committee on Production Guidelines
for Book Longevity of the Council on Library Resources.

Maps 2–11 drawn by Richard Stinely, after Ralph T.
Whitelaw, *Virginia's Eastern Shore: A History of
Northampton and Accomack Counties* (Richmond, Va.,
1951).

This volume received indirect support from an unrestricted
book publications grant awarded to the Institute by the
L. J. SKAGGS AND MARY C. SKAGGS FOUNDATION
of Oakland, California.

Dedicated to John Briggs

Acknowledgments

I AM GRATEFUL to a number of people and organizations that, respectively, provided substantive advice and crucial financial support during the research and writing of this book.

First, I thank Jack P. Greene, who advised me during the writing of the dissertation on which this book is based. His suggestions improved the organization and tightened the presentation of the arguments.

A series of editors at the Institute of Early American History and Culture made useful comments for revisions and encouraged me to persevere. Specifically, I acknowledge Norman S. Fiering, Philip D. Morgan, A. Roger Ekirch, and Thomas Purvis. Also, I would like to thank Gil Kelly, Fredrika Teute, and Suzanne Coffman (particularly in composing the index) for the care and patience they displayed in shepherding the manuscript through to publication.

A number of other historians of the seventeenth-century Chesapeake provided valuable advice. In particular, I acknowledge Lois Green Carr for her comments and constant encouragement. Also of great help were suggestions made by Brooks Miles Barnes, Joseph Douglas Deal III, John M. Hemphill, Jon Kukla, Jean M. Mihalyka, Darrett B. Rutman, and W. Elliott Wilkins, Jr.

Two institutions provided financial support for my research. The Johns Hopkins University provided assistance while I was a graduate student there. Subsequently, I received a National Endowment for the Humanities Summer Stipend, which allowed me to complete important supplemental research.

In addition to professional peers and organizations, I would like to extend my thanks to a number of individuals who provided encouragement. First, I appreciate the support of my family, who have stood behind my seemingly quixotic pursuit of history. Second, I acknowledge Joseph Maier, a close friend I met during graduate school; Jody was a valuable sounding board for me as I shaped and reshaped my understanding of the results of my investigations into the records of the Eastern Shore of Virginia. Third, I want to thank Tom Hickey, a close friend who provided encouragement at every step of the prolonged process of revision and publication. Finally, I acknowledge the paramount importance of my oldest and dearest friend, John Briggs, to whom this volume is dedicated. His friendship and humanity have provided me with an unshakable foundation for many, many years.

Contents

Maps and Tables

Maps

Tables

Abbreviations

*The Formation
of a Society
on Virginia's
Eastern Shore,
1615–1655*

Introduction

HISTORIANS KNOW very little about the development of society in Virginia during its first half-century and, particularly, in the generation following the dissolution of the Virginia Company in 1624. Especially important is the question, What held Virginia local society together? In the absence of a strong religious bond, contractual foundation, or nuclear settlement pattern—all of which characterized early New England towns—what formed the basis of social cohesion at the local level in Virginia? This question assumes added significance when juxtaposed to the relative autonomy of Virginia localities, largely free of oversight and coercion from either James City or England.[1] Social cohesion in Virginia would, of necessity, have to result from a local organic development.

Until the 1960s, most historians of early Virginia ignored the development of society in the generation after the fall of the Virginia Company. Typically, their treatment of these crucial formative years took the shape of a sketchy political narrative organized around highly visible events at the provincial level. Robert Beverley first used this framework in *The History and Present State of Virginia* in 1705, and most subsequent historians followed his lead.[2]

Those historians who attempted to study Virginia society concerned

1. Wesley Frank Craven, *The Southern Colonies in the Seventeenth Century, 1607–1689* (1949; reprint ed., Baton Rouge, La., 1970), 150–172, 269–291; Warren M. Billings, "The Growth of Political Institutions in Virginia, 1634 to 1676," *WMQ*, 3d Ser., XXXI (1974), 225–242; Steven Douglas Crow, " 'Left at Libertie': The Effects of the English Civil War and Interregnum on the American Colonies, 1640–1660" (Ph.D. diss., University of Wisconsin–Madison, 1974); Edmund S. Morgan, *American Slavery, American Freedom: The Ordeal of Colonial Virginia* (New York, 1975), 146–147.

2. Robert Beverley, *The History and Present State of Virginia*, ed. Louis B. Wright (Chapel Hill, N.C., 1947); Edmund Randolph, *History of Virginia*, ed. Arthur H. Shaffer (Charlottesville, Va., 1970); John Daly Burk, *History of Virginia*, 2 vols. (Petersburg, Va., 1804–1816); John W. Campbell, *A History of Virginia from Its Discovery till the Year 1781* (Petersburg, Va., 1813); Robert R. Howison, *A History of Virginia, from Its Discovery and Settlement by Europeans to the Present Time*, 2 vols. (Philadelphia, 1846–1848); Charles Campbell, *History of the Colony and Ancient Dominion of Virginia* (Philadelphia, 1860); John Fiske, *Old Virginia and Her Neighbors*, 2 vols. (Boston, 1902); Thomas J. Wertenbaker, *Virginia under the Stuarts,*

themselves mostly with questions other than social cohesion. Their studies—of land and labor, of Indians, servants, and slaves, of social structure and general conditions of life—were supported by data from throughout Virginia and failed to convey a sense of a specific population in one
locale. Moreover, their evidence was largely from the period after 1660.[3]

Since the mid-1960s, there has been an explosion of research on the
seventeenth-century Chesapeake, appearing in papers, dissertations, articles, collections of essays, and monographs. Although a considerable
proportion of this work has been concerned with political and institutional history, the vast majority has been in the area of economic and
social history, including studies of immigration, demography, family,
social mobility, conditions of life, social order, religion, servants, race
and intercultural relations, prices, wealth distribution, agriculture, merchants, and trade.[4]

The range and quality of this research is remarkable and has illumi-
nated the development of society in the Chesapeake in the seventeenth
century. In particular, this literature casts light on issues relating to the
study of social cohesion in the early Chesapeake. Thus, historians have
documented a population characterized by an extreme morbidity, a high
mortality, and a sex ratio heavily weighted with male immigrants. These

1607–1688 (Princeton, N.J., 1914); Richard L. Morton, *Colonial Virginia*, 2 vols.
(Chapel Hill, N.C., 1960). Alf J. Mapp, Jr., in *The Virginia Experiment: The Old
Dominion's Role in the Making of America, 1607–1781* (La Salle, Ill., 1974), continued this tradition into the 1970s. For a valuable overview of trends in Virginia historiography, see Thad W. Tate, "The Seventeenth-Century Chesapeake and Its Modern
Historians," in Tate and David L. Ammerman, eds., *The Chesapeake in the Seventeenth Century: Essays on Anglo-American Society* (Chapel Hill, N.C., 1979), 3–50.

3. Lyon Gardiner Tyler, *England in America, 1580–1652* (New York, 1904), esp.
chap. 6; Philip Alexander Bruce, *Social Life of Virginia in the Seventeenth Century*
(Richmond, Va., 1907); Thomas J. Wertenbaker, *Patrician and Plebeian in Virginia;
or, The Origin and Development of the Social Classes of the Old Dominion* (Charlottesville, Va., 1910); Thomas J. Wertenbaker, *The Planters of Colonial Virginia*
(Princeton, N.J., 1922), esp. chaps. 3, 4; Craven, *Southern Colonies*. For a review of
the literature, see Tate, "The Seventeenth-Century Chesapeake and Its Modern Historians," in Tate and Ammerman, eds., *Chesapeake in the Seventeenth Century*, 6–32.

4. For an overview of developments in the economic and political history of 17th-
century Virginia, primarily post-1660, see Warren M. Billings, "Towards the Rewrit-
ing of Seventeenth-Century Virginia History," *VMHB*, LXXXIII (1975), 184–189.
For a more extensive review of Chesapeake research appearing between the mid-
1960s and 1979, see Tate, "The Seventeenth-Century Chesapeake and Its Modern
Historians," in Tate and Ammerman, eds., *Chesapeake in the Seventeenth Century*,
32–50. For a comprehensive review of developments in Chesapeake studies after
1979, see the introduction to Lois Green Carr, Philip D. Morgan, and Jean B. Russo,
eds., *Colonial Chesapeake Society* (Chapel Hill, N.C., 1988), 1–46.

factors combined to restrict family formation and disrupt those families that did form. The result was a society with a disproportionately youthful, single, and male population. Some historians have concluded that society in the early Chesapeake was fragile and lacking in cohesion and that social instability had a disruptive impact on political stability. Other historians have argued that, even in the demographically hostile conditions of the early Chesapeake, social cohesion was possible. This latter view stresses the proliferation of kin ties (as mortality and remarriage led to the subsequent linking of previously unrelated individuals), the strength of kin and neighborhood support networks, and the stabilizing influence of local religious and governmental institutions.[5]

In an attempt to reconcile these opposing views, one notable survey of the literature concludes: "Closer attention to variations across space and time may help resolve seeming differences of interpretation. The disruptive forces in seventeenth-century Chesapeake society were strongest, of course, in the earliest years, and the stabilizing influences gradually exerted themselves as the century proceeded. We need further analysis of how long the forces of instability held sway and how quickly the countering networks of support arose." The present study addresses this very question by examining the formation of society on Virginia's Eastern Shore between 1615 and 1655. Other studies that have explored pre-Restoration Chesapeake society have been largely thematic; and those works that have focused on the development of society in particular locales have, for the most part, concerned themselves with the second half of the seventeenth century.[6] This study of the Eastern Shore exam-

5. For a masterful thumbnail sketch of this literature, see Carr, Morgan, and Russo, eds., *Colonial Chesapeake Society*, 4–6. See also Jack P. Greene, *Pursuits of Happiness: The Social Development of Early Modern British Colonies and the Formation of American Culture* (Chapel Hill, N.C., 1988), 13–18.
6. Quotation in Carr, Morgan, and Russo, eds., *Colonial Chesapeake Society*, 6. For thematic studies, see Tate, "The Seventeenth-Century Chesapeake and Its Modern Historians," in Tate and Ammerman, eds., *Chesapeake in the Seventeenth Century*, 32–35; Carr, Morgan, and Russo, eds., *Colonial Chesapeake Society*, 4–6. It should be noted that much of the best work has focused on Maryland. For studies of particular locales, see Kevin Peter Kelly, "Economic and Social Development of Seventeenth-Century Surry County, Virginia" (Ph.D. diss., University of Washington, 1972); Robert Anthony Wheeler, "Lancaster County, Virginia, 1650–1750: The Evolution of a Southern Tidewater Community" (Ph.D. diss., Brown University, 1972); Carville V. Earle, *The Evolution of a Tidewater Settlement System: All Hallow's Parish, Maryland, 1650–1783* (Chicago, 1975); Lorena Seebach Walsh, "Charles County, Maryland, 1658–1705: A Study of Chesapeake Social and Political Structure" (Ph.D. diss., Michigan State University, 1977); James P. P. Horn, "Social and Economic Aspects of Local Society in England and the Chesapeake: A Comparative Study of the Vale of

ines the extent to which social cohesion characterized the people who settled across the Chesapeake Bay from James City during the first generation after the fall of the Virginia Company.[7]

The method chosen for this study is shaped by network analysis, an approach that focuses on individuals, their interactions with other individuals, and the patterns formed as a result of such contacts. These features, combined with the explicit understanding that "the whole network of relations so formed is in a state of flux," make network analysis particularly appropriate for the study of the development of a colonial society, where continuous immigration introduced new individuals into the social setting and thus affected the development of patterns of interaction.[8] A special advantage of an approach based on network analysis is that it allows a maximum exploitation of Virginia's county court records, the main primary source for the colony before 1660. It enables the historian to mine the county court books—basically a record of economic and social interaction—systematically rather than anecdotally. This approach requires a tedious attention to individuals and their contacts in a geographic context, but it rewards perseverance with new insights.

In 1980 Darrett B. Rutman published an important article proposing network analysis as a method for the study of local society. Moreover, he laid a firm theoretical foundation for further local studies by surveying the methods, models, and assumptions of sociologists, anthropologists, and historians who have attempted to explore local societies. His efforts have helped to highlight several points crucial to anyone undertaking such a study. For example, in order to clarify the term "community study," he emphasized the distinction between the conception of community as a field for social interaction and the conception of community as a reified ideal frequently distorted by fuzzy definitions and value judgments. For the most part, New England historians have conceived of

Berkeley, Gloucestershire, and the Lower Western Shore of Maryland, c. 1660–1700" (Ph.D. diss., University of Sussex, 1982); Darrett B. Rutman and Anita H. Rutman, *A Place in Time*, I, *Middlesex County, Virginia, 1650–1750*, and II, *Explicatus* (New York, 1984).

7. Although the Eastern Shore includes portions of the present states of Virginia, Maryland, and Delaware, the term "Eastern Shore" in this study refers to that part of the peninsula located in Virginia.

8. Jeremy Boissevain, preface, in Boissevain and J. Clyde Mitchell, eds., *Network Analysis: Studies in Human Interaction* (The Hague, 1973), viii. This is a useful introduction to the range of questions susceptible to investigation with network analysis.

community as a reified ideal and therefore generated studies whose foundations are subjective and whose results are difficult to compare in any systematic way. Rutman, advocating an approach stressing the patterning of social interaction, turned to the method of network analysis. Though admitting that historians of early America rarely would be able to meet the rigorous and highly quantified demands of formal network analysis, Rutman argued cogently that they could still be guided by the logic of the analysis. That logic includes a concern for geographic setting, conditions for travel, interpersonal networks (both familial and nonfamilial), nodes for interaction (for example, church and court), and extralocal contact.[9] It is these concerns that have shaped the following study of social cohesion on the Eastern Shore of Virginia from 1615 to 1655.

The work of several historians confirms the value of network analysis in understanding local societies in the seventeenth century. Focusing on England, New England, and the post-Restoration Chesapeake, these studies depict local societies bound together by geographically restricted neighborhood networks, which were supported by kin networks and institutional bonds of church and state. Most important, these studies provide evidence that, even in the fluid social environment of the Chesapeake, these interpersonal and institutional networks—which formed the societal network, or web—provided cohesion. This study of the Eastern Shore of Virginia before 1660 complements and supports the conclusions of these earlier studies and extends them back in time.[10]

9. Darrett B. Rutman, "Community Study," *Historical Methods*, XIII (1980), 29–32. See also Rutman and Rutman, *A Place in Time: Middlesex County*, 21–30. Darrett B. Rutman had earlier written about some of the same concerns in "The Social Web: A Prospectus for the Study of the Early American Community," in William L. O'Neill, ed., *Insights and Parallels: Problems and Issues of American Social History* (Minneapolis, Minn., 1973), 57–89. For another interesting view of the study of community, see Richard R. Beeman, "The New Social History and the Search for 'Community' in Colonial America," *American Quarterly*, XXIX (1977), 422–443.

10. Linda Auwers Bissell, "Family, Friends, and Neighbors: Social Interaction in Seventeenth-Century Windsor, Connecticut" (Ph.D. diss., Brandeis University, 1973); Walsh, "Charles County, Maryland, 1658–1705"; Horn, "Social and Economic Aspects of Local Society in England and the Chesapeake"; Rutman and Rutman, *A Place in Time: Middlesex County*; James Horn, "Adapting to a New World: A Comparative Study of Local Society in England and Maryland, 1650–1700," and Lorena S. Walsh, "Community Networks in the Early Chesapeake," both in Carr, Morgan, and Russo, eds., *Colonial Chesapeake Society*, 133–175, 200–241.

LOCATED ACROSS THE Chesapeake Bay from the original Virginia settlements, the Eastern Shore is a narrow peninsula with a mean breadth of
eight miles. Its bayside is indented by numerous creeks and branches; its
seaside, which takes the full force of Atlantic storms, has a less stable,
more shifting geography of sandbars and offshore islands. The Eastern
Shore's flat terrain is densely wooded, with a large proportion of pines;
the soil is a rich, sandy loam, remarkably free of rocks.[11]

The Eastern Shore is a rewarding locale for a network study. First, it
provides a view of the development of a pre-Restoration local society in
Virginia from the earliest years of settlement. English settlers initially
located on the peninsula during the Virginia Company period, and the
growth and spread of population proceeded rapidly in the thirty years
after the dissolution of the Company. Of corollary importance are the
Eastern Shore's particularly fine series of county court records, which
extend continuously from January 1633.[12] In the absence of tithable
lists, church records, private correspondence, diaries, and personal business accounts for the period before 1660, these court records are the
main source of knowledge about English settlement on the Eastern
Shore. They record land transactions, debtor and creditor relationships,
wills and inventories, criminal prosecutions, civil complaints, and—most
valuable of all—a profusion of depositions that richly document individual networks.

One of the attractions in choosing to study the formation of society on
the Eastern Shore is the quality of historical research already available to
build on and amplify. Susie M. Ames's *Studies of the Virginia Eastern
Shore in the Seventeenth Century* provides valuable insights into the
society, economy, politics, and institutions of the peninsula's inhabitants
during the first century of English settlement. Even more important for
any historian seeking to plot individual interactional networks is Ralph
T. Whitelaw's *Virginia's Eastern Shore: A History of Northampton and
Accomack Counties*; this ambitious and prodigious study attempts to
map the location of patents as well as to trace much of their subsequent
histories, including sales, bequests, escheats, gifts, and the like.[13] (It

---

11. Jennings Cropper Wise, *Ye Kingdome of Accawmacke; or, The Eastern Shore of
Virginia in the Seventeenth Century* (Richmond, Va., 1911), 1–3.

12. Throughout this volume, Old Style dates have been adjusted to New Style, so
that the new year begins on January 1 rather than March 25.

13. Susie M. Ames, *Studies of the Virginia Eastern Shore in the Seventeenth Century* (Richmond, Va., 1940); Ralph T. Whitelaw, *Virginia's Eastern Shore: A History
of Northampton and Accomack Counties*, 2 vols. (Richmond, Va., 1951).

should be noted here that, in the original division into counties, Virginia's Eastern Shore was called Accomack County; in 1643, it was renamed Northampton County, a name it retained until the division of the peninsula into two counties, Northampton and Accomack, in 1663.)

The population that forms the core of this study is the group of landholders that acquired land before or during 1655. They are an obvious focus for a study of social cohesion; they were, after all, those settlers who were committed enough to want to develop the land resources and financially in a position to do so. The county court records document the lives of landholders far more fully than any other group, thereby making it possible to construct brief biographies by stripping the county court books for every reference to them. Also, it is easier to identify residences for landholders than for nonlandholders, a prerequisite to studying the network of contacts linking individuals.

Inevitably, there are limitations inherent in the decision to study any defined population or specific locale. The focus on landholders allows for only limited insights about the lives of nonlandholders, including most women, children, blacks, Indians, servants, and individuals on the margins of society. But, as noted above, in a network analysis of a local society—and particularly in a study examining the basis of social cohesion—the initial focus on landholders is necessary and provides valuable insight into a very important and influential segment of the society.

How representative is Virginia's Eastern Shore of developments in other early seventeenth-century Chesapeake locales? Only time will tell, time during which other detailed network studies appear that allow comparisons. Certainly, local geographies vary and populations of immigrants differ; but there is nothing to suggest that either the geography or population of settlers specific to the Eastern Shore would have influenced significantly the networks and level of social cohesion observed there. One factor that may have been unique to the Eastern Shore in the first half of the seventeenth century was a native population that was, for the most part, friendly and supportive. (The impact of the native population on Eastern Shore settlement is discussed at length in the text.) Until the completion of additional studies allows more detailed comparisons, I have cited, where appropriate, relevant work on the seventeenth-century Chesapeake. Similarities between the Eastern Shore and other Chesapeake societies are noted throughout.

THIS STUDY BEGINS with an overview of the Eastern Shore during the Virginia Company period: Why and where did settlement occur, and what do we know about the people who came? It then focuses on the growth of population and spread of settlement on the Eastern Shore through 1655, in particular the patterns of land settlement and their influence on physical contact among the settlers. Chapter 3 discusses the extent and development of ties of kinship in the lives of Eastern Shore settlers, and Chapter 4 examines the networks connecting friends and neighbors.

Chapter 5 analyzes the local economic network and the impact of occupational and official position on the extent of individual economic ties. Chapter 6 traces economic contacts off the Eastern Shore and how they tied the Eastern Shore into a larger Chesapeake and Atlantic network. Chapter 7 analyzes how local institutions of government, religion, and militia drew individuals outside their personal networks. Chapter 8 relates the societal network, including both personal and institutional ties, to exercise of authority on the Eastern Shore, then relates both, in turn, to social stability on the peninsula. An overview of potentially destabilizing developments, both internal and external, reveals the strength and importance of the local societal network and the effective exercise of authority in promoting social stability.

The final chapter places this study into a larger framework, that of English-speaking populations in the Chesapeake, New England, and England itself. Three commonalities dominate: the spatial restriction of individual networks, the intense localism exhibited by local cultures, and the importance of the effective exercise of local authority. Evidence of these commonalities on the Eastern Shore, with a detailed examination of personal networks and the role of institutions, establishes that, earlier than previously suspected, Chesapeake local societies were marked by a cohesion sufficient to underpin local stability—and, indeed, sustained a sense of community.

1 The Virginia Company and the Eastern Shore

ON MAY 24, 1624, the Court of King's Bench withdrew the charter of the Virginia Company of London. Financial problems and intense factionalism had prevented the Company from providing effective support and direction for its settlement in Virginia, which was still reeling from an Indian attack of March 1622. The decision of the court gave England its first royal colony.[1]

The nascent society that James I inherited from the Virginia Company in 1624 was not what the promoters of the Company had envisioned before settlement began in 1607.[2] The Company's leaders, in their quest for profits, initially had conceived of the settlement as a commercial organization. According to their plan, the colonists (as Company employees) would discover precious minerals, trade with the natives, and find a water passage to the Orient. The profits resulting from these efforts would accrue to the benefit of Company investors. Although other objectives may have mingled with this economic motive from the beginning, the Company's members were primarily interested in receiving a substantial return on their initial investment. But the profit never materialized. By 1624 the promoters of the dissolved Virginia Company could look back on eighteen years of corporate effort, during which they had failed to reap the fantastic wealth that they had expected.

---

1. Wesley Frank Craven, *Dissolution of the Virginia Company: The Failure of a Colonial Experiment* (New York, 1932), is the most complete account of the fall of the Company. For the history of the settlement of Virginia during the Company period, see Charles M. Andrews, *The Colonial Period of American History*, I, *The Settlements* (1934; reprint ed., New Haven, Conn., 1964); and Wesley Frank Craven, *The Southern Colonies in the Seventeenth Century, 1607–1689* (1949; reprint ed., Baton Rouge, La., 1970).

2. The interpretation presented here is especially influenced by Sigmund Diamond, "From Organization to Society: Virginia in the Seventeenth Century," *American Journal of Sociology*, LXIII (1958), 457–475; and Irene W. D. Hecht, "The Virginia Colony, 1607–1640: A Study in Frontier Growth" (Ph.D. diss., University of Washington, 1969). See also Andrews, *Colonial Period*, I, *Settlements*; Craven, *Dissolution of the Virginia Company*, and *Southern Colonies*.

Instead, a complex interweaving of their expectations, policies, and actions had transformed Virginia from a corporate organization into an embryonic society. Trying to attract an increased labor force to further their own corporate interests, the Company had established policies that allowed individuals to live outside corporate control. Changes in regulations concerning land, trade, government, and immigration permitted an increasing number of men and women to relate to one another outside the formal organizational structure. Thus, more and more individuals became landholders, traded freely, took part in government, and formed families.[3]

The early history of settlement on the Eastern Shore of Virginia from 1615 to 1624 is inseparable from the shifting policies of the Virginia Company. An early description of the Eastern Shore appears in an account by Captain John Smith. In June 1608 Smith and an exploring party landed on Cape Charles at the southern tip of the peninsula and immediately encountered two Indians. Smith allayed the suspicions of the natives, who led him to Accomack, where the Indian werowance (king) resided. The werowance treated his guests well and entertained them with descriptions of Chesapeake Bay, its islands and rivers. Smith noted the "pleasant fertill clay-soile" of the Eastern Shore and then continued "along the coast, searching every inlet, and bay fit for harbours and habitations."[4]

In 1612 Smith published an account of his explorations in *A Map of Virginia, with a Description of the Countrey, the Commodities, People, Government, and Religion*. By that date, the Virginia Company had revised its unrealistic expectations of quick wealth. Company managers had turned their attention instead to the exploitation of Virginia's natural resources. In *A Map of Virginia* Smith noted many commodities that might be produced in Virginia. Of special importance for the future settlement of the Eastern Shore, he included fish and salt.[5] His advocacy of the fishing industry and of salt production, combined with his report

3. Diamond, "From Organization to Society," *Am. Jour. Soc.*, LXIII (1958), 471–475.
4. John Smith, *The Proceedings of the English Colonie in Virginia, [1606–1612]* . . . , in Philip L. Barbour, ed., *The Complete Works of Captain John Smith (1580–1631)*, 3 vols. (Chapel Hill, N.C., 1986), I, 225 (hereafter cited as *Works*).
5. "Virginia Council Instructions to Sir Thomas Gates, May, 1609," in Samuel M. Bemiss, ed., *The Three Charters of the Virginia Company of London, with Seven Related Documents, 1606–1621* (Williamsburg, Va., 1957), 66–67; John Smith, *A Map of Virginia, with a Description of the Countrey, the Commodities, People, Government, and Religion*, in *Works*, I, 159. When Company managers first proposed a

of the exploration of the Eastern Shore, may have been responsible for bringing the peninsula to the attention of the Company.

In November 1612, the same year that Smith's *Map of Virginia* was printed, Captain Samuel Argall carried Sir Thomas Dale to Smith's Island off the southern tip of the Eastern Shore

> to have his opinion of the inhabiting of it; who, after three dayes march in discovering it, approved very well of the place: and so much the better, because we found abundance of fish there, and very great Cod . . . of which we are in hope to get a great quantitie this Summer, for the reliefe of our men.

At that time, fish formed an important part of the settlers' diet because crop production was meager, trade with the Indians unreliable, and supplies from the Company inadequate.[6]

The following May, Argall again explored the Eastern Shore, which he described as having

> many small Rivers in it, and very good harbours for Boats and Barges, but not for ships of any great burthen; and also great store of Inhabitants, who seemed very desirous of our love. . . . We also discovered a multitude of Ilands bearing good Medow ground, and as I thinke, Salt might easily be made there, if there were any ponds digged, for that I found Salt kerned where the water had over-flowne in certain places. Here is also great store of fish, both shel-fish and other.[7]

Thus Argall confirmed Smith's observations about the fertility of the land, the friendliness of the natives, the felicitous proximity of fish as well as the salt to cure it, and the favorable nature of the geography—a landscape interlaced with navigable waterways.

Finally, in an account of affairs in Virginia through June 1614, Ralph

---

program of product diversification, they included 10 fishermen and 2 saltmakers in the list of laborers needed in Virginia. "A True and Sincere Declaration of the Purpose and Ends of the Plantation Begun in Virginia [1609]," in Alexander Brown, ed., *The Genesis of the United States*, 2 vols. (1890; reprint ed., New York, 1964), I, 352–353.

6. "A Letter of Sir Samuell Argoll Touching his Voyage to Virginia, and Actions There: Written to Master Nicholas Hawes, June 1613," in Brown, ed., *Genesis of the United States*, II, 640–641; Smith, *Proceedings*, in *Works*, I, 263–264; Edmund S. Morgan, *American Slavery, American Freedom: The Ordeal of Colonial Virginia* (New York, 1975), chap. 4.

7. "A Letter of Sir Samuell Argoll," in Brown, ed., *Genesis of the United States*, II, 644. *Kern*: "to crystallize" (*Oxford English Dictionary*).

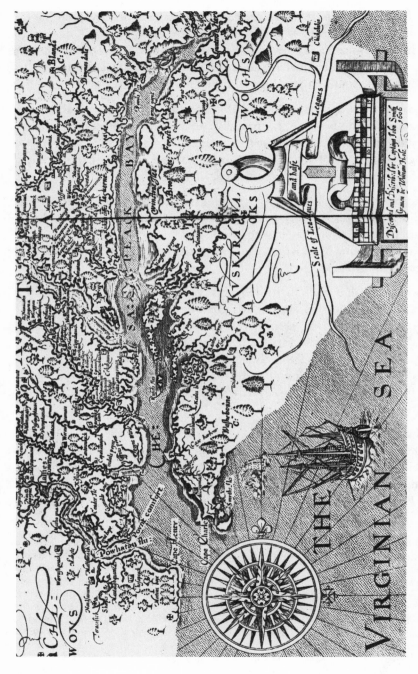

Map 1. The Eastern Shore: John Smith's Map of 1612. Detail. *Courtesy of the Newberry Library, Chicago*

Hamor, secretary of Virginia, also noted the abundance of fish in the waters off the Eastern Shore and emphasized the importance of salt for their preservation.

> For fish the Rivers are plentifiully stored, with . . . diverse . . . kindes, of all which my selfe have seene great quantity taken, especially . . . at *Smiths Island* . . . and even at that very place which is not above fifteene miles from *Pointcomfort*, if we had beene furnished with salt, to have saved it, wee might have taken as much fish as would have served us that whole yeere.[8]

Encouraged by these accounts of the abundance of fish and salt, the Virginia Company established a settlement on the peninsula. In 1616 John Rolfe reported that the Eastern Shore was one of six places "possessed and inhabited" in Virginia. "At Dales-Gift (being upon the sea, neere unto Cape Charles . . .) are seventeen, under the command of one lieutenant Cradock; all these are fedd and maintayned by the colony. Their labor is to make salt and catch fish at the two seasons aforementioned [spring and fall]." The saltworks was located on Smith's Island, and the Company's employees were housed on the nearby mainland at Dale's Gift.[9]

This first effort at settlement did not last long. By 1619 the saltworks had ceased production. The venture had probably suffered the same fate as the rest of the Virginia Company's ambitious plans to produce iron, glass, lumber, pitch, silk, wine, and a number of other products. Failure

---

8. Ralphe Hamor, the younger, *A True Discourse of the Present Estate of Virginia* (1615; facsimile reprint ed., New York, 1971), D3. For the importance of salt in the fishing industry, see also John Smith, *The Generall Historie of Virginia, New-England, and the Summer Isles . . .* , in *Works*, II, 267.

Quotations from 17th-century sources have been modernized typographically. Thus, where modern usage dictates, *u* has been changed to *v*, and vice versa, *i* has been changed to *j*, and *vv* has been changed to *w*; finally, ampersands have been expanded.

9. John Rolf[e], "Virginia in 1616," *Virginia Historical Register, and Literary Advertiser*, I (1848), 106, 110. Although most historians cite 1614 as the year of first European settlement on the Eastern Shore, the exact timing is uncertain. It is clear that the saltworks had been established at least by 1615. Historians who give an earlier date do so either on the basis of Rolfe's report, which does not support this reading, or by citation to other historians who have relied on Rolfe.

Historians have disputed the site of Dale's Gift, but this placement seems most consistent with the available evidence (Ralph T. Whitelaw, *Virginia's Eastern Shore: A History of Northampton and Accomack Counties*, 2 vols. [Richmond, Va., 1951], I, 53–54).

Map 2. People and Places during the Company Period

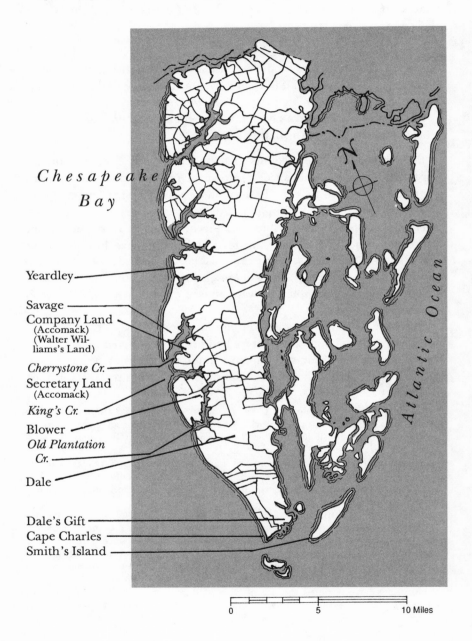

Chesapeake Bay

Atlantic Ocean

Yeardley

Savage

Company Land
(Accomack)
(Walter Williams's Land)

Cherrystone Cr.

Secretary Land
(Accomack)

King's Cr.

Blower

Old Plantation Cr.

Dale

Dale's Gift

Cape Charles

Smith's Island

0   5   10 Miles

was inevitable. The Company lacked both the knowledge and the funds necessary to succeed in such an extensive program of development. Nor had the technological limitations of a frontier setting been considered. Furthermore, high mortality swept away hundreds of laborers as well as the skilled craftsmen whose job was to direct the production of commodities. Most important, the cost of recruiting, transporting, supplying, and replacing workers inflated the price of any product resulting from their labor far over the existing market rate in England.[10]

The saltworks on the Eastern Shore also may have fallen victim to the rush to plant tobacco, which was the only exception to the unprofitability of Virginia products. First sent to England in 1613, tobacco enjoyed an increasing demand. Exports rose from twenty-three hundred pounds in 1615 to forty-one thousand in 1618, and average annual prices hovered around three shillings per pound. Unlike any other commodity produced in Virginia, the difference between the cost of producing tobacco in Virginia and the market price in England resulted in a quick and substantial profit. The Company tried to control the production of tobacco and to advance its program of product diversification, but those colonists who had finished their terms of service to the Company (and some who hadn't) turned to the cultivation of tobacco. Evidence of the boom was everywhere.[11] Meanwhile, Company members were impatient for some sort of return on their investment.

In 1618 the Company's managers realized that a drastic change in corporate policy was necessary to save the Virginia venture from financial collapse. The resulting reforms loosened the grip of corporate control and had a profound impact on the future development of society in Virginia. First, there was a radical change in land policy. As early as 1609 the promise of land had been used to attract laborers as well as investment capital. The promise had been subject to conditions and remained

10. On saltworks, see "The Court Book, May 17, 1620," in Susan Myra Kingsbury, ed., *The Records of the Virginia Company of London*, 4 vols. (Washington, D.C., 1906–1935), I, 350–351; H. R. McIlwaine, ed., *Journals of the House of Burgesses of Virginia, 1619–1658/59* (Richmond, Va., 1915), 35. On other problems, see Hecht, "Virginia Colony," 103–119, 124–125. See Morgan, *American Slavery, American Freedom*, 84–86, for a discussion of the problem of overspecialization of the work force.

11. Melvin Herndon, *Tobacco in Colonial Virginia: "The Sovereign Remedy"* (Williamsburg, Va., 1957), 2, 26, 46; Hecht, "Virginia Colony," 164–166, 192; Smith, *Generall Historie*, in *Works*, II, 262; "The Court Book, May 17, 1620," in Kingsbury, ed., *Records of the Virginia Company*, I, 350–351.

largely unfulfilled; nevertheless, many settlers had use of a few acres each. In 1618 the Company established a new land policy that was intended to fulfill past obligations and to provide incentives to future investment and immigration by ending the Company's stranglehold on land. Thereafter, people could acquire land in exchange for transporting individuals into Virginia—that is, the headright system. The second reform loosened the Company's virtual monopoly of trade into and out of Virginia. Third, the Company relaxed its complete control over the government of Virginia.[12] In order to encourage immigration, the Company instituted a "laudable form of Government by Majestracy and just Laws for the happy guiding and governing of the people" in Virginia. The "laudable form of Government" included the first representative body in America.[13]

12. For the Company's early land policy, see [Robert Johnson], *Nova Britannia* (1609; facsimile reprint ed., New York, 1969), D4, D4 verso; "A Letter from the Councill and Company of the Honourable Plantation in Virginia to the Lord Mayor, Aldermen, and Companies of London," in Brown, ed., *Genesis of the United States*, I, 253; Richard Rich, *Newes from Virginia* (1610; facsimile reprint ed., New York, 1970), B3, B3 verso; Robert Johnson, *The New Life of Virginia* (1612; facsimile reprint ed., New York, 1971), E3 verso, E4; Hamor, *True Discourse*, 17, 19; "A Briefe Declaration of the Present State of Things in Virginia, 1616," in Brown, ed., *Genesis of the United States*, II, 776–777. For the reforms of 1618, see "Virginia Company Instructions to George Yeardley, November 18, 1618," and "A Declaration of the State . . . in Virginia, June 22, 1620," in Kingsbury, ed., *Records of the Virginia Company*, III, 100–101, 107–108, 359–362.

For the earlier monopoly on trade, see "The First Charter, April 10, 1606," and "Articles, Instructions, and Orders, November 20, 1606," in Bemiss, ed., *Three Charters of the Virginia Company*, 7–9, 18–21; [Johnson], *Nova Britannia*, D4 verso. Only the small minority of individuals who had finished their terms of service to the Company were free to trade independently (Craven, *Southern Colonies*, 125). For the relaxation of trade restrictions after 1619, see Morgan, *American Slavery, American Freedom*, 95.

For the original organization of government, see "The First Charter, April 10, 1606," "Articles, Instructions, and Orders, November 20, 1606," and "Ordinance and Constitution, March 9, 1607," in Bemiss, ed., *Three Charters of the Virginia Company*, 5–6, 9, 13–15, 23–26. In 1609 the Company's managers reorganized the government under the second charter and gave greater power to the governor in Virginia ("The Second Charter, May 23, 1609," "Virginia Council Instructions to Sir Thomas Gates, May, 1609," in Bemiss, ed., *Three Charters of the Virginia Company*, 44–48, 56–59, 64–66; "Lord De La Warr's Commission," in Brown, ed., *Genesis of the United States*, I, 382). In 1612 the Company attempted to consolidate control over its employees in Virginia (*For the Colony in Virginea Britannia, Lawes Divine, Morall and Martiall, etc.* [1612], 11–21, in Peter Force, ed., *Tracts and Other Papers, Relating Principally to the Origin, Settlement, and Progress of the Colonies in North America, from the Discovery of the Country to the Year 1776*, 4 vols. [Washington, D.C., 1836–1847], III).

13. "Virginia Company Instructions to George Yeardley, November 18, 1618," in

Taken together, these three reforms altered irrevocably the corporate organization of Virginia. Thereafter, free of Company control, men could hold land, trade independently, and participate in government. In other words, their relations with one another could be as individuals within a society rather than as employees within a corporate setting. But one important element of a society was still in short supply: women. The Company therefore undertook to transport women to Virginia to be wives for the planters. Thereby the settlers might be induced to remain in Virginia rather than leave after making a quick profit.[14]

But having made these reforms, the Company's leaders did not abandon their earlier plans for ambitious product diversification, including the production of salt. They declared that the Eastern Shore saltworks, "having been lately suffered to decay; we now intending to restore in so great plenty, as not onely to serve the Colony for the present, but as is hoped, in short time, the great fishings on those Coasts." The governor and Council of Virginia were to choose twenty corporate tenants to renew the saltworks and fishing station on Smith's Island. The tenants would each be rented fifty acres on the island. For five years, they would collect one-half of the profits from their cultivation of this land as well as from their efforts in the salt and fishing industries. Yet after endless planning and encouragement, the revival of the saltworks was a fiasco.[15]

Kingsbury, ed., *Records of the Virginia Company*, III, 98–99; Craven, *Southern Colonies*, 133–136.

14. "The Court Book, November 3, 1619," "Virginia Company Letter to the Governor and Council in Virginia, August 12, 1621," "Discourse of the Old Company, April (?) 1625," in Kingsbury, ed., *Records of the Virginia Company*, I, 256–257, III, 493–494, IV, 522.

15. "A Broadside, May 17, 1620," *ibid.*, III, 279–280. John Pory, secretary of Virginia, disapproved of the proposed plans to renew the saltworks. He derided the choice of planting the tenants on 50-acre plots on Smith's Island, which he depicted as barren land, far inferior to that which was nearby on the Eastern Shore mainland and which Sir Thomas Dale had bought for the Company from the Indians. Pory also encouraged the production of salt by means of the evaporation of the liquid from seawater rather than by the laborious procedure of boiling it in kettles as had been done previously. "John Pory to Sir Edwin Sandys, June 7, 1620," *ibid.*, III, 304.

For efforts to revive the saltworks over the next three years, see the following: "The Court Book, July 7, 1620 and June 11, 1621," *ibid.*, I, 393, 483; "A Declaration of the State . . . in Virginia, June 22, 1620," "Virginia Company Instructions to the Governor and Council of State in Virginia, July 24, 1621," "Virginia Council and Company Letter to Governor and Council in Virginia, September 11, 1621," "Council of the Virginia Company Letter to the Governor and Council in Virginia, December 5, 1621," "Council in Virginia Letter to Virginia Company of London, January 1621/22," " 'A Note of the Shipping, Men, and Provisions Sent and Provided for Virginia . . . in the Yeere 1621,' " *ibid.*, III, 315, 476, 507, 532, 586, 642; [Edward

In 1623 a report circulated that "there hath beene soe little done that the Collonie . . . buyes all theire salt for theire necessarye use." By the end of that year, the effort to revive the saltworks had collapsed.[16] The rest of the Company's elaborate program for product diversification also failed. Success was prevented by the same factors that had doomed the Company's earlier efforts: undercapitalization, uninformed planning, high mortality, and the cost of labor.[17]

The Virginia Company was more successful in other aspects of its reforms, and the nucleus of settlement on the Eastern Shore resulted from those reforms. In establishing a participatory government, the Company had attempted to alleviate the burden of taxation needed to support it. They did so by providing for tenants to be settled on special allotments of land designated for the support of particular government officials, the same method that had been used to support a college, ministers, and the Company itself. In 1620 the London leadership of the Company allotted five hundred acres and twenty tenants to provide an income for the secretary of Virginia. When the first group of ten tenants arrived in the fall, Secretary John Pory, on the advice of Governor George Yeardley, seated them near Accomack, located on the bayside of the Eastern Shore about twelve miles from the tip of the peninsula. A settlement of Company tenants had already been made on land adjacent to that suggested to Pory.[18]

The Eastern Shore may have been chosen as the site for these settle-

Waterhouse], *A Declaration of the State of the Colony and Affaires in Virginia* (1622; facsimile reprint ed., New York, 1970), 7.

16. "An Answere to a Declaraĉon of the Present State of Virginia, May 1623," and "The Court Book, November 19, 1623," in Kingsbury, ed., *Records of the Virginia Company*, II, 497, IV, 144. Even after the dissolution of the Virginia Company, efforts to set up a saltworks continued (H. R. McIlwaine, ed., *Minutes of the Council and General Court of Colonial Virginia, 1622–1632, 1670–1676* [Richmond, Va., 1924], 480).

17. "Parts of Drafts of a Statement touching the Miserable Condition of Virginia, 1623," in Kingsbury, ed., *Records of the Virginia Company*, IV, 176; Hecht, "Virginia Colony," 124–125; Craven, *Southern Colonies*, 145–146.

18. "Virginia Company Instructions to George Yeardley, November 18, 1618," "The Court Book, May 17, 1620," and "Council in Virginia Letter to Virginia Company of London, January, 1621/22," in Kingsbury, ed., *Records of the Virginia Company*, I, 349, III, 99–101, 585; *A Declaration of the State of the Colonie and Affaires in Virginia* (1620; facsimile reprint ed., New York, 1973), C1 verso, C2; McIlwaine, ed., *Minutes of the Council and General Court*, 148; Whitelaw, *Virginia's Eastern Shore*, I, 167–168. Secretary Pory noted that he had planted near the Company land so that the two groups of tenants could provide security and assistance to one another (Whitelaw, *Virginia's Eastern Shore*, I, 175–176). "Extracts of All the Titles and Estates of Land, Sent Home by Sir Francis Wyatt, May 1625" notes that, although the

ments because of its fertile land and numerous rivers and creeks, convenient for transportation. Both of these advantages had been noted by visitors to the peninsula. Also important may have been the friendly relations the English enjoyed with the natives there. The Virginia settlers had found the Eastern Shore Indians to be an important source of corn, around which developed a mutually beneficial trade. This shift of valuable trade had provoked the Indians across the Chesapeake Bay against those on the Eastern Shore. It also may have exacerbated existing irritations. John Pory observed in 1621, "There may be on [the Eastern Shore] about two thousand [Indians]: they on the West would invade them, but that they want Boats to crosse the Bay, and so would divers other Nations, were they not protected by us." Despite mutual hostility, however, the natives on the Western Shore in the summer of 1621 sought the help of those on the Eastern Shore in an attempt to poison the English. The Eastern Shore Indians refused. In the same year, they also reported to the English the plans for an uprising that was aborted because of their warning.[19]

But the attack had only been postponed. In March 1622, Western Shore Indians rose against the English. The relationship between the two groups had never been cordial. Although the Company had originally intended—ethnocentrically—to provide the natives with a religious education and to incorporate them into the English settlement, what had happened was quite different. Murder, torture, and cheating had marked the interaction between Indians and settlers, and the result was mistrust and hatred. The English outpost had gradually developed into a permanent settlement that increasingly threatened the Indians. They responded in the spring of 1622. During a surprise attack, almost 350 men, women, and children were slain in the course of one day. Chaos reigned as the settlers grouped together and tried to provide themselves with supplies. A brutal war ensued between settlers and natives.[20]

Company's and secretary's tenants were seated on the Eastern Shore, no land had ever been ordered to be laid out for them there (Kingsbury, ed., *Records of the Virginia Company*, IV, 559).

19. "John Martin's 'The Manner Howe to Bringe the Indians into Subjection,' December 15, 1622," in Kingsbury, ed., *Records of the Virginia Company*, III, 705; Smith, *Generall Historie*, in *Works*, II, 291; [Waterhouse], *A Declaration of the State of the Colony and Affaires in Virginia* (1622), 21; "Council in Virginia Letter to Virginia Company of London, January 20, 1622/23," in Kingsbury, ed., *Records of the Virginia Company*, IV, 10.

20. See Morgan, *American Slavery, American Freedom*, chaps. 3–5, for a comprehensive discussion of English-Indian contact during the Company period.

The Indians on the Eastern Shore did not attack the English there; but, while the Eastern Shore settlers were spared the devastation wrought on their countrymen over the bay, they were not unaffected by the repercussions of the disaster.[21] During the period of panic immediately following the terrible slaughter, the Council in Virginia wrote to the London leadership that, for the purpose of fortification, another chief city might have to be established.[22] The Eastern Shore was considered a possible location. But the Company managers replied that James City could be sufficiently reinforced and that a move from there would upset all of the progress to date as well as the expectations of the investors, the king, and the public. They concluded that the Council in Virginia would "do well so wholie to abandon the thought thereof, as in this point not to returne us any answer." The Council wrote back that a move had never been seriously entertained. But in private correspondence, George Sandys, treasurer of Virginia, revealed that the governor and he had agreed that the land on the Eastern Shore should "be survaid for the planting of a Partie there as better furnished with all sortes of provisions and fit thereafter for fortificaçon." Sandys added in another letter that the Eastern Shore "had beene better, at the first, to have seated on, in regard of fertilitie, Convenience, all sorts of provision and strength both against the Native and fforreiner."[23]

The Company, seeking some explanation for the debacle of 1622, turned to the weakness caused by the dispersion of settlement resulting from the reforms of 1618.[24] After an initial burst of corporate energy

21. [Waterhouse], *A Declaration of the State of the Colony and Affaires in Virginia* (1622), lists the colonists who were killed, and there are no names for the Eastern Shore. A letter from Richard Frethorne to his parents, however, related how a group of Western Shore Indians had failed in their attack on a ship and had then turned toward Accomack. If this is true, there is no indication that any destruction resulted. This group of intruders would probably have received a cool reception from their Eastern Shore brethren. Kingsbury, ed., *Records of the Virginia Company*, IV, 61.

22. Kingsbury, ed., *Records of the Virginia Company*, III, 612–613. Shortly before the Indian attack, the Council in Virginia had suggested to the Company managers that the chief city might have to be moved to a more defensible location. *Ibid.*, III, 583.

23. *Ibid.*, III, 667, IV, 11–12, 67, 73–74. Sandys added in both letters that he personally opposed abandoning the settlements already established on the Western Shore.

24. "The Court Book, July 17, 1622," "The Court Book, April 30, 1623," "Sir Francis Wyatt Commission to Sir George Yeardley, June 20, 1622," "George Sandys Letter to Sir Miles Sandys, March 30, 1623," "George Sandys Letter to Sir Samuel Sandys, March 30, 1623," "Parts of Drafts of a Statement touching the Miserable

following the reforms, the bulk of immigrants had come to Virginia under private rather than public auspices. While the Company's efforts at product diversification had failed, the private sector had grown.[25] The area of settlement had expanded steadily as the English sought more land for tobacco cultivation. Exports of tobacco leapt from 41,000 pounds in 1618 to 500,000 pounds in 1626, and the average annual price fluctuated between two and three shillings.[26]

By the early 1620s, private individuals also had begun to acquire acreage on the Eastern Shore. One of these was Ensign Thomas Savage, who had arrived in Virginia in 1608 at the age of thirteen. Left with the Indians for three years in order to learn their language, Savage won the affection of the natives and later served as an interpreter and guide for the English. After living in Virginia for more than ten years, he received from the Eastern Shore werowance a grant for land on Cherrystone Creek across from where the public plantations were later established. The English subsequently recognized his claim, and by 1625 he lived there with two servants and his wife Hannah, who had come to Virginia in 1621.[27]

At the same time that Savage received his grant of land from the Indians, so too did Sir George Yeardley, a grant confirmed by the Virginia Company. In his early thirties when he arrived in Virginia in 1610, he held several military positions in succession before being designated deputy governor in 1616 and governor two years later. As governor and

Condition of Virginia," *ibid.*, II, 96, 383, III, 656–657, IV, 70–71, 73, 178. See also [Waterhouse], *A Declaration of the State of the Colony and Affaires in Virginia* (1622), 12–13.

25. Craven, *Southern Colonies*, 139. The private sector sometimes prospered at the expense of the public (Smith, *Generall Historie*, in *Works*, II, 292).

26. Herndon, *Tobacco in Colonial Virginia*, 46; Hecht, "Virginia Colony," chap. 7; Morgan, *American Slavery, American Freedom*, chap. 6.

27. John Smith, *A True Relation of Such Occurrences and Accidents of Noate as Hath Hapned in Virginia . . .* , in *Works*, I, 69; Edward Arber and A. G. Bradley, eds., *Travels and Works of Captain John Smith, President of Virginia, and Admiral of New England* (Edinburgh, 1910), cii–ciii; Hamor, *True Discourse*, 37–38; "The Court Book, July 10, 1621," "Sir George Yeardley Answer to the Demand of Captain John Martin, February 4, 1624/25," "Extracts of All the Titles and Estates of Land, Sent Home by Sir Francis Wyatt, May 1625," in Kingsbury, ed., *Records of the Virginia Company*, I, 504, IV, 514, 559; Nell Marion Nugent, ed., *Cavaliers and Pioneers: Abstracts of Virginia Land Patents and Grants*, I, 1623–1666, II, 1666–1695 (Richmond, Va., 1934, 1977), I, 24; CCR-2, 399–400; Annie Lash Jester and Martha Woodruff Hiden, comps., *Adventurers of Purse and Person: Virginia, 1607–1625* ([Richmond, Va.], 1964), 67.

later as a member of the Virginia Council, Yeardley maintained an extensive plantation on the Western Shore. He lived in James City. Although he visited his large tract to the north of Ensign Savage's on the Eastern Shore, Yeardley probably never developed the land.[28]

Another absentee landowner was Lady Elizabeth Dale, widow of Sir Thomas Dale. Her husband had held official Company posts in Virginia, including the position of deputy governor, before he left the colony in 1616. Five years later, the Virginia Company granted his widow's request for a patent. Lady Elizabeth probably based her claim for land on an action of the Company in 1611 when Sir Thomas Dale received the equivalent of fifty-six shares of the joint stock, equal to fifty-six hundred acres. An Eastern Shore plantation was established at Old Plantation Creek, with supervision of the estate assigned to overseers. The work, however, did not proceed smoothly. Within a year of her 1621 patent, Lady Dale requested that the Company grant a letter of recommendation so that the governor would aid a specially assigned agent in the recovery of the profits of her land. Her servants in Virginia were cheating her.[29]

While Savage, Yeardley, and Dale all held extensive tracts of land, William Williams and John Blower owned more modest amounts. Williams, who patented 100 acres on September 13, 1621, was living on his land with his wife three years later, but they either died or left the Eastern Shore during the next year. Blower patented 150 acres on the north side of Old Plantation Creek in 1623. He had resided in Virginia since 1610, and his wife arrived in 1620. Two years after he received his patent, Blower, his wife, and two servants were living on the land.[30]

28. Whitelaw, *Virginia's Eastern Shore*, I, 287; Nugent, ed., *Cavaliers and Pioneers*, I, 96; "Extracts of All the Titles and Estates of Land, Sent Home by Sir Francis Wyatt, May 1625," in Kingsbury, ed., *Records of the Virginia Company*, IV, 559; Brown, ed., *Genesis of the United States*, II, 1065; Morgan, *American Slavery, American Freedom*, 122–123; Jester and Hiden, comps., *Adventurers of Purse and Person*, 27, 42–43, 378–379; Arber and Bradley, eds., *Travels and Works of Captain John Smith*, 595.

29. Brown, ed., *Genesis of the United States*, II, 869–874; "The Court Book, June 11 and 13, 1621 and May 20, 1622," in Kingsbury, ed., *Records of the Virginia Company*, I, 483, 491–492, II, 15; Nugent, ed., *Cavaliers and Pioneers*, I, 163. Charles E. Hatch, Jr., in *The First Seventeen Years: Virginia, 1607–1624* (Williamsburg, Va., 1957), 93, claims that Lady Elizabeth moved to the Eastern Shore, but there is no evidence that she ever lived in Virginia after the death of her husband.

30. On Williams: CCR-2, p. 14; "A List of Names of the Living in Virginia, February the 16th 1623 [Old Style]," in John Camden Hotten, ed., *The Original Lists of Persons of Quality; Emigrants . . . Who Went from Great Britain to the American Plantations 1600–1700* (New York, 1874), 189; Jester and Hiden, comps., *Adventur-*

Governor Francis Wyatt noted in a report sent to England in May 1625 that, in addition to the above landholders on the Eastern Shore, "certaine others have planted their but no pattents have bine graunted them." Where did these "others" settle? Apparently they stayed near the original settlements on the Company's and secretary's land. Later geographic patterns in the spread of land claims point to the conclusion that the Eastern Shore colonists planted lands within a tightly confined area no more than one or two miles from the official tracts.[31]

Some information about these people can be pieced together from the Muster (or census) taken in early 1625. Authorized by royal commission and by act of the Virginia Assembly, the Muster was intended to provide information needed by the king in order to plan for the future of Virginia. It included data on the sex, age, and date of immigration of settlers as well as on the number of servants, houses, boats, and stores. For the Eastern Shore, the Muster listed fifty-one individuals living and two who had died during 1624. These people were listed in nineteen separate musters, which ranged in size from one to fifteen people.[32]

Number in individual musters	1	2	3	4	15
Number of individual musters (total = 19)	9	3	3	3	1
Number of people (total = 51)	9	6	9	12	15

Thus, nine people were listed individually while nine headed musters of two, three, or four persons, and one, Captain William Epes, commanded a muster of fifteen. The size of Epes's muster reflected his privileged position as first commander of Accomack, an office giving him the power to act in the name of the central government as a chief magistrate.

---

ers of Purse and Person, 66–69. On Blower: Whitelaw, *Virginia's Eastern Shore*, I, 139; Jester and Hiden, comps., *Adventurers of Purse and Person*, 67; "Extracts of All the Titles and Estates of Land, Sent Home by Sir Francis Wyatt, May 1625," in Kingsbury, ed., *Records of the Virginia Company*, IV, 559; Nugent, ed., *Cavaliers and Pioneers*, I, 121.

31. "Extracts of All the Titles and Estates of Land, Sent Home by Sir Francis Wyatt, May 1625," in Kingsbury, ed., *Records of the Virginia Company*, IV, 559. See Chapter 2 on land patterns as well as McIlwaine, ed., *Minutes of the Council and General Court*, 156.

32. Jester and Hiden, comps., *Adventurers of Purse and Person*, 3–4; data on the Eastern Shore Muster, 66–69.

The thirteen servants in his muster probably represented the labor force assigned to the public lands. Two other musters listed two servants each.[33] The age structure reveals a very youthful population, especially so for servants. The Muster specifies ages for sixteen servants (of seventeen listed), with an average of 21.7 and a median of 23 (range 12–30); for nonservants, the Muster gives ages for twenty-two (of thirty-four listed), with 25 years as both the average and median (range 19–36).

Virginia Company policies, in addition to being responsible for the original settlement of the Eastern Shore, also shaped certain characteristics of the population. Of the forty-six inhabitants whose date of arrival in Virginia is known, thirty-eight came after the Company established new incentives for immigration after 1618.[34] The six women on the Eastern Shore had all arrived in Virginia after 1618, when the Company began to encourage the immigration of women. In addition, reflecting the Company's efforts to promote marriages and the formation of families, the Muster noted that all six women were married and two of them had a child each. Thus, although the population was predominantly young, single, and male and thereby reflected the Company's need for laborers, one-third of the musters included a husband and wife, the basis of familial society.

No information has survived to characterize the background, wealth, or daily life of the people on the Eastern Shore during the Company period. Frustratingly little remains to sketch out their living conditions. Each of the individual musters seems to have maintained a separate residence. Sixteen musters mention a house, another had none, one had two, and one (Epes again) had two and a fort. Fourteen had a store, or stock of goods; Epes had three stores. He also was one of the five heads of musters who owned a boat. These bare facts hide the probability of small, roughly built dwellings, few and simple tools and household utensils, and very limited stocks of food, clothing, and other necessities.[35]

33. "Governor in Virginia Warrant Granted to Richard Bolton, November 21, 1623," in Kingsbury, ed., *Records of the Virginia Company,* IV, 404; Craven, *Southern Colonies,* 167. Other musters may include servants who are not identified as such.

34. The date of arrival is not known for three residents, and two were born in Virginia.

35. For an imaginative reconstruction of such conditions, see Aubrey C. Land, "The Planters of Colonial Maryland," *MHM,* LXVII (1972), 111–112. For a review of literature on the standard of living of English settlers in the early Chesapeake, see James Horn, "Adapting to a New World: A Comparative Study of Local Society in England and Maryland, 1650–1700," in Lois Green Carr, Philip D. Morgan, and Jean B. Russo, eds., *Colonial Chesapeake Society* (Chapel Hill, N.C., 1988), 146–164.

If the living conditions of this small, compact population were simple, so too were its institutions of government and religion. Captain William Epes, the only government official, provided daily leadership. But the inhabitants had a voice in shaping legislation affecting themselves by the choice of representatives to the Assembly. The settlement also boasted the services of a minister. In 1621 Richard Bolton had been recommended to the Virginia Company as a minister for "some vacant place in Virginia." By November 1623 Bolton had taken a place on the peninsula, and the inhabitants provided his maintenance.[36]

A trend toward private landholdings, family organization, and local governmental and religious institutions—this was the legacy of the Virginia Company. These developments marked a change in the colony from a corporate organization of laborers working for the good of the Company to the beginnings of a society of individuals pursuing their own interests. On the Eastern Shore, approximately fifty of these individuals lived in proximity. Tracing the spread of settlement can help us understand the subsequent development of Eastern Shore society and, particularly, what held it together.

36. McIlwaine, ed., *Journals of the House of Burgesses*, viii; "The Court Book, July 10, 1621," "Governor in Virginia Warrant Granted to Richard Bolton, November 21, 1623," in Kingsbury, ed., *Records of the Virginia Company*, I, 506, IV, 404.

2 Land and Landholders

PATTERNS OF LAND SETTLEMENT on the Eastern Shore profoundly influenced contact among the colonists. How loosely or densely interconnected the societal network would be was affected by whether settlers claimed land that was contiguous or noncontiguous and whether they situated themselves to take advantage of available modes of transportation. Other factors also influenced the development of a local society, including how long people lived on the peninsula before claiming land, what they did before they became landholders, and where they claimed their first acreage. Answers to these questions suggest the extent to which new landholders disrupted or fitted into a developing societal web.

By 1622 settlement on the Eastern Shore centered on three creeks located on the bayside of the peninsula: Old Plantation Creek (about eight miles from Cape Charles), King's Creek, and Cherrystone Creek (both four miles further north). The majority of settlers were located on King's Creek and Cherrystone Creek. With favorable climate and geography, friendly Indians, and the encouragement of the Virginia Company, the Eastern Shore colonists seemed to enjoy promising prospects for developing the abundant land resources of the peninsula.

But this promise remained unfulfilled for several years. John Blower's 1623 patent for 150 acres was the last title granted for land on the Eastern Shore until 1627. The reason for this hiatus was the Indian attack on the Western Shore in the spring of 1622. Although spared the death and destruction that the natives inflicted across the bay, the Eastern Shore settlers did not escape the repercussions of that brief attack. Initially the colony responded chaotically and then with a policy of retrenchment. Actions by the Assembly, governor, and Council as well as directions from England discouraged dispersal of population and spread of settlement. In England, reports of the calamity intensified the division between supporters and opponents of the Virginia Company's leadership.[1]

1. See Edmund S. Morgan, *American Slavery, American Freedom: The Ordeal of Colonial Virginia* (New York, 1975), chaps. 3–5, for a complete discussion of the English-Indian contact. For contemporary comments concerning the spread of settlement, see J. Frederick Fausz and Jon Kukla, eds., "A Letter of Advice to the Governor

As actions in London led toward the dissolution of the Virginia Company, the colonists were uncertain whether their titles to land would be recognized. In *A Proclamation for Setling the Plantation of Virginia*, Charles I in 1625 sought to alleviate this anxiety by assuring landholders that he would "by any course that shall be desired of Us, settle and assure the particular rights and interests of every Planter and Adventurer, in any of those Territories, which shall desire the same, to give them full satisfaction for their quiet and assured enjoying thereof." With previous land grants thus confirmed, the colonists next sought a continuation of the already existing methods of patenting land. But no such confirmation was immediately forthcoming. Not until mid-1634 did the Privy Council end almost ten years of uncertainty by authorizing a return to the system of granting patents instituted by the Virginia Company. The colonists responded with a flood of applications for land.[2]

On the Eastern Shore in the decade following the dissolution of the Virginia Company, uncertainty about the colony's land policy was reflected in the concentration of settlement.[3] Faced with rich land re-

---

of Virginia, 1624," *WMQ*, 3d Ser., XXXIV (1977), 118. "The Court Book, July 17, 1622," "The Court Book, April 30, 1623," "Sir Francis Wyatt Commission to Sir George Yeardley, June 20, 1622," "George Sandys Letter to Sir Miles Sandys, March 30, 1623," "George Sandys Letter to Sir Samuel Sandys, March 30, 1623," "Parts of Drafts of a Statement touching the Miserable Condition of Virginia," in Susan Myra Kingsbury, ed., *The Records of the Virginia Company of London*, 4 vols. (Washington, D.C., 1906–1935), II, 96, 383, III, 656–657, IV, 70–71, 73, 178; see also [Edward Waterhouse], *A Declaration of the State of the Colony and Affaires in Virginia* (1622; facsimile reprint ed., New York, 1970), 12–13. For the reaction and subsequent events in England, see Wesley Frank Craven, *The Dissolution of the Virginia Company: The Failure of a Colonial Experiment* (New York, 1932), chaps. 7, 9, 10.

2. Charles I, *A Proclamation for Setling the Plantation of Virginia* (facsimile reprint ed., Charlottesville, Va., 1946); "Governor and Council in Virginia Letter to the Privy Council, April 6, 1626," in Kingsbury, ed., *Records of the Virginia Company*, IV, 572; H. R. McIlwaine, ed., *Minutes of the Council and General Court of Colonial Virginia, 1622–1632, 1670–1676* (Richmond, Va., 1924), 481; Fairfax Harrison, *Virginia Land Grants: A Study of Conveyancing in Relation to Colonial Politics* (Richmond, Va., 1925), 24–25; Manning Curlee Voorhis, "The Land Grant Policy of Colonial Virginia, 1607–1774" (Ph.D. diss., University of Virginia, 1940), 40–43. See also Wesley Frank Craven, *The Southern Colonies in the Seventeenth Century, 1607–1689* (1949; reprint ed., Baton Rouge, La., 1970), 175–176; and Craven, *White, Red, and Black: The Seventeenth-Century Virginian* (Charlottesville, Va., 1971), 10. For a brief description of the method of patenting land under Virginia's headright system, see Edmund S. Morgan, "Headrights and Head Counts," *VMHB*, LXXX (1972), 362.

3. The analysis of landholding that follows is heavily indebted to Ralph T. Whitelaw, who mapped all of the original patents for land on the Eastern Shore in *Virginia's*

sources, the colonists there cautiously claimed small holdings in a limited area. Thus, patents of from twenty to fifty (occasionally one hundred) acres, for lease periods rarely more than ten years, accounted for nine of the sixteen claims for new land between 1625 and 1634.[4] Furthermore, the colonists patented only in the immediate vicinity of the established settlements on Old Plantation, King's, and Cherrystone creeks.

Following the Privy Council's clarification of the conditions for patenting land, however, this situation changed dramatically. Land claims soared. In 1635 alone, patentees on the Eastern Shore took up 5,750 acres of new land, a sharp contrast to the 2,190 acres claimed during all of the nine previous years. A comparison of the average (and median) acreage of new claims reveals a similar increase in size: 479 acres average (200 median) in 1635, versus 137 acres average (100 median) for the rest of the post-Company period.[5] This high growth rate did not continue. It represented a one-time release of demand held in check during a decade of ill-defined land policy. Most significant about this surge of claims,

---

Eastern Shore: A History of Northampton and Accomack Counties, 2 vols. (Richmond, Va., 1951). Whitelaw divided the Eastern Shore into hundreds of tracts, each of which represented an original patent or, sometimes, more than one patent. He then tried to trace the subsequent transactions (sales, bequests, escheats) that subdivided or combined tracts. Whitelaw's achievement was substantial, but the result is limited by the nature of the land records themselves. Patents and deeds during the 17th century were remarkable for the vagueness of their boundaries. They relied on very impermanent natural and man-made markers—creeks, trees, fences. Directions "into the woods" were ambiguous and acreages often estimates. Reference to the boundaries of another landholder's acreage only compounded the problem. These factors contributed to the boundary disputes that litter the court record. And if confusion and controversy reigned at the time, then there can be little wonder that Whitelaw sometimes had to estimate and make educated guesses in order to locate the original grants and trace their subsequent history. After checking Whitelaw's conclusions against a close reading of all available primary sources, I have made necessary corrections and adopted his system for my own purposes. In the analysis that follows, the term "tract" always refers to one of the pieces of land delineated according to Whitelaw's division.

4. The Council of Virginia in December 1633 authorized the colony's secretary to lease his land on the Eastern Shore for 21-year periods (McIlwaine, ed., *Minutes of the Council and General Court*, 480).

The statistics on landholding presented throughout this chapter result from an examination of all relevant primary sources, including patents, county court records, Council and General Court minutes, and so forth. By collating information from these diverse sources, I have sought to establish the date, amount, and location of as many land transactions as possible. Because of the scope of reconstructing the landholdings of 422 individuals, however, an effort to document each bit of evidence and each decision involved would result in extremely burdensome annotation. No such effort has been made.

5. All calculations involving acreages have been rounded to the nearest acre.

Map 3. Land Settlement through 1635

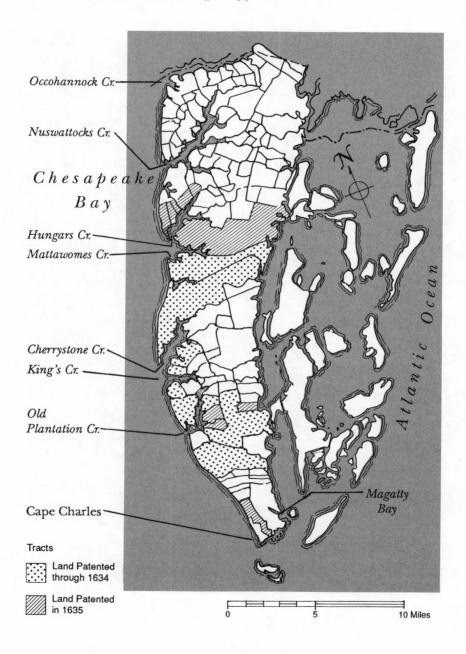

Occohannock Cr.

Nuswattocks Cr.

Chesapeake Bay

Hungars Cr.
Mattawomes Cr.

Cherrystone Cr.
King's Cr.

Old Plantation Cr.

Cape Charles

Atlantic Ocean

Magatty Bay

Tracts

Land Patented through 1634

Land Patented in 1635

0   5   10 Miles

Map 4. Land Settlement South of Occohannock Creek through 1645

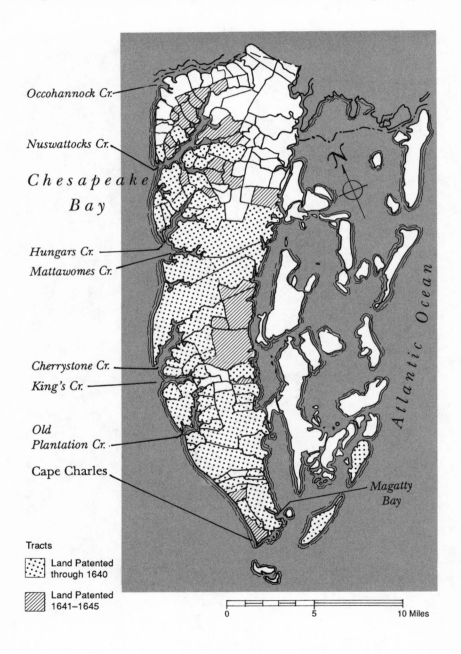

Occohannock Cr.

Nuswattocks Cr.

Chesapeake Bay

Hungars Cr.

Mattawomes Cr.

Cherrystone Cr.

King's Cr.

Old Plantation Cr.

Cape Charles

Atlantic Ocean

Magatty Bay

Tracts

Land Patented through 1640

Land Patented 1641–1645

0   5   10 Miles

Map 5. Land Settlement North of Occohannock Creek through 1645

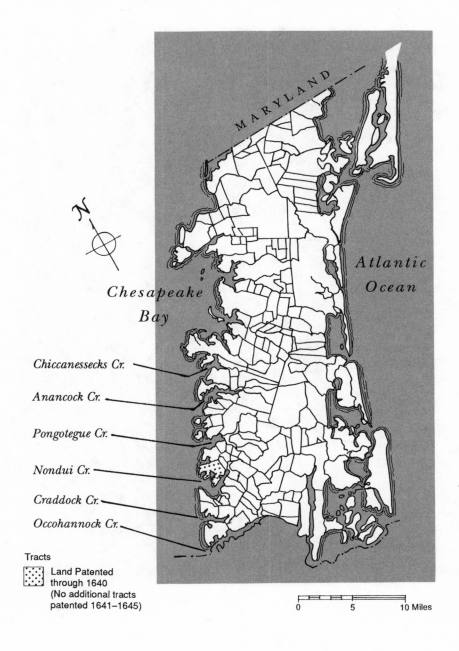

Chesapeake Bay

Atlantic Ocean

MARYLAND

Chiccanessecks Cr.

Anancock Cr.

Pongotegue Cr.

Nondui Cr.

Craddock Cr.

Occohannock Cr.

Tracts

Land Patented
through 1640
(No additional tracts
patented 1641–1645)

0   5   10 Miles

Map 6. Land Settlement South of Occohannock Creek through 1655

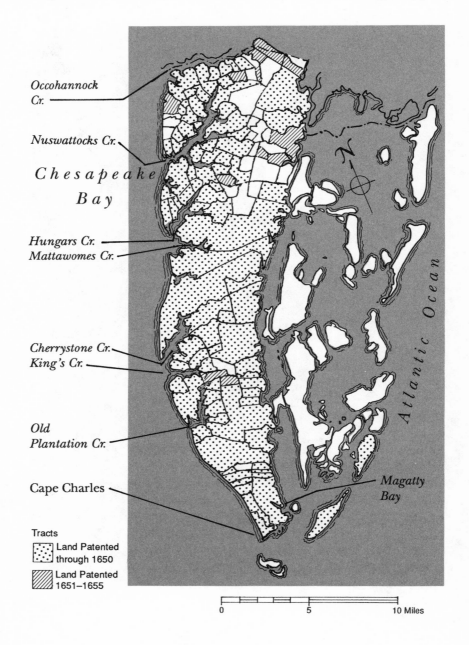

Occohannock Cr.

Nuswattocks Cr.

Chesapeake Bay

Hungars Cr.
Mattawomes Cr.

Cherrystone Cr.
King's Cr.

Old Plantation Cr.

Cape Charles

Atlantic Ocean

Magatty Bay

Tracts

Land Patented through 1650

Land Patented 1651–1655

0   5   10 Miles

Map 7. Land Settlement North of Occohannock Creek through 1655

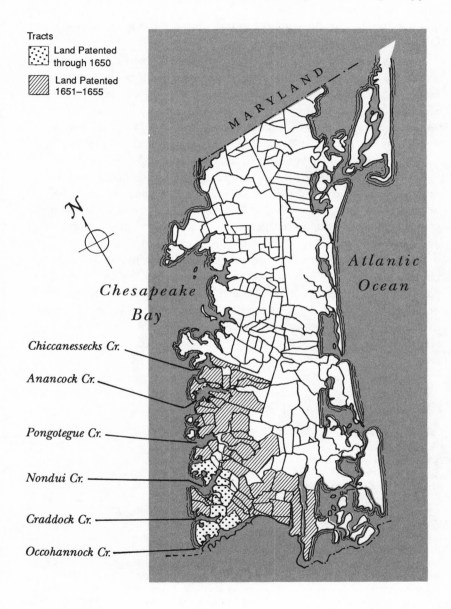

however, is that it initiated a pattern of orderly land development that had an important impact on the nascent Eastern Shore society, revealing a population whose expansive impulse did not undermine the possibility for contact among its members.

Some of the land claimed in 1635 represented a further expansion of settlement around Old Plantation Creek, but several of the new patents marked the directions that land claims would take through 1655. The first of these patents, granted to Edmund Scarburgh on November 28, 1635, was a claim for two hundred acres located in the southern part of the peninsula. During the next five years virtually all of the land from Cape Charles to Old Plantation Creek was claimed.[6]

Another patent for two hundred acres granted to Scarburgh on the same day set the trend for the development of seaside property. For the next twenty years, colonists patented land on the seaside in a steady sweep north from this initial grant.[7] As with Scarburgh's original acreage, however, patents on the seaside always lay to the south of the furthest point of settlement on the bayside. This distinction reflected the relative merits of the two sides of the peninsula for the colonists. Compared to the seaside, the bayside was more sheltered from the severity of ocean storms, it was closer to the seat of government at James City, and its many creeks and inlets were more easily navigable and hospitable to settlement than the treacherous waters and exposed islands of the seaside.

Development along the bayside creeks began to move north in 1635, when three colonists received patents for land on Hungars Creek, the next major waterway to the north of Cherrystone Creek.[8] Thus began a

6. Nell Marion Nugent, ed., *Cavaliers and Pioneers: Abstracts of Virginia Land Patents and Grants*, I, *1623–1666*, II, *1666–1695* (Richmond, Va., 1934, 1977), I, 36. Settlers may have avoided claiming land there before because of the vague boundaries of a large parcel of land granted to Sir Thomas Dale. It was rumored that his widow, Lady Elizabeth Dale, owned all the land from Cape Charles to Old Plantation Creek. The first tentative encroachment in this area was a 1628 claim for land by Charles Harmar, formerly an overseer of Lady Elizabeth Dale. Whitelaw, *Virginia's Eastern Shore*, I, 96–97; McIlwaine, ed., *Minutes of the Council and General Court*, 48, 179.

7. Nugent, ed., *Cavaliers and Pioneers*, I, 35–36. This generalization ignores two anomalies: the earlier grants to Thomas Savage and George Yeardley extended from the bayside to the seaside. It also ignores an apparent anomaly in a tract of land between Mattawomes and Hungars creeks to the north of George Yeardley's. This tract is a combination by Ralph T. Whitelaw of several different patents (see Whitelaw, *Virginia's Eastern Shore*, I, 318–320). The grant of land to William Stone in 1635 was, in fact, for land in the western, or bayside, portion.

8. The three patentees were William Andrews, William Stone, and William Gayny. Nugent, ed., *Cavaliers and Pioneers*, I, 23, 27–28, 31.

steady trend of patenting land along the bayside creeks, in order, from south to north. From 1636 to 1640, colonists first claimed land on Nuswattocks Creek; from 1646 to 1650, on Occohannock, Craddock, and Nondui creeks; and from 1651 to 1655, on Pongotegue, Anancock, and Chickanessecks creeks. At the same time that the edge of settlement moved northward, colonists also patented land on unclaimed tracts along those creeks already settled. For example, on Hungars Creek, colonists continued to claim land on new tracts for ten years after the initial claim in 1635, and on Nuswattocks Creek, for eight years after the initial claim.[9]

This patenting of land along the bayside creeks is one aspect of another general pattern marking the development of settlement. From the very beginning of colonization on the Eastern Shore, those individuals claiming land preferred waterside locations. They patented land so that water formed one of the boundaries for the overwhelming majority of tracts.[10] When tracts were landlocked, they were left unclaimed for lengthy periods as colonists patented land elsewhere on the bayside or seaside. For example, when William Waters claimed a landlocked tract near the head of Old Plantation Creek, it was ten years after almost all patent activity had shifted northward. In 1655, as colonists were claiming land north of Occohannock Creek, fifteen of the thirty-one unclaimed, less desirable tracts south of that creek were landlocked (twelve more were on the seaside). Only under special circumstances would someone be interested in acreage without access to water. In one of the few cases of an individual's patenting a landlocked tract, Obedience Robins claimed 450 acres adjacent to a tract he already held on the seaside. The reason for the colonists' preference for tracts with water access is

9. See patent to John Nuthall for last land patented on a new tract on Hungars Creek (*ibid.*, I, 158). For the first claim on Nuswattocks Creek, see Stephen Charlton's patent of May 10, 1638; for the last, see Thomas Johnson's patent of June 4, 1646 (*ibid.*, I, 82, 163).

Although a claim for land on the last untouched tract is not the same as a claim for the last available land, the former has been used here as a guide to the progress of taking up land. The latter may distort the overall picture by postponing the last claim until some unnoted and undesirable bit of land was patented.

10. This generalization is not affected by Ralph T. Whitelaw's occasional combination of patents into one tract. In two respects, however, his tract maps may be deceptive. First, the seemingly landlocked tracts on the peninsula between Nuswattocks and Occohannock creeks were originally included as part of a large grant to Francis Yardley (CCR-2, pp. 228–229). Second, in a very few cases, a tract that does not appear to be on water is in fact on a very small branch of a larger creek. For an example, see the patent to Michael Ricketts for land on a small branch of Hungars Creek (Nugent, ed., *Cavaliers and Pioneers*, I, 287).

obvious: it was far easier to ship Virginia's staple crop, tobacco, if it could be loaded directly onto an oceangoing vessel or transshipped on a smaller boat.[11]

In addition to preferring land near water, the settlers overwhelmingly preferred to patent land on tracts contiguous to those previously patented. The few exceptions to this rule after 1635 fall into one of two categories. The first of these included land claimed on only a handful of seaside tracts. The second, a result of the active land market from 1651 to 1655, involved several patents for land slightly beyond the northern edge of development.[12] These exceptions, however, represent a very small fraction of the total number of land claims.

The presence of Indians on the Eastern Shore may have prevented a more random patenting by instilling caution in the settlers. Although a mutually advantageous trade encouraged the maintenance of ties between the colonists and Indians, the two cultures did not coexist without friction.[13] Thus, when the Virginia Assembly passed an act in 1632 restricting contact between colonists and natives on the Western Shore, the legislators recognized the uniquely friendly situation across the bay and ordered the commanders on the Eastern Shore "to observe all good termes of amitie"; but they also cautioned local officials there that

they cause the planters to stand uppon theire guard, and not to suffer the Indians especially the Mattawombes to make any ordi-

11. Nugent, ed., *Cavaliers and Pioneers*, I, 225, 260. Transshipment by boats was common on the Eastern Shore, because many of its creeks were too shallow to accommodate larger ships. For another discussion of the preference for waterside settlement in Virginia and Maryland, see Lorena S. Walsh, "Community Networks in the Early Chesapeake," in Lois Green Carr, Philip D. Morgan, and Jean B. Russo, eds., *Colonial Chesapeake Society* (Chapel Hill, N.C., 1988), 200–201.

12. Land claimed directly across a creek from a previously patented tract has been considered contiguous. For examples of first exception, see the grants to John Foster in 1643, Charles Scarburgh in 1647, and Edward Harrington in 1653 (Nugent, ed., *Cavaliers and Pioneers*, I, 35–36, 152, 174, 285). For examples of second exception, see the patents to William Taylor in 1651, to July Gardner in 1652, and to Littleton Scarburgh and Edmund Scarburgh, Jr., in 1655. Finally, see the reference to a 1652 grant to John Robinson in a patent of Nicholas Waddelowe in 1661 (*ibid.*, I, 213, 260, 307, 414). A very early example of a grant north of Occohannock Creek was a patent received by Nathaniel Littleton in 1636 for acreage on the north bank of Nondui Creek. This was the site of a trading outpost. For a discussion of this, see Whitelaw, *Virginia's Eastern Shore*, I, 675–676.

13. McIlwaine, ed., *Minutes of the Council and General Court*, 48, 50, 104. The fullest treatment of the contact between Indians and settlers on the Eastern Shore is Joseph Douglas Deal III, "Race and Class in Colonial Virginia: Indians, Englishmen, and Africans on the Eastern Shore during the Seventeenth Century" (Ph.D. diss., University of Rochester, 1981), chap. 1.

narie resort or aboade in theire houses, and yf any English without leave resort unto theire townes, the commanders to bynd them over to the next quarter cort.[14]

Although the presence of Indian settlements may have slowed and contained the spread of the colonists' land claims, it did not stop the expansion. Thus, by 1640, as the English claimed land north of Matta-womes Creek, the Indians located on that waterway became a threat by dividing the area of white settlement into two parts. The Mattawomes, formerly feared and respected by the English, were probably the major concentration of Indians south of Occohannock Creek. And yet, with very little effort, the colonists relocated them to a seaside tract for which the Indians received a patent. In the mid-1640s, when Indians on the Western Shore attacked the English there, the Eastern Shore colonists escaped unharmed as they had in 1622. Having taken precautionary steps earlier, local officials on the peninsula, possibly in a conciliatory frame of mind, ordered several landholders to pay the Indians for the land they held.[15]

In the late 1640s and 1650s, however, relations deteriorated between the natives and the colonists, who were now pressing far north of Occo-hannock Creek. From 1648 to 1655, the official county court record reveals many Indian grants of land to the colonists. Attempting to regu-larize these transactions and maintain a semblance of fairness, the Vir-ginia Assembly in 1654 ordered Eastern Shore officials to allow the natives to sell their land to the colonists only if the majority in each Indian "towne" agreed.[16] Despite indications of the peaceful transfer of land, however, there were also references to the colonists' unfair dealings with the natives. In these cases, the Indians resorted to the county court for justice. At other times, they appeared before the local officials as supplicants: "Att this Court Ochiwamp, with other Indyans presented themselves desireinge protection and especial care of Land for their Live-inge." But nothing could stop English encroachment. Excited by rumors of impending attack by the Indians north of Occohannock Creek in the

14. William Waller Hening, ed., *The Statutes at Large: Being a Collection of All the Laws of Virginia . . . ,* I (New York, 1823), 167, 192–193. For the spatial location of the Indians on the Eastern Shore, see C. A. Weslager, "Indians of the Eastern Shore of Maryland and Virginia," in Charles B. Clark, ed., *The Eastern Shore of Maryland and Virginia,* 3 vols. (New York, 1950), I, 44; Whitelaw, *Virginia's Eastern Shore,* I, 18; and Deal, "Race and Class in Colonial Virginia," chap. 1.

15. Whitelaw, *Virginia's Eastern Shore,* I, 281–282; CCR-2, pp. 235, 265, 289.

16. CCR-3, pp. 135a, 166, 179, fol. 192, p. 223, fol. 226–p. 227, CCR-4, pp. 35, 125, fol. 225; Hening, ed., *Statutes at Large,* I, 391.

early 1650s, some of the colonists on the Eastern Shore launched a preemptive assault of their own and crushed the Indians, who never thereafter presented a serious military challenge to white usurpation.[17]

The Indians faced a numerical increase, as well as a geographical spread, of colonists. In 1625, 51 settlers lived on the peninsula. By 1634, when the Assembly designated the Eastern Shore settlement as Accomack County (renamed Northampton County in 1643), the number had increased almost eightfold to 396 men, women, and children.[18] Over the same period, the population of the Eastern Shore rose from 4.2 percent to 8 percent of the total number of colonists in Virginia and stayed close to the latter proportion of the colony's total population for the next twenty years. During those years, the total number of settlers on the Eastern Shore increased from 396 to just above 1,000.[19]

A detailed, statistical breakdown of the post-1625 English population on the Eastern Shore, although highly desirable, is impossible in the absence of necessary primary sources. For the period between 1625 and

17. CCR-3, fols. 207, 209, CCR-4, fols. 90, 225, CCR-7, fol. 13, p. 14, fol. 51 (for quotation). See Chapter 8 for a fuller treatment of the attack.

18. Annie Lash Jester and Martha Woodruff Hiden, comps., *Adventurers of Purse and Person: Virginia, 1607–1625* ([Richmond, Va.], 1964), 66–69; Warren M. Billings, ed., *The Old Dominion in the Seventeenth Century: A Documentary History of Virginia, 1606–1689* (Chapel Hill, N.C., 1975), 117–118. This was the lowest population of the eight newly formed shires. Hening, ed., *Statutes at Large*, I, 224, 249.

19. These figures are from Morgan, *American Slavery, American Freedom*, appendix tables 1, 3, 4. There is some problem in estimating the population of Northampton County by 1655. According to *A Perfect Description of Virginia* ..., 7, the Eastern Shore was inhabited by 1,000 colonists in 1649 (in Peter Force, ed., *Tracts and Other Papers, Relating Principally to the Origin, Settlement, and Progress of the Colonies in North America from the Discovery of the Country to the Year 1776*, 4 vols. [Washington, D.C., 1836–1847], II). But taking the reported Northampton County tithables for 1653 (500) and using Morgan's tithable multiplier for that year (1.88) results in a population of 940. This figure is probably low. Morgan's tithable multipliers are based on population and tithable totals for all of Virginia and do not take into account regional variation. Thus, the Eastern Shore, an area settled for almost 40 years by the mid-1650s, probably had a higher proportion of women and children (that is, untithables) than frontier areas where the population was generally characterized by more single males. In 1699 the ratio of total population to tithables ranged from 1.86 in Northumberland County to 3.54 in Isle of Wight County. Northampton County and Accomack County (formed to the north of Northampton County in 1663) had ratios of 3.01 and 3.11, respectively. Both were above the overall Virginia ratio of 2.69. Assuming, not without reason, that the Northampton County ratio was higher also in 1653, we must conclude that the population of the Eastern Shore was slightly more than 1,000 in that year.

1655, there are no records of births, marriages, or deaths and no detailed militia, census, or tithable lists. The county court record constitutes the single most important primary source, and it does not allow a usable reconstruction of the peninsula's entire population, because a person's appearance there is entirely random, depending on that person's being a plaintiff, defendant, witness, or casual participant in an action. As a result, there are too many gaps and uncertainties to allow a reliable demographic picture to emerge. In particular, the lives of servants, women, and children are seriously underrepresented in the county court record, which is overwhelmingly a record of economic transactions. There is no evidence, however, that the Eastern Shore was demographically different from English settlements elsewhere in the early seventeenth-century Chesapeake region. A portrait of the English population in the Chesapeake area can be briefly sketched: a sex ratio heavily weighted toward men, an unusually youthful population, and a high mortality rate.[20]

It is possible to recover the landholding subpopulation with some confidence. From the beginning of settlement until the end of 1655, 422 individuals are known to have held land; 315, or three-quarters of the total, were resident adults at the time of first landholding.[21] The breakdown for all landholders is as follows:

Adult residents	315
Minors	55
Nonresidents	29
Questionable residents	23
Total	422

When these individuals first acquired land is noted as well:

20. For a summary statement of the demographic situation in the 17th-century Chesapeake, see Daniel Blake Smith, "Mortality and Family in the Colonial Chesapeake," *Journal of Interdisciplinary History*, VIII (1977–1978), 410–418. See also Lorena S. Walsh, " 'Till Death Us Do Part': Marriage and Family in Seventeenth-Century Maryland," in Thad W. Tate and David L. Ammerman, eds., *The Chesapeake in the Seventeenth Century: Essays on Anglo-American Society* (Chapel Hill, N.C., 1979), 127–128; the substantial literature on demography is cited in the same volume by Thad W. Tate, "The Seventeenth-Century Chesapeake and Its Modern Historians," 34–35. Finally, see Daniel Blake Smith, "The Study of the Family in Early America: Trends, Problems, and Prospects," *WMQ*, 3d Ser., XXXIX (1982), 9–10; and introduction to Carr, Morgan, and Russo, eds., *Colonial Chesapeake Society*, 4.

21. The date of first landholding can be either the date of a person's first land transaction or the date when a person is first mentioned as holding land.

1620–	1636–	1641–	1646–	1651–
1635	1640	1645	1650	1655
68	72	87	82	113

The focus of the rest of this study is the lives of these landholders.

Thus far, the analysis of English settlement on the Eastern Shore has depicted the general directions of land claims. It has also stressed the overwhelming preference for patenting contiguous acreage with access to water, patterns conducive to keeping the growing number of colonists in contact with one another and therefore important for the development of a societal network. Equally important were the modes of transportation that determined the range of interpersonal contact. The state of overland travel can be summarized briefly. In order to visit another Eastern Shore resident, an individual normally would have walked, probably following the most direct route through fields and woods. This pedestrian mode of travel was necessary for two reasons. First, very few individuals had access to a horse. Not until 1639 was the first license issued to furnish Virginia with horses and other beasts of carriage. No evidence exists of horses' being in use on the Eastern Shore until 1642, when Argoll Yardley bought one from George Ludlow. By 1650 only six more landholders are known to have acquired one. This figure represents 2.9 percent of the total number of adult resident landholders up to that time. The situation was marginally better by 1655, at which time twenty-two landholders, or 6.8 percent of the total number of adult resident landholders to that date, are known to have owned, or at least had the use of, a horse. Nevertheless, horses remained an expensive luxury until later in the seventeenth century.[22]

A related reason for the overwhelming reliance on walking rather than riding may have been the lack of convenient roadways. It is difficult to determine to what extent paths that were perfectly adequate for walking were also satisfactory for riding. But stray references reveal some problems. When Richard Hill and Edmund Scarburgh rode together, they could ride at a gallop "only in the playne path betweene Dunn and Pimminoe." Certain paths were distinguished from others as "horse paths," presumably because they were more convenient for transit by horse. Yet

22. "Virginia in 1639–40," *VMHB*, XIII (1905–1906), 380–381; CCR-2, p. 250; Carville V. Earle, *The Evolution of a Tidewater Settlement System: All Hallow's Parish, Maryland, 1650–1783* (Chicago, 1975), 144–145. An order of the county court in 1655 indicates that some individuals used the horses of others without permission (CCR-5, p. 135).

it is indicative of the scarcity of horses until the early 1650s that the distinction of a horse path from any other path did not appear in the record until 1655.[23]

Why were so few paths convenient for travel by horse? Part of the answer is that the colonists were more concerned with planting crops and constructing houses and outbuildings than with developing and maintaining roads, a commitment that would have required expenditure of scarce capital and labor. In the early years, when settlement was not too spread out and access not a problem, footpaths sufficed. But after the first years of struggle were over and as the area of settlement spread, another obstacle hindered the development of roads: the geography of the Eastern Shore. Numerous creeks, some of them quite wide, and innumerable branches made the terrain particularly inconvenient for long trips by horse. Paths frequently connected the heads of different waterways.[24] But problems arose when a path reached the bank of a creek. References to bridges reveal the nature of the difficulty.

As people claimed land on the bayside creeks from south to north, bridges were built to carry traffic over the heads of the larger waterways: first Hungars Creek, then Nuswattocks and Occohannock creeks, and finally the creeks further north. At some crossings, the colonists used bridges built by the Indians.[25] But these structures, like those built by the colonists, were not permanent and required continual maintenance and rebuilding. The bridge at the head of Hungars Creek is a good example. There had been a bridge at that crossing for at least five years when the churchwardens presented John Towlson for destroying it in 1648. The commissioners of the county court ordered that the inhabitants living near Hungars Creek build a bridge sufficient "either for horsemen or footemen to passe over." Three years later, however, Towlson appeared before the court again for failing in his obligation to replace the bridge that he had ruined. The commissioners ordered him to erect a bridge and allocated one hogshead of tobacco (a fine owed by Benjamin Mathews in another case heard at the same court) to help toward the cost of construction.[26] But problems continued in the maintenance of a bridge over

23. CCR-3, p. 111 (for quotation), CCR-5, fol. 40–fol. 41, CCR-7, p. 67–fol. 67.

24. CCR-3, fol. 166, CCR-4, p. 184, CCR-5, fol. 40–fol. 41, fol. 91–p. 92, CCR-7, p. 67–fol. 67; Nugent, ed., *Cavaliers and Pioneers*, I, 339.

25. CCR-2, pp. 302–304, CCR-3, p. 45, fol. 149, p. 150, fol. 192, CCR-4, p. 57, fol. 58, pp. 137, 184, CCR-5, p. 33, CCR-7, p. 14; Nugent, ed., *Cavaliers and Pioneers*, I, 204–205 (for quotation), 233, 324.

26. CCR-3, p. 150 (for quotation), CCR-4, p. 57, fol. 58.

Hungars Creek. In 1653 William Greening petitioned on behalf of himself, other travelers, and the public good that the commissioners take some action to replace the "rotten sticke or 2 left for a Bridge; The same beinge a high roadewaye, and necessary passage for Travillors; soe that eyther the passenger must bee constrayned to goe 3 or 4 myles aboute, or adventure both health and lyfe in goeinge over." The court ordered that a bridge be built there as quickly as possible and that the whole county contribute to the expense. William Whittington, a commissioner who lived on Hungars Creek, was to manage and oversee the business.[27]

The precarious condition of bridges must have made it difficult to travel north and south by land for those living on the more populous bayside of the peninsula. But there was an alternative: travel by water. The county supported public ferries from a very early date. The first evidence of such support in 1634 indicates that a ferry provided transportation for colonists on either side of King's Creek, the center of settlement. At one time or another ferries also plied the waters of Old Plantation and Hungars creeks.[28]

Although the convenience, reliability, and continuous operation of public water transportation are questionable, private water carriers provided an alternative for some.[29] It is impossible to determine exactly how many landholders owned a boat, but an analysis of every reference to water carriers before 1655 suggests that they were not uncommon. Wills or inventories exist for sixty-two resident adult landholders who died before 1655. Four inventories and one will include a boat as part of the estate, for 8 percent of the total.[30] Yet a thorough search of the official record reveals that, among adult resident landholders who died before 1655, 27 percent of those who left a will on record or whose estate was inventoried owned a water carrier at some point during their lives; the figure was 23 percent for those forty-seven individuals without a will or inventory. Contemporaries thought the ownership of boats to be widespread. According to a passage published in *A Perfect Description of*

27. CCR-3, fol. 212–p. 213, CCR-4, p. 117–p. 118, p. 184.
28. CCR-1, pp. 24, 129, CCR-2, pp. 141, 392, CCR-3, fol. 13, pp. 123, 170.
29. The problem of public carriers was funding. Hening, ed., *Statutes at Large*, I, 348.
30. For only one of these five decedents, however, does the court record reveal a reference to possessing a boat before death. By comparison, four wills or inventories included a horse as part of the estate, and for three of these individuals, the official record contains evidence of their ownership of horses. Clearly, the county court books were more likely to include references to an individual's owning a horse than a boat.

Virginia in 1649: "They have in their Colony Pinnaces, Barkes, great and small Boats many hundreds, for most of their Plantations stand upon the Rivers sides or up little Creeks, and but a small way into the Land so that for transportation and fishing they use many Boates."[31]

In addition to traveling on a public ferry or owning a vessel, an individual had two other ways to travel by water. First, individuals could ride to their destination in someone else's craft. For example, of the 109 adult resident landholders who died before 1655, at least 28 owned a water carrier at some time. There are, however, references to another 13 riding in the boats of other individuals. This figure is, of course, a minimum. Second, individuals could borrow or rent a water carrier from someone who owned one. Instances of this usually appear in the court record in connection with litigation to recover damages.[32]

Of crucial importance to the feasibility of water transport were craftsmen who could build and repair water carriers. No one on the Eastern Shore identified himself as a shipbuilder until 1637. Significantly, five of the eight men identified as shipbuilders appeared in the official record in 1637, just at the time when the spread of settlement created a need for transportation more convenient than that by land. The other three shipbuilders arrived by 1643. Six of the eight became landholders; the other two were associates of William Stephens, the most important boatwright on the Eastern Shore.[33] With the exception of these two nonlandholders, who left after a few years, and one shipbuilder who died in 1651, the other five lived and worked past 1655. Moreover, self-proclaimed boatwrights were not the only craftsmen qualified to work on water carriers. Some carpenters also earned part of their living in this way.[34] Thus thirteen landholding carpenters and six nonlandholding carpenters must

31. *A Perfect Description of Virginia*, 6, in Force, ed., *Tracts and Other Papers*, II. Also reflecting the importance of water transportation was legislation intended to prevent people from stealing or "loosing" the boats of others (Hening, ed., *Statutes at Large*, I, 170, 264).

32. CCR-1, pp. 8, 18, 85, 91, 95, 99, 153, CCR-2, pp. 82, 231–232, 268, CCR-3, fol. 13, CCR-4, pp. 52, 53, 175.

33. The six landholding boatwrights were John Towlson, William Berry, William Stephens, James Bruce, Ambrose Dixon, and Walter Price. The two associates of Stephens were Roger Williamson and Roger Hensfield (also called Richard Hanser). For the association among the last three (and the confusion over the name of Hensfield / Hanser), see CCR-1, pp. 102–104, 107, 126, 128, CCR-2, p. 213.

34. CCR-2, p. 259. It was not uncommon for boatwrights to refer to themselves as carpenters; John Towlson, William Berry, and William Stephens all did so at one time or another.

be included in the work force available for the supply and maintenance of boats.

Combining information on modes of transportation and on geographic expansion of settlement suggests the possibilities for contact among the colonists. Through the 1630s, the area settled on the Eastern Shore was small enough that nearly all of the inhabitants were mutually accessible either by means of an overland walk or a water carrier. The latter could have been a public ferry or a private vessel that was rented, owned, or borrowed. After 1640 the extent of settlement made overland contact very difficult for inhabitants living far apart. Travel by horse might have reduced the time required to reach distant settlers, but (as noted above) few colonists on the Eastern Shore owned horses before 1655. Furthermore, the condition of roads in this frontier society and, more important, the geographic fragmentation caused by numerous waterways hindered the widespread use of horses. It was to these waterways that the settlers turned, by necessity for long trips, by convenience for shorter. The availability of water carriers as well as craftsmen to build and maintain them reduced to some extent the obstacles to long-distance travel.

The physical possibility for contact was an important factor shaping the interactional networks linking the colonists, but the most crucial factor in the formation of local society was the human element, the settlers themselves. Who were they, and what motivated them to move to Virginia? Unfortunately, the available data fail to address these questions directly. Historians trying to grapple with them have relied for the most part on information from the lists of servants who moved to the English colonies. One historian concludes that servants "came from a variety of backgrounds covering the whole range of social rank below the peerage" and that they moved in search of work and opportunity.[35] These conclusions, useful as they are for characterizing servants in the aggregate, cannot be applied unreservedly to a specific population consisting of

35. James Horn, "Servant Emigration to the Chesapeake in the Seventeenth Century," in Tate and Ammerman, eds., *Chesapeake in the Seventeenth Century*, 94–95. For another analysis of migration and the factors shaping the movement of people, see Russell R. Menard's superb essay, "British Migration to the Chesapeake Colonies in the Seventeenth Century," in Carr, Morgan, and Russo, eds., *Colonial Chesapeake Society*, 99–132. Menard concludes "that the incentives [to move] were primarily economic and that those who moved to Maryland and Virginia did so in large part because they thought migration promised greater opportunities and a more comfortable life than staying at home" (132).

Table 1. Patent Activity

	Before 1626	1626– 1630	1631– 1635	1636– 1640	1641– 1645	1646– 1650	1651– 1655
				Number			
New patents	4	14	13	57[a]	29[b]	27	83
Repatents with new land included			1	3	4	4	5
Repatents		1	1	6	6	3	3
				Total Amount, in Acres			
New patents	12,950	1,790	5,200	17,525	14,800	13,750	49,681
Repatents with new land included			100 + 950	600 + 450	1,950 + 700	1,050 + 1,250	2,200 + 1,169
Repatents		9,000	9,000	14,850	2,850	500	3,750
				Median Size, in Acres			
Patents	1,925	75	200	250	300	450	500

[a] Includes 2 of questionable amount.   [b] Includes 1 of questionable amount.

servants and nonservants. The English backgrounds and reasons for migration of Eastern Shore landholders remain a mystery. But their lives after settlement provide some indication of the range of their hopes and the effects of their individual decisions on the development of the peninsula's society.

The trends in size of patents and total acreage involved reveal a population optimistic about the future of land investments. During the Company period, technically the colonists patented 12,950 acres on the Eastern Shore, a figure distorted by a 9,000-acre grant to Thomas Savage and a 3,700-acre grant to George Yeardley. The period 1626–1640 manifested a steady increase in the number of acres patented.[36] Thus the 6,150 acres granted between 1631 and 1635 represented a 344 percent increase over the 1,790 acres given out during the preceding five years; the 17,975 acres claimed between 1636 and 1640 roughly tripled the total of the first half of the decade. From 1641 through 1650, the total acreage claimed by the colonists decreased slightly and then leveled off. The first half of the sixth decade, however, saw a 339 percent increase over the acreage patented between 1646 and 1650. This pattern in the total acreage involved in claims for land on the Eastern Shore resembles that for all of Virginia. The land boom of the late 1630s probably reflected renewed confidence following the clarification of land policy, and the increase of the early 1650s is probably an indicator of a sharp rise in immigration. It should also be noted that both of these booms corresponded to periods of relatively high prices for tobacco.[37] This correlation is not surprising. Tobacco cultivation formed the basis of the Eastern Shore economy, which responded to changes in the price of its staple commodity.

As the total acreage involved in land patents fluctuated, one indicator showed a constant upward trend: the median acreage of land patents. From 75 acres in the period 1626–1630 to 500 acres in the period 1651–1655, the rising median reflected the increasing optimism, expanding opportunities (including available labor and capital), and rising commitment of the Virginia colonists.[38]

This same pattern emerges from an analysis of the first landholdings

36. For the purposes of this comparison of total acreage claimed, land previously granted and then repatented has been eliminated. For example, in 1639 Henry Williams patented 200 acres on Old Plantation Creek; but, because 150 acres of this was a repatent of a 1636 grant, only 50 acres are counted as new land. Nugent, ed., *Cavaliers and Pioneers*, I, 46, 101.

37. Craven, *White, Red, and Black*, 10, 14–15; Russell R. Menard, "A Note on Chesapeake Tobacco Prices, 1618–1660," *VMHB*, LXXXIV (1976), 402.

38. Susie M. Ames, *Studies of the Virginia Eastern Shore in the Seventeenth Century* (Richmond, Va., 1940), chap. 2, includes a very brief discussion of the trend in the size of patents. But her analysis is based on a sampling approach, and on occasion this leads to an unfortunate choice of years to sample. For example, Ames generalizes for the 1630s and early 1640s on the basis of patents granted from 1635 to 1637, an unusually active period of patenting following the newly announced patent policy (23). Nevertheless, although basing her conclusions on an unsystematic sampling, Ames also found an increase in the size of patents through the third quarter of the 17th century. Ronald Eugene Grim found the median acreage of patents in York County during the 1630s to be 250 acres, the same as the Eastern Shore figure ("The Absence of Towns in Seventeenth-Century Virginia: The Emergence of Service Centers in York County" [Ph.D. diss., University of Maryland, 1977], 73).

of those claiming land on the Eastern Shore through 1655. For this analysis, a first landholding could be a long-term lease, a purchase or other transfer, or a patent. With the exception of the Company period (again complicated by the large grants to Savage and Yeardley) and with the elimination of those first landholdings that were bequests, the average size of first landholding showed a continuous rise from 1626 to 1655.[39] Thus, those receiving their first land in the period 1626–1630 averaged 99 acres, and those in the 1651–1655 cohort averaged 430 acres. Of some interest is the fact that the average (excluding bequests) leveled off somewhat after reaching 393 acres in the period 1641–1645. Over the next ten years, it increased by only 37 acres. The pattern for median first acreages on the peninsula is similar to that for averages: with the exception of the period before 1630, the median acreage for the first landholding increased steadily and then leveled off by 1655.

While growth reflected optimism, commitment, and the opportunity to act on both feelings, it was not the product of a boom mentality, marked by a random exploitation of the available land resources. As we have seen, landholders on the Eastern Shore through 1655 overwhelmingly chose sites for their first holdings contiguous to land claimed earlier.[40] The exceptions to this rule tend to support it. For example, in 1636 Nathaniel Littleton patented one thousand acres at the mouth of Nondui Creek, far north of the existing line of settlement. But unlike those colonists who sought land for the purpose of settlement and farming, Littleton wanted the land at Nondui Creek as an outpost for Indian trade, a purpose that necessitated a leap over the boundary of existing claims.[41] Another exception to the general rule of contiguity lends it support. In 1636 Robert Drake received a patent for two hundred acres on the bayside in the southern part of the peninsula. Yet Drake could not have settled this land; he was still a minor. Evidently he had just arrived in Virginia with his father, mother, and sister when his father had died.

39. Bequests have been eliminated, because they were often of large acreages that represented the total of the decedents' land accumulation over a considerable period of time. This outsized acreage distorts analysis of the land accumulation pattern of the ordinary landholder.

40. Left out of this analysis as well as analyses that follow are landholders whose first holding was mentioned in primary sources but not located on Ralph T. Whitelaw's tract maps. It is not possible to determine whether these individuals acquired land contiguous to the land of another colonist.

41. See Whitelaw, *Virginia's Eastern Shore*, I, 675–676, for a discussion of Littleton's claim to this land.

Table 2. First Landholding

First Landholding	No. of New Landholders	Size of First Landholding in Acres (No. of Landholders)			
		Bequests Included		Bequests Excluded	
		Average	Median	Average	Median
Before 1626	6	3,238 (4)	1,925 (4)	3,238 (4)	1,925 (4)
1626–1630	25	328 (16)	100 (16)	99 (14)	75 (14)
1631–1635	37	502 (24)	50 (24)	136 (22)	50 (22)
1636–1640	72	235 (45)	150 (45)	214 (42)	150 (42)
1641–1645	87	345 (49)	250 (49)	393 (32)	250 (32)
1646–1650	82	414 (43)	300 (43)	421 (34)	300 (34)
1651–1655	113	507 (83)	300 (83)	430 (73)	300 (73)

Note: All acreages have been rounded to the nearest whole acre.

Table 3. Residency before Landholding

First Landholding	Median Residency in Record at First Land Claim (No. of Claimants)		
	Area of Settlement		
	First	Second	Third
1636–1645	3 years[a] (61)	4 years[a] (23)	
1646–1650	5 years (7)	6.5 years (16)	7 years (11)
1651–1655	9 years (17)	7.5 years (6)	7 years (29)

Note: Calculations exclude nonresidents, minors, and some individuals with common names.

[a]Because court records began in 1633, this figure is low.

The patent was taken out in the name of Robert Drake, but it probably represented an investment for when he came of age. These are the only examples of individuals' claiming noncontiguous land for their first landholding until the late 1640s, when a small number of new landholders claimed land near Occohannock Creek and farther north.[42]

Despite the possibility for an explosion of settlement up and down the Eastern Shore, the evidence for contiguity of first land ownership overwhelmingly indicates that the colonists followed a more orderly pattern. The same conclusion results from an examination of the location of first landholdings in successive time periods. For this analysis, the Eastern Shore has been divided into three regions. The first extends from the tip of the peninsula north to Cherrystone Creek, encompassing the area of settlement through 1635. The second region reaches from the northern edge of the first to the northern shore of Nuswattocks Creek and includes the area touched by claims during the next decade. The third region, from the southern shore of Occohannock Creek north, was first broached in the period 1646–1655. Settlers on the Eastern Shore revealed a marked preference for claiming land in the more established areas. Thus, from 1636 to 1645, when the colonists first claimed land on the shores of Hungars and Nuswattocks creeks in the second region, 73 percent of adult resident landholders chose their first acreage in the original area of settlement.[43] Similarly, in the period from 1646 to 1655, when land was being claimed north of Occohannock Creek, 27 percent of adult resident landholders chose their first landholding in the original area of settlement, and another 33 percent chose their first landholding in the second area south of Occohannock Creek.

What impact did these new landholders have on the Eastern Shore's nascent society? A useful indicator is the number of years they had lived there before claiming land. Were they more likely to be newcomers or

42. Nugent, ed., *Cavaliers and Pioneers*, I, 46; CCR-2, p. 72; Whitelaw, *Virginia's Eastern Shore*, II, 986. By 1653 Robert Drake, no longer a minor, had moved to London. He was involved in a lengthy lawsuit to recover his claim to this land. CCR-4, fol. 3, CCR-5, p. 20, CCR-7, fols. 49, 50.

Of the nine whose first landholding was not contiguous from 1647 through 1655, John West and Charles Scarburgh were minors, Randall Herle was nonresident, and John Hinman was living on the land of his wife's first husband. All of these claims would seem to have been speculative ventures.

43. This analysis excludes nonresidents, minors, and anyone whose residency on the Eastern Shore is questionable, because the first land claimed by or for them would not reflect a consideration that they would be taking up residence on the land chosen.

longtime inhabitants? In the first region—the area of original settlement—an adult resident claiming land between 1636 and 1645 had appeared in the record a median of 3 years. The median climbed from 5 to
9 years during the following two five-year periods. The same upward
trend is evident for those claiming land in the second region of settlement, from Hungars Creek to the northern bank of Nuswattocks Creek,
where the median rose from 4 years in the decade 1636–1645 to 6.5 and
then 7.5 during the next two five-year periods. In the third and last
region of settlement, the median remained constant at 7 years in the two
five-year periods after 1646, when development there had just begun.
These figures establish that the new landholders, before deciding on the
location of their first acreage, had lived on the Eastern Shore for several
years. During this period they would have had time to become accus-
tomed to the developing pattern of local interaction and behavior. This
was extremely important. It meant that, before taking on the responsible
position of landholder, these individuals had established contacts and at
least begun to learn the developing customs of Virginia.[44]

Two trends are observable from the data on length of residency before
first landholding. The first relates to developments within each of the
three regions of settlement. In the first two areas of settlement, the median number of years that an individual had appeared as a resident
before claiming land increased steadily.[45] The older the area of settlement, the longer the period of socialization before an individual became
a landholder; this tendency suggests a reduced possibility for the disruption of developing networks of interaction linking the settlers. The second trend focuses on the relationship among the three regions. Comparing the three areas of settlement in the years through 1650 reveals that
the newer the area of settlement, the longer was the median time of
residence for those claiming their first land there. In terms of the development of the society, this meant that those individuals socialized in the
local patterns for the longest time were the ones most involved in expanding the spatial bounds of the society. While this trend was broken

44. The nature of some of these contacts and customs will be explored in the next
few chapters.
45. One reason for this pattern could be that, as land was developed and became
more expensive in these areas, a prospective landholder would have required a longer
period to accumulate the resources necessary to claim any acreage. A second reason
might be that the newcomers represented a lower class of immigrants, who may have
needed more time to raise the needed capital.

from 1651 through 1655, the period of residence before landholding was still a lengthy seven years or more, whatever the area chosen.[46]

Under what circumstances did those who came to the Eastern Shore live during the years until they became landholders? Available records do not provide data as systematic and quantifiable as those for landholdings, but fragments pieced together from depositions, deeds, bills of sale, suits, and other records entered in the county court books provide strong evidence of certain common experiences. Of the 269 post-1635 landholders who were residents but not minors, at least one-tenth (28) had worked as servants for other Eastern Shore landholders. They appeared a median number of ten years in the available record before becoming landholders themselves.[47] During this prolonged period of dependence, a servant could acquire skills to prosper in Virginia, most importantly in the cultivation of tobacco. He could also learn local patterns of behavior as well as begin to form a network of contacts that could continue and spread in the years following servitude.

David Dale is an interesting study of a servant who became a landholder. First mentioned in 1636, Dale worked as a servant for John Neale, a prominent merchant with extensive landholdings on the southern tip of the Eastern Shore and a store in Kicoughtan across the Chesapeake Bay. In 1644 Neale assigned Dale three hundred acres of his own land, thereby enabling Dale to continue to have contact with the same people as he had while he was Neale's servant. After his former master's death, Dale married his widow and assigned the acreage formerly given to him by Neale to his new stepdaughter, Margaret Neale.[48]

46. The unusually large number of new resident landholders first acquiring land from 1651 to 1655 may have put a strain on the land market in the older areas of settlement and pushed first-time landholders to the north.

47. The county court record is not extensive enough to sustain a similar analysis before 1635. Also, it should be emphasized that, because of the nature of the records used, all of the figures cited for servants, laborers, tradesmen, professionals, and relatives are minima.

The figure of 28 does not include those individuals who were claimed by others as headrights. Despite the probability that in a large number of cases these individuals were servants, it is difficult to establish that relationship for any given individual.

Appearance for 10 years does not mean that the service was 10 years. A former servant could, after his period of servitude, become a laborer or tradesman, marry the heir to other land and wait to claim his own, or become a squatter, sharecropper, or tenant. Sharecropping, tenancy, and other arrangements that gave nonlandholding planters access to land will be discussed more fully in Chapter 5.

48. Dale as servant and Neale's background: CCR-1, pp. 85, 110, CCR-2, p. 390, CCR-3, p. 212, CCR-6, fol. 13; Nugent, ed., *Cavaliers and Pioneers*, I, 18, 43, 54, 55,

Another two-tenths of the 269 post-1635 adult resident landholders were laborers, tradesmen, overseers, or professionals. These individuals appeared in the record a median number of four years before claiming their first land. The separate figure for laborers was two years higher than this, so that they would have had at least six years during which to accustom themselves to local ways. Tradesmen such as smiths, carpenters, bricklayers, tailors, shoemakers, and tanners as well as overseers and professionals such as ministers, merchants, chirurgeons (or doctors), and storekeepers had two fewer years of residency than the laborers. But the nature of their occupations would have required a greater degree of continuing interaction with the local population and so would have compensated for the shorter period of socialization.

Carpenters far outnumbered tradesmen of any other craft, and William Stephens can be taken as a representative of that trade. The first reference to Stephens, a boatwright as well as a carpenter, was in connection with some tar that he had lent and wanted returned by Grace Robins, the wife of Obedience Robins. Stephens may have lived near the Robins home on Cherrystone Creek, because six years later Obedience Robins leased to him twenty acres with the housing "whereupon the said Stephens is now seated." Stephens contracted with William Hensley to plant on his ground with the help of one of Stephens's servants in return for one-half of Hensley's crop.[49]

Moreover, at least 19 percent of the post-1635 landholders who were residents and of age were related in some way to earlier landholders, who could have cushioned and guided their entry into the local society.[50] Looked at from this perspective, the four and one-half years during which these individuals appeared in the record before their first landholding seems even more significant. Focusing on those appearing for two years or less—that is, below the median—reveals the nature and importance of this type of relationship. Several married into local families and thereby received land. For example, John Baldwin described

---

68, 80, 225. Dale's own land: CCR-1, pp. 74–75, CCR-2, pp. 11, 22–26, 389, 440. Dale's marriage: CCR-2, p. 399, CCR-3, p. 106, fol. 171, CCR-4, p. 194, CCR-5, p. 108.

49. CCR-1, p. 88, CCR-2, pp. 78–81, 182, 188–189, 272–273 (for quotation), CCR-4, fol. 116.

50. This 19% does not include those individuals who were servants, laborers, tradesmen, overseers, or professionals and who were related to other landholders. They have already been discussed under other categories.

himself in 1647 as a "sojourner" at the house of John Little. Within two years Baldwin had married Mary Wilkins, the daughter of John Wilkins, who had been a resident on the Eastern Shore for at least twenty-five years. John Wilkins gave livestock, household goods, and 150 acres of land to his new son-in-law.[51]

Similarly, in 1653 Edmund Scarburgh, a resident for more than twenty-four years, gave all of his land, housing, and cattle at his Magatty Bay plantation to John Smart, the man who had just married Scarburgh's daughter Tabitha. Other men, such as Nathaniel Eaton, Andrew Jacob, and Thomas Sprigg, married widows of earlier landholders. Other relationships bound those below the median to longtime residents. Francis Pettit, George Puddington, and Thomas Teackle were all related to Obedience Robins, a prominent early resident on the Eastern Shore. John Custis was the brother of Ann Custis, who had married Argoll Yardley, a son of the former governor George Yeardley and a native of Virginia. Yardley gave his brother-in-law a twenty-one year lease to plant an orchard and to build on Yardley's extensive holdings.[52] Because of the nature of these kin relationships and the prominence of many of the landholders involved, the shorter period of socialization for this group seems less crucial to their integration into the local society.

Although the extant primary sources do not allow a complete recovery of prelandholding experiences, the known patterns for servants, laborers, tradesmen, professionals, and overseers as well as for kinsmen of earlier landholders are probably representative. Combined with the earlier analysis of timing and choice of location for first landholding, they suggest that, while the population expanded geographically and numerically, it did so in an orderly manner with minimal disruption to the developing societal network.

A brief analysis of claims for second landholding provides additional

51. CCR-3, pp. 177, 233, fol. 236; Jester and Hiden, comps., *Adventurers of Purse and Person*, 69.
52. Smart: CCR-4, p. 152. Eaton, Jacob, Sprigg: CCR-2, p. 43, CCR-4, p. 14–fol. 14; Nugent, ed., *Cavaliers and Pioneers*, I, 135. Robins: CCR-1, pp. 57–58, CCR-3, fol. 107–p. 108; Whitelaw, *Virginia's Eastern Shore*, I, 639. Yardley: Whitelaw, *Virginia's Eastern Shore*, I, 108, 289. (Note that George Yeardley's sons spelled the name as Yardley, and I have adopted the latter spelling for the sons.) Other men fitting the same pattern are Leonard Peddock, who was related to Stephen Charlton, and Francis Pott, who was related by marriage to John Severne, Stephen Charlton, and, possibly, Edmund Scarburgh and Randall Revell (CCR-3, p. 195; Nugent, ed., *Cavaliers and Pioneers*, I, 157–158; Whitelaw, *Virginia's Eastern Shore*, I, 625).

Table 4. Second Landholding

	First Acquisition of Landholding					
Measure	1626–1630	1631–1635	1636–1640	1641–1645	1646–1650	1651–1655
Second Landholding						
No. receiving	13	21	42	35	28	20
Proportion receiving	52%	57%	58%	40%	34%	18%
No. receiving within 5 years of first landholding	3	6	23	10	a	a
No. receiving within 5 years as proportion of those receiving second landholding for whom elapsed time known	33% of 9	55% of 11	85% of 27	63% of 16	a	a
Size, in acres						
Including bequests						
Average	1,338	337	335	591	311	363
Median	400	300	250	300	250	300
(No. calculated)	(13)	(16)	(35)	(27)	(20)	(15)
Excluding bequests						
Average	700	337	335	520	274	363
Median	350	300	250	275	225	300
(No. calculated)	(12)	(10)	(30)	(26)	(18)	(15)
Total Acres Held to Date[b]						
Average	1,645	323	459	679	624	508
Median	400	300	400	375	300	393
(No. calculated)	(13)	(19)	(36)	(28)	(20)	(18)
1st and 2d Landholdings						
No. contiguous	10	5	10	10	6	6
No. known noncontiguous	0	10	17	10	10	9
Median miles between		3.25	6.5	7.75	5.75	13

Note: No landholders of the before-1626 cohort claimed land twice.

[a]Because of the reduced time in which to claim second land, this figure would be distorted.   [b] These figures are minima, because all questionable acreage has been omitted.

support for this view of orderly expansion. From 1626 through 1640, slightly more than a majority of those who claimed land once received land a second time, usually within five years. After 1640 the proportion of each five-year cohort receiving more acreage declined further below a majority. This decline can be explained in two ways. First, the number of years during which to claim more land became less with each successive cohort after 1640 because of the cutoff date of 1655. But this fact would not explain the declining proportion entirely, because that proportion began to fall from 1641 to 1645, when there were still ten years or more to claim additional acreage. More important were the dramatic rise and then stabilization in the size of first landholdings from 1640 to 1655. This dramatic rise meant that those becoming landholders in this period would have had less need to increase their acreages very quickly. Their median acreage of 250–300 acres was only 100–150 acres less than the median size of all landholdings for those claiming land twice. Combining this information with the surprisingly constant median size of second landholding (250–300 acres after 1631) and of all land held to date (300–400 acres) suggests a similarity in the land opportunities and range of expectations for each five-year cohort.[53]

An analysis of the location of second landholdings also suggests regularity in development. The first point to emphasize is the proportion of landholders receiving their second landholding on an adjacent tract.[54] For the 1626–1630 cohort, all of those claiming more land did so on an adjacent tract. Between a third and a half of those in the five-year cohorts after 1630 did the same. This constant proportion claiming land near their first acreage was complemented by a slightly higher proportion claiming second holdings on tracts not adjacent to their first. The median distance between tracts of first and second landholding was 3.25 miles for the 1631 to 1635 cohort; it increased to and then hovered between 5.75 and 7.75 miles for the next three five-year cohorts. This constancy indicates a common range of experience for landholders seeking to expand their landholdings. Also, inasmuch as people were most likely to claim land with which they were familiar, it suggests the spatial context of interpersonal contacts.[55]

53. This is not meant to suggest an equality of land distribution. For more on this, see Table 9 and explanatory text.

54. Because of the difficulty of identifying land claims precisely, the following analysis is based on locating the claims according to Ralph T. Whitelaw's tract system. All distances cited are distances between the nearest edges of tracts involved.

55. This contention will be corroborated by subsequent evidence on the range of personal networks of interaction.

For the 1651–1655 cohort, the median distance to second landholding increased to thirteen miles. It reflected an effort by landholders to take advantage of the expanding land market north of Occohannock Creek. In this effort, they were following the practice of earlier landholders who had sought land in developing areas on the northern bayside creeks. For example, in the 1631–1640 cohorts virtually all landholders who claimed their second acreage at a distance above the median for their group did so in the areas then under development. Originally having settled on Old Plantation, King's, or Cherrystone creeks, they sought new or more land on Hungars or Nuswattocks creeks. Likewise, those in later cohorts, having settled in the older area or slightly to the north, were claiming land on Occohannock, Craddock, Nondui, and other northerly creeks.[56] This practice was complemented by the phenomenon of those claiming their first acreage on a northern creek then claiming their second to the south in areas of earlier settlement.[57]

Trends in size and location of first and second landholdings as well as in length of residency and personal background reveal important insights about the possibilities for contact, the attitudes and opportunities of settlers, and the preconditions for the development of a societal network. Two final sets of data help to focus attention on population and landholding by dropping in on the Eastern Shore at five-year intervals beginning in 1635 and ending in 1655. They provide valuable observations on the society by separating into cohorts those individuals who first held land through 1635, then 1636–1640, 1641–1645, and so on for a total of five cohorts by 1655. Each cohort's contribution to overall population and landholding statistics can then be measured at five-year intervals.

Five-year persistence rates—comparing the number who held land at the end of each cohort period to the total number acquiring land during

56. For a few examples of the 1631–1640 cohorts, see Jonathan Gills (CCR-2, pp. 15, 447–448; Nugent, ed., *Cavaliers and Pioneers*, I, 534–535), Thomas Smith (Nugent, ed., *Cavaliers and Pioneers*, I, 43, 115), Francis Martin (CCR-1, pp. 80, 94; Nugent, ed., *Cavaliers and Pioneers*, I, 118, 123), Elias Hartry (CCR-3, fol. 20–p. 21; Nugent, ed., *Cavaliers and Pioneers*, I, 103), and James Perrin (Nugent, ed., *Cavaliers and Pioneers*, I, 110, 139).

A few examples of later cohorts include John Johnson (CCR-2, pp. 278–279; Nugent, ed., *Cavaliers and Pioneers*, I, 260), Charles Scarburgh (Nugent, ed., *Cavaliers and Pioneers*, I, 174, 264), and George Hack (CCR-4, fol. 120; Nugent, ed., *Cavaliers and Pioneers*, I, 265).

57. See Christopher Kirke (Nugent, ed., *Cavaliers and Pioneers*, I, 119, 139) and William Whittington (CCR-3, fol. 212–p. 213; Nugent, ed., *Cavaliers and Pioneers*, I, 170).

Table 5. Numbers of Landholders

	Cohort				
Landholders	Through 1635	1636– 1640	1641– 1645	1646– 1650	1651– 1655
Total no. first hold- ing during period	68	72	87	82	113
No. holding at end of period of first holding	47	57	63	60	95
Proportion holding at end of period	69%	79%	72%	73%	84%

that period—ranged from just above two-thirds in the first cohort to just above four-fifths in the last. Thus 69 percent of those who acquired land before or during 1635 were still landholders at the end of 1635. For each of the next three cohorts, about three-quarters of new landholders persisted; for the last cohort, 84 percent. Two factors contributed to the lower rate of persistence for the initial cohort. First, because the cohort's time span ranged from about 1620 to 1635 (compared to five-year time spans for the rest of the cohorts), the landholders in the former group had a longer period during which to die, move, or lose their land. Second, landholdings for this cohort were smaller than for any subsequent group, and more of them were held as leases, an arrangement that probably contributed to individuals' falling out of the landholding group because of their tenuous position within it. Reversing these arguments helps to explain the increase in persistence from 1651 through 1655; thus, a greater initial commitment, reflected in larger first landholdings, was probably most influential in this increase. These statistics on persistence demonstrate the fluidity of population with which the Eastern Shore's developing society had to come to terms.

Tracing changes in each cohort's makeup at five-year intervals provides another perspective on population fluctuation. In particular, statistics on adult resident landholders focus attention on that group whose actions determined the shape of society on the Eastern Shore. In any given year, adult residents represented 78–87 percent of the total number of landholders. Within the first cohort, five-year persistence rates were 59–70 percent; within the second cohort, 64–76 percent; within the

Table 6. Landholders Surviving to End of Each Cohort Period

Cohort	No. Surviving				
Status	1635	1640	1645	1650	1655
Through 1635					
Minors	6	4	2	0	0
Nonresidents	4	1	1	2[a]	1
Adult residents	37	27[b]	20[c]	14[c]	10
Total	47	32	23	16	11
1636–1640					
Minors		5	5	5	1
Nonresidents		2	1	1	2[d]
Adult residents		50	37	28	20[b]
Total		57	43	34	23
1641–1645					
Minors			11	10	6
Nonresidents			5	5	4
Adult residents			47	31	30[e]
Total			63	46	40
1646–1650					
Minors				12	12
Nonresidents				0	0
Adult residents				48	37
Total				60	49
1651–1655					
Minors					21
Nonresidents					1
Adult residents					73[f]
Total					95
Overall					
Minors	6	9	18	27	40
Nonresidents	4	3	7	8	8
Adult residents	37	77	104	121	170
Total	47	89	129	156	218

[a] Includes one adult resident who became nonresident.   [b] Includes two minors who became adult residents.   [c] Includes one minor who became adult resident.
[d] Includes one minor who became nonresident.   [e] Includes three minors and one nonresident who became adult residents.   [f] Includes three questionable residents.

Table 7. Persistence of Adult Resident Landholders

Cohort	Adult Resident Landholders				
	1635	1640	1645	1650	1655
Through 1635					
No.	37	25[a]	17	10[b]	7[c]
(Deaths)		(10)	(8)	(5)	(2)
Proportion of preceding date		68%	68%	59%	70%
Proportion of total	100%	33%	17%	9%	4%
1636–1640					
No.		50	37[d]	28[e]	18[c]
(Deaths)			(10)	(6)	(9)
Proportion of preceding date			74%	76%	64%
Proportion of total		67%	37%	24%	11%
1641–1645					
No.			47	31[f]	26[b]
(Deaths)				(8)	(3)
Proportion of preceding date				66%	84%
Proportion of total			47%	27%	16%
1646–1650					
No.				48	37[g]
(Deaths)					(3)
Proportion of preceding date					80%
Proportion of total				41%	23%
1651–1655					
No.					73
(Deaths)					
Proportion of preceding date					
Proportion of total					45%

Note: Minors and nonresidents who became adult residents have been eliminated.
[a]Plus 2 disappearances. [b]Plus 1 disappearance and 1 move. [c]Plus 1 move. [d] Plus 3 disappearances. [e] Plus 2 moves and 1 person with no land left. [f] Plus 1 move, 5 disappearances, and 3 with no land left. [g] Plus 3 moves, 4 disappearances, and 1 with no land left.

Table 8. Landholdings of Adult Resident Landholders

	1635	1640	1645	1650	1655
First Landholding, through 1635					
No. of landholders	37	27	20	14	10
No. with acreage that can be estimated	24	18	16	11	8
Average acreage					
Minimum	239	902	1,602	1,478	1,351
Maximum	239	927	1,666	1,537	1,383
Median acreage					
Minimum	92	550	600	560	530
Maximum	92	600	755	700	650
First Landholding, 1636–1640					
No. of landholders		50	37	28	20
No. with acreage that can be estimated		33	21	17	12
Average acreage					
Minimum		337	383	485	487
Maximum		361	417	515	496
Median acreage					
Minimum		200	300	300	400
Maximum		250	300	340	450
First Landholding, 1641–1645					
No. of landholders			47	31	30
No. with acreage that can be estimated			18	14	17
Average acreage					
Minimum			256	629	1,459
Maximum			256	657	1,488
Median acreage					
Minimum			175	300	800
Maximum			175	325	800

Table 8. *Continued*

	1635	1640	1645	1650	1655
First Landholding, 1646–1650					
No. of landholders				48	37
No. with acreage that can be estimated				22	21
Average acreage					
Minimum				323	592
Maximum				323	632
Median acreage					
Minimum				275	400
Maximum				275	400
First Landholding, 1651–1655					
No. of landholders					73
No. with acreage that can be estimated					50
Average acreage					
Minimum					409
Maximum					417
Median acreage					
Minimum					300
Maximum					300
Overall					
No. with acreage that can be estimated	24	51	55	64	108
Average acreage					
Minimum	239	536	696	632	688
Maximum	239	560	728	656	708
Median acreage					
Minimum	92	300	300	300	400
Maximum	92	300	300	345	400

Note: There are several qualifications to the above data. (1) Land identified as "parcel" or "neck" or similar terms—and not by number of acres—is excluded, even though the dates of acquisition and sale might be known. If this were a person's only landholding in a particular year, the acreage held would be unknown; if it were one of several holdings, the total acreage would be reduced by the amount of this unknown holding, and calculations

third cohort, 66–84 percent; and within the fourth cohort, 80 percent. On average, mortality accounted for 67 percent of those lost in any five-year period. Computing ten-year persistence rates allows comparison with other studies. The persistence rate for the period 1646–1655 was 51 percent overall for all cohorts. Breaking this rate down reveals a persistence rate of 41 percent for the first cohort, 49 percent for the second, and 55 percent for the third. The persistence rate for the initial ten-year period for the first cohort was 46 percent; for the second cohort, 56 percent; and for the third cohort, 55 percent. This rate is slightly higher than that found for Surry County, Virginia, where, based on tithable lists, persistence for the first ten years of residence was 45–47 percent. But Surry's lower rate may be accounted for by the fact that tithables included both landholders and nonlandholders, the latter a more mobile element in the population. The persistence rate for Surry is, therefore, broadly comparable with that on the Eastern Shore. They both, in turn, compare to rates discovered in contemporary England. The population turnover in Virginia was not a foreign experience to these transplanted Englishmen.[58]

58. Kevin Peter Kelly, "Economic and Social Development of Seventeenth-Century Surry County, Virginia" (Ph.D. diss., University of Washington, 1972), 22–24. Kelly surveys the literature on population turnover for both old and New England.

---

for average and median holdings would also be reduced. (2) In cases of transfer without an official record thereof, ownership is assigned to the first owner for the dubious interim. (3) Acreage whose ultimate disposition is unknown is excluded from the minimum calculations and included in the maximum.

Note that the averages and medians in this table are probably high, because, for any given year, a substantial proportion of landholders held an unidentifiable amount of land. Thus the figures for the cohorts:

Cohort	Proportion Whose Acreage Is Unknown in Any Given Year
Through 1635	20%–35%
1636–1640	34%–43%
1641–1645	43%–62%
1646–1650	43%–54%
1651–1655	32%

Examining the landholding record, economic transactions, and other evidence about these individuals suggests they were probably smaller landholders. Thus, omitting them from the calculations would tend to offset the reduction caused by omitting holdings defined only as "parcel" or "neck." The resultant figures, not perfect as acreage totals, strongly suggest relationships and trends.

Table 9. Distribution of Land among Adult Resident Landholders

Decile of Landholders	1635	1640	1645	1650	1655
Top					
No. of holders	2	5	5	6	11
Low range					
No. of acres	1,050– 1,800	1,500– 3,700	1,600– 9,000	1,600– 5,100	1,300– 5,100
Percent of total	49.8	40.6	50.8	47.6	43.1
High range					
No. of acres	1,050– 1,800	1,700– 3,700	1,800– 9,000	1,950– 5,100	1,300– 5,100
Percent of total	49.8	39.5	49.5	47.2	42.7
2d					
No. of holders	3	5	6	7	11
Low range					
No. of acres	200– 800	860– 1,250	700– 1,500	700– 1,300	800– 1,200
Percent of total	24.5	19.8	17.5	15.2	14.6
High range					
No. of acres	200– 800	1,000– 1,250	800– 1,700	700– 1,600	850– 1,300
Percent of total	24.5	19.5	17.6	15.7	15.0
3d and 4th					
No. of holders	5	10	11	13	22
Low range					
No. of acres	100– 200	400– 800	400– 600	400– 600	500– 800
Percent of total	11.4	19.0	15.3	16.5	18.6
High range					
No. of acres	100– 200	400– 800	400– 800	400– 700	500– 800
Percent of total	11.4	19.9	16.3	16.4	18.9
5th and 6th					
No. of holders	5	10	11	13	22
Low range					
No. of acres	50– 100	274– 400	250– 400	300– 400	300– 500
Percent of total	6.9	11.6	9.1	10.5	12.1
High range					
No. of acres	50– 100	300– 400	300– 400	300– 400	318– 500
Percent of total	6.9	12.1	9.1	10.5	11.9

Table 9. *Continued*

Decile of Landholders	1635	1640	1645	1650	1655
7th and 8th					
No. of holders	5	10	11	13	21
Low range					
No. of acres	50	100– 250	150– 250	165– 250	200– 300
Percent of total	4.4	6.5	5.2	6.9	8.0
High range					
No. of acres	50	100– 274	150– 300	165– 300	250– 300
Percent of total	4.4	6.5	5.4	6.9	7.9
9th and 10th					
No. of holders	4	11	11	12	21
Low range					
No. of acres	30– 50	12– 100	30– 150	30– 165	30– 200
Percent of total	3.1	2.5	2.0	3.3	3.6
High range					
No. of acres	30– 50	12– 100	42– 150	42– 165	42– 200
Percent of total	3.1	2.5	2.1	3.3	3.6
Overall					
No. of holders	24	51	55	64	108
No. of acres					
Low	5,724	27,351	38,255	40,416	74,354
High	5,724	28,579	40,017	41,978	76,416

Note: See note to Table 8 for an explanation of how land was totaled for individuals and how low and high totals were calculated.

Especially significant for the continuity of a societal network are figures that indicate a given cohort's proportion of the total number of adult resident landholders in a specified year. Inevitably, with each five-year report, the proportion for any one cohort fell as its numbers dwindled and new landholders increased the total. Thus in 1655, 4 percent of the total number of adult resident landholders were from the oldest cohort, and 45 percent from the newest. Focusing on the proportion of total population for each new cohort is even more important for an understanding of the process of socialization and of the impact of new landholders on the Eastern Shore. The second cohort at first represented

67 percent of the total number of adult resident landholders to date. For the third cohort that share was 47 percent; for the fourth cohort, 41 percent; and for the fifth, 45 percent. Thus, after 1640, each new cohort represented less than half of the total number of adult resident landholders. Conversely, more than half had held land for more than five years and could provide a stabilizing influence for the newcomers. This is especially significant when viewed in conjunction with the fact that new landholders had generally resided on the Eastern Shore for several years before claiming their first land. Lengthy prelandholding residency and the stabilizing influence of a majority of settlers who had held land for more than five years helped to reduce the potentially disruptive impact of population fluctuation.

A final look at landholding focuses on total landholdings at five target dates. As with average and median size of first landholdings, the data on total landholdings reveal the same early jump in acreage followed by a leveling of averages and medians. More important, the median landholding for all cohorts on the Eastern Shore reveals a fairly constant total of three hundred to four hundred acres. The constancy of this figure not only indicates a constant experience of landholding but also suggests a commonly held perception of the optimal amount of land required to establish a plantation. This median size of landholding is comparable to that in other Chesapeake areas in a similarly early stage of development.[59]

59. For York County, Virginia, during the 1630s, see Grim, "The Absence of Towns in Seventeenth-Century Virginia," 73; for the area south of the Rappahannock River in the late 1650s, see Darrett B. Rutman and Anita H. Rutman, *A Place in Time: Middlesex County, Virginia, 1650–1750* (New York, 1984), 54; for Charles County, Maryland, in 1659 and for Somerset County, Maryland, in 1671, see Russell Robert Menard, "Economy and Society in Early Colonial Maryland" (Ph.D. diss., University of Iowa, 1975), 242; for All Hallow's Parish, Maryland, in 1675, see Earle, *The Evolution of a Tidewater Settlement System*, 203–205; for the Restoration Eastern Shore of Maryland, see Paul G. E. Clemens, "The Settlement and Growth of Maryland's Eastern Shore during the English Restoration," *Maryland Historian*, V (Fall 1974), 67–78. Menard notes a lower median of 100 acres for St. Mary's County in 1640, during a period when that county was characterized by an unusually rigid hierarchy, but the median rose to 250 acres by 1659 ("Economy and Society in Early Colonial Maryland," 242). It is also worth noting that in Surry County, Virginia, between 1660 and 1690 the size of patents that were kept intact and probably intended as plantations averaged 433 acres. This figure is not directly comparable to the averages for all landholdings on the Eastern Shore, which not surprisingly range from 100 to 300 acres higher. See Kevin P. Kelly, " 'In Dispers'd Country Plantations': Settlement Patterns in Seventeenth-Century Surry County, Virginia," in Tate and Ammerman, eds., *Chesapeake in the Seventeenth Century*, 190.

This is not to suggest that land was evenly distributed among land-holders. In any given year, the top tenth of landholders was in possession of 40.6–50.8 percent of the minimum attributable acreage (39.5–49.8 percent of the maximum). The next tenth held 14.6–24.5 percent of the minimum (15–24.5 percent of the maximum). The lowest fifth of land-holders, on the other hand, held 2–3.6 percent of the minimum (2.1–3.6 percent of the maximum). Obviously, land was not distributed equally on the Eastern Shore or elsewhere in the Chesapeake region.[60] But one point is worth noting in conjunction with these figures on land distribution. After 1640 the proportion of land held by the top fifth of landholders fell steadily from 68.3 percent to 57.7 percent minimum (from 67.1 percent to 57.7 percent maximum). As a result, each fifth below the top showed some increase in its share of the total land held. In sum, there was some shift toward the center of the landholding spectrum.

As the data on land and landholders indicate, the patterns of settlement on the Eastern Shore were conducive to the development of a societal network. In general the colonists established plantations of modest size, next to one another and on waterways. All of these patterns maximized the possibility for contact in a nonnuclear settlement. But it is important to stress that the settlement was in fact nonnuclear. Although holdings were smaller and population denser in the area of earliest settlement on Old Plantation, King's, and Cherrystone creeks, elsewhere settlers on larger holdings were more separated from their neighbors. Landholders were seated on plantations large enough to put them out of sight of their nearest neighbors. The need for sufficient acreage to allow tobacco-worn fields to lie fallow for a lengthy period before being rotated back into production may have influenced this settlement pattern. But the consequent residential isolation did not imply self-sufficiency or an antisocial attitude.[61]

60. The Eastern Shore's inequitable distribution is quite similar to that found by Lorena Seebach Walsh in Charles County, Maryland: "Charles County, Maryland, 1658–1705: A Study of Chesapeake Social and Political Structure" (Ph.D. diss., Michigan State University, 1977), 394–395.

61. Kelly, " 'In Dispers'd Country Plantations,' " in Tate and Ammerman, eds., *Chesapeake in the Seventeenth Century*, 183, 191. For a discussion of tobacco cultivation and the long-fallow system, see Morgan, *American Slavery, American Freedom*, 141–142; Rutman and Rutman, *A Place in Time: Middlesex County*, 40–41; and Earle, *Evolution of a Tidewater Settlement System*, 216–217. These historians provide a corrective to the older view that tobacco farming in the Chesapeake was slovenly and wasteful. See Philip Alexander Bruce, *Economic History of Virginia in the Seventeenth Century: An Inquiry into the Material Condition of the People Based*

Finally, certain trends cushioned the disruptive effect of a continual addition of new landholders. The tendency for more recent residents to locate in older areas of settlement, and for more long-term residents to claim in newer areas, would have allowed the development and spread of a common social pattern. The lengthy period of socialization for the average landholder would have achieved this same result by exposing the servant, laborer, tradesman, overseer, professional, or kinsman to the developing local patterns of interaction and behavior. Finally, after the initial period of settlement, new landholders in any five-year cohort never exceeded half of the total number of landholders. Therefore, despite the population's high level of mortality, the rate of persistence for landholders was sufficient to provide continuity of personnel for social interaction.

---

upon Original and Contemporaneous Records, 2 vols. (New York, 1896), I, 323; Craven, *Southern Colonies*, 220–222.

Contact despite residential isolation will be discussed in later chapters. See also Walsh, "Charles County, Maryland, 1658–1705," 9–10.

3 Family and Kinship

DEMOGRAPHIC FACTORS characteristic of the Chesa-
peake colonies conditioned the development of a societal web on the
Eastern Shore. High mortality, a preponderance of men in the population, and a late age at marriage had a powerful influence, particularly on
the formation and continuance of ties of kinship. Yet, although fragile,
these ties were not insignificant. It is important to know what proportion
of new landholders had relatives on the Eastern Shore, what proportion
formed kin networks after claiming land. It is essential to determine
whether relatives lived near one another and how the kin network functioned. These factors defined the role played by family and kinship in
binding the local population together.[1]

In June 1636 Thomas Smith received a patent for 150 acres on Old
Plantation Creek. This was his first land on the Eastern Shore. He substantiated his claim by presenting the names for three headrights: one for
himself, one for his wife Sarah, and one for his daughter Ann.[2] At this

1. For some of the literature on 17th-century Chesapeake demography and family,
see Irene W. D. Hecht, "The Virginia Muster of 1624/5 as a Source for Demographic
History," *WMQ*, 3d Ser., XXX (1973), 65–92; Lorena S. Walsh and Russell R.
Menard, "Death in the Chesapeake: Two Life Tables for Men in Early Colonial
Maryland," *MHM*, LXIX (1974), 211–227; Edmund S. Morgan, *American Slavery,
American Freedom: The Ordeal of Colonial Virginia* (New York, 1975), 158–179;
Lois Green Carr, "The Development of the Maryland Orphans' Court, 1654–1715,"
and Russell R. Menard, "Immigrants and Their Increase: The Process of Population
Growth in Early Colonial Maryland," in Aubrey C. Land et al., eds., *Law, Society,
and Politics in Early Maryland* (Baltimore, 1977), 41–64, 88–110; Daniel Blake
Smith, "Mortality and Family in the Colonial Chesapeake," *Journal of Interdisciplin-
ary History*, VIII (1977–1978), 403–427; Lorena S. Walsh, " 'Till Death Us Do Part':
Marriage and Family in Seventeenth-Century Maryland," and Darrett B. Rutman and
Anita H. Rutman, " 'Now-Wives and Sons-in-Law': Parental Death in a Seventeenth-
Century Virginia County," in Thad W. Tate and David L. Ammerman, eds., *The
Chesapeake in the Seventeenth Century: Essays on Anglo-American Society* (Chapel
Hill, N.C., 1979), 126–182. Daniel Blake Smith, "The Study of the Family in Early
America: Trends, Problems, and Prospects," *WMQ*, 3d Ser., XXXIX (1982), 3–28;
introduction to Lois Green Carr, Philip D. Morgan, and Jean B. Russo, eds., *Colonial
Chesapeake Society* (Chapel Hill, N.C., 1988), 4–6.
2. Nell Marion Nugent, ed., *Cavaliers and Pioneers: Abstracts of Virginia Land
Patents and Grants*, I, 1623–1666, II, 1666–1695 (Richmond, Va., 1934, 1977), I,
43; see also the patents of James Berry, William Jones, William Whittington, and

time he had no other ties of kinship on the Eastern Shore. His situation was not unusual; it characterized about one-quarter of the 315 individuals who became landholders through 1655 and who were residents and adults at the time of first landholding. Some of them already had a spouse; some also had children; some had children with no spouse. Whatever the combination, the rudiments of a nuclear family were present.

Another quarter of the pre-1655 resident adult landholders had more extensive kin relationships at the time when they first acquired acreage. Although sometimes married and sometimes parents as well, what distinguished these individuals was the existence of ties of kinship outside a nuclear family. Aunts, uncles, nieces, nephews, cousins, siblings, and in-laws proliferated in varied combinations. Sometimes only one other relative appeared; at other times, a new landholder was related to several other residents on the Eastern Shore. An example was George Parker, who patented his first land in 1650. Just the year before, his brother Robert Parker had patented his own first land on the Eastern Shore. In addition, George Parker was a cousin of Anthony West, whose son John became a landholder in 1650. Through Anthony West, Parker also was related to Ralph Barlow, the husband of West's daughter Kathryne and a patentee in 1649.[3]

These ties of kinship influenced the decision of where to acquire a first landholding. With very few exceptions, a new landholder with relatives already on the Eastern Shore located on either an adjacent tract or one nearby. When John Custis first arrived, he actually leased land from his brother-in-law Argoll Yardley. William Cotton, minister on the Eastern Shore in the 1630s, married Ann, the daughter of Thomas Graves, who held land on the same tract as the glebe land. Cotton patented his first land across a creek from that of William Stone, who had married Verlinda Graves, the sister of Ann (Graves) Cotton.[4]

William Westerhouse, 43, 123, 170, 294. Finally, see Richard Bunduch: CCR-3, fol. 163; Nugent, ed., *Cavaliers and Pioneers*, I, 296.

3. CCR-2, pp. 115–116, CCR-4, p. 83, fol. 219–p. 220; Nugent, ed., *Cavaliers and Pioneers*, I, 185, 193; Ralph T. Whitelaw, *Virginia's Eastern Shore: A History of Northampton and Accomack Counties*, 2 vols. (Richmond, Va., 1951), I, 649.

4. Whitelaw, *Virginia's Eastern Shore*, I, 140, 289; CCR-1, pp. 10–11; Nugent, ed., *Cavaliers and Pioneers*, I, 13, 27–28, 59; Annie Lash Jester and Martha Woodruff Hiden, comps., *Adventurers of Purse and Person: Virginia, 1607–1625* ([Richmond, Va.], 1964), 190. Darrett B. Rutman and Anita H. Rutman also note the phenomenon of relatives living near one another: *A Place in Time: Middlesex County, Virginia, 1650–1750* (New York, 1984), 49–51.

Although almost one-half of the adult residents who acquired land before 1655 had either nuclear or other kinship ties with individuals on the Eastern Shore at the time of acquisition, slightly more than one-half did not. Yet more than half of this latter group formed such ties before 1655. For most of these landholders, the newly formed relationships were those of marriage and parenthood. Such was the case for Christopher Kirke. At the time he first patented land in 1640, he had no local relatives. By the time of his death thirteen years later, he left bequests to his wife Alice and his children, Christopher, Mary, and Rebecca.[5]

Christopher Kirke's experience illustrates the nascent kin network of the vast majority of those individuals forming their first kin ties after they became landholders, but another, smaller group exhibited developing networks that extended beyond the nuclear family.[6] For example, when Obedience Robins bought his first acreage on Cherrystone Creek, he was not related to any other Eastern Shore inhabitant. He was not a bachelor for long, however, before he married Grace Waters, the widow of Edward Waters, formerly of Elizabeth City County, Virginia. Grace Waters-Robins already had two children by her earlier marriage, William and Margaret Waters. As the years passed, she bore at least five Robins children: Dorothy, John, Mary, Frances, and Obedience Robins, Jr. Meanwhile, by the mid-1630s, several other inhabitants on the Eastern Shore had identified themselves as relatives of Obedience Robins. Francis Pettit referred to himself in 1636 as the "brother" of Robins. Whether he meant stepbrother or brother-in-law is uncertain, because both usages were common. But a kin relationship was definitely involved, because in later years another Eastern Shore resident, Mrs. Frances Flood, the aunt of Francis Pettit, Jr., also referred to Robins as "brother." Of a less questionable nature is the relationship of Obedience Robins to Edward Robins, definitely a brother. Edward, although not a full-time resident on the Eastern Shore, did own land there that his daughters Elizabeth and Rachel Robins inherited after his death in 1641. In addition, by the mid-1640s Jane Puddington, the sister-in-law of Richard Robins (Obedience Robins's brother who was still in England), had appeared in Northampton County with her husband George. A final kin connection was

5. CCR-4, p. 134; Nugent, ed., *Cavaliers and Pioneers,* I, 119. Of the 80 who appear to have had no relatives on the Eastern Shore by 1655, 35 lived beyond that date and may have formed kinship ties then.
6. It is possible that some of those for whom only a nuclear family tie can be found before 1655 may have formed a more elaborate kin network after that date.

formed by 1650, when Dorothy, the daughter of Obedience and Grace Robins, married Mountjoy Eveling.[7]

A landholder whose kin network developed in this way generally saw his relatives settle nearby. This observation mirrors the earlier one that newly arrived settlers usually located near their relatives. Focusing on the already resident landholder, however, reveals a different perspective on this phenomenon. Consider again the example of Obedience Robins and his elaborating kin network. By 1647 Robins held a large acreage from Cherrystone Creek to the seaside. His brother Edward Robins leased land on a tract that was at the mouth of that creek and adjacent to a tract owned by Obedience. When Edward died in 1641, his daughters Elizabeth and Rachel inherited 1,000 acres that their father had bought at the head of Cherrystone Creek near their uncle. Meanwhile, Francis Pettit, the "brother" of Obedience Robins, had arrived in the mid-1630s and purchased land and housing from an earlier resident. Although the location of this acreage cannot be determined, Pettit definitely lived on Cherrystone Creek by 1644. Likewise, George and Jane Puddington, related to Obedience Robins through his brother Richard in England, held land on the same waterway. When Dorothy, the daughter of Obedience Robins, married Mountjoy Eveling, her father gave them 450 acres contiguous to his own holdings. Mountjoy added to this a purchase of 200 acres on the adjacent tract, sold to him by Elizabeth and Rachel Robins, cousins of Dorothy (Robins) Eveling. Elizabeth and Rachel also leased land there to Dorothy's stepbrother William Waters.[8]

Relatives probably settled near one another for two reasons. First, settlement near relatives—near people known and trusted—provided a bit of security in the New World. As will be demonstrated shortly, kin relied on one another for everyday support as well as in emergencies. Second, individuals who had immigrated more recently turned naturally to their already resident relatives for advice on the best land and location available. The latter in turn knew most about the area within a limited radius of their own tracts, a fact suggested already by the distance be-

7. CCR-1, pp. 57–58, CCR-2, pp. 65, 85–86, 460–461, CCR-3, fol. 107–p. 108, fol. 221–fol. 222, CCR-5, fol. 25–p. 26; Nugent, ed., *Cavaliers and Pioneers*, I, 167; Jester and Hiden, comps., *Adventurers of Purse and Person*, 256–257; Whitelaw, *Virginia's Eastern Shore*, I, 176, 218; "The Randolph Manuscript," *VMHB*, XVIII (1910), 21.

8. CCR-1, pp. 105, 110, 113, 130, CCR-2, pp. 14, 359–360, 460–461, CCR-4, fol. 174, CCR-7, p. 67–fol. 67, fol. 71; Nugent, ed., *Cavaliers and Pioneers*, I, 152, 224–225; Whitelaw, *Virginia's Eastern Shore*, I, 178.

tween first and second landholdings. (This observation will be reinforced later by additional evidence of the short radius that circumscribed the interactional world of the colonists.) Thus, when asked by their relatives where to settle, the old-timers probably suggested locations near themselves.

The general tendency to settle near already resident relatives facilitated contact among kin. Examples of interaction among relatives appear frequently in the county court record. John Pott, related to John Severne through his uncle Francis Pott, mentioned in the course of a deposition that he had been "at his brothers John Seavernes house" when he heard a slanderous statement made by another visitor. In a separate case concerning slander, Sarah Hinman revealed several such contacts. She recounted how, after Sunday sermon, she and her husband John and her daughter Ann (by then married to John Tilney and living apart from her parents) had dined together at a friend's house. Sarah also told of a visit at the house of her cousin Richard Baily. Although such comments are almost invariably brief, their profusion throughout the court record testifies to an active sociability among kin.[9]

Another, more cryptic type of evidence for the contact among relatives was the frequency with which individuals witnessed legal instruments involving their relatives. For example, John Custis witnessed several transactions involving his brother-in-law Argoll Yardley: a lease of land from Yardley to Nicholas Granger, a confirmation by Yardley of a sale of land by his brother Francis Yardley, and a power of attorney granted to Argoll Yardley by Thomas Burbage. Similarly, Leonard Peddock appeared as a witness to a number of legal instruments involving his relative Stephen Charlton.[10]

Highly visible throughout the official record are references to favors

9. For Pott: CCR-2, pp. 59–60; Whitelaw, *Virginia's Eastern Shore*, I, 397. For Hinman: CCR-3, fol. 142, CCR-5, p. 12–p. 13, p. 16–p. 17, p. 74–p. 75. Other examples include the contact between Obedience Robins and his "brother" Francis Pettit (CCR-1, pp. 57–58), between John Foster and his brother Armstrong Foster (CCR-2, pp. 191–194), and between Robert Berry and his father-in-law David Wheatley (CCR-4, fol. 11, p. 18).

10. For Yardley: CCR-4, p. 172–p. 173, CCR-5, pp. 51, 70. For the Peddock-Charlton contacts, see CCR-3, fols. 26, 67, CCR-4, fol. 28. For similar contacts between William Berriman and his sister Jane Jackson, see CCR-2, p. 367, and Whitelaw, *Virginia's Eastern Shore*, I, 444; between Thomas Butteris and his kinsman John Johnson, see CCR-4, p. 172–p. 173; and among members of the Barlow-West-Parker-Elsey clan, see CCR-4, p. 136–fol. 136, CCR-5, pp. 51, 70, 107, fol. 151, and CCR-7, p. 2.

and gifts exchanged among relatives. A quick overview of such actions gives an idea of their range and variability. When John Parramore had to put up a recognizance for his appearance at the next county court in connection with a case at suit, Thomas Hunt, the stepfather of Parramore's wife Jane, put up security with him. Bridgett Billiott, recently widowed, called on Armstrong Foster, the brother of her first husband John Foster, to act as feoffee-in-trust for a gift of cattle to her children. James Barnaby gave a calf to his "Cosine and godson" John Whitehead and provided "that the male Cattle shalbe disposed withall for his good and godlie education and the female to run on for a stocke till hee . . . come to maturitye of yeares att Sixteene yeares of age." Similarly John Stringer gave two cows to his niece Mary Games with the stipulation that in the event of her death the livestock and its increase would revert to his son Richard. When Mary Games did die in her minority, however, father and son both agreed that the cows should go to Ann Games, mother of Mary and sister of John Stringer.[11]

In addition to such favors and gifts, kin also exchanged informal loans. John Dorman recounted in a deposition how he had gone with William Melling, a land surveyor, to the house of Edmund Scarburgh, Melling's cousin and also a land surveyor. After confirming that a particular tract had not been taken up earlier, Scarburgh encouraged Melling: "Therefore (Coussen Mellinge) . . . proceed on; I will not bee your hinderance; but will further you in what I can; And take my instruments agayne alongst with you (which . . . Melling did then carrye to deliver him)." Another example of lending is George Parker's loan of "one case of English stronge waters" to his kinsman Ralph Barlow.[12]

Exchanges of a more material nature also marked contact among relatives. The sale or leasing of land to kin has been mentioned already. Other marketable commodities also changed hands. As might be expected in the labor-intensive economy of Virginia, servants were an important part of exchange among relatives. In fact, on occasion, individuals actually appeared as servants for their kin. Francis Stockley transported his brother John Stockley into Virginia in return for John's labor for three years "as his proper servant." John Pott claimed part of the

11. For Parramore-Hunt, see CCR-2, pp. 202–203; for Billiott-Foster, see CCR-2, pp. 191–194, CCR-5, p. 8–fol. 8; for Barnaby-Whitehead, see CCR-4, p. 34; for Stringer-Games, see CCR-5, fol. 41, p. 49–fol. 49.

12. For Scarburgh-Melling, see CCR-5, p. 125; for Barlow-Parker, see CCR-4, p. 158.

estate of his kinsman John Severne in payment for "his service and Labour spent in the said Severns imployment." Although not a servant, William Waters was employed on a voyage to Holland by his stepfather Obedience Robins as well as by Argoll Yardley and John Wilkins. Besides land and labor, many transactions among relatives involved livestock, another sine qua non for a developing rural economy. The most common indicator of economic contact, however, appears in the form of tobacco or currency due on the death of one of the parties to the deal.[13]

On rare occasions relatives clashed over such contracts and exchanges. Inasmuch as evidence for economic contact among kin comes from the official record of the county court, such conflicts assume an inordinate visibility. To put them into perspective, it should be noted that these conflicts represent a very small fraction of the total number of economic contacts. Two deals that went awry involved the construction of housing. One was summarized in the course of a deposition by Francis Pettit, who related how he had arrived at the house of John Savage with the latter's cousin Thomas Savage. On arrival Thomas

> Asked the said John Savage saying how is it cozen. And John Savage replyed saying I am much dampnifyed for want of my house. . . . Then the said Tho: Savage replyed saying I think I did give you a courtesie in not comeing, for I should have but eaten upp your Victualls the weather being soe vehement cold.

A month later Thomas Savage was working on the house. The other difference concerning construction occurred between John Wilkins and his son-in-law John Baldwin over the latter's nonperformance of a building contract.[14]

Although mentioned in depositions, neither of the preceding conflicts seems to have prompted action by the county court. There may have been some hesitancy to prosecute relatives unless the stakes were high. Two cases involving Stephen Charlton illustrate this point. In the spring

13. Servants exchanged: CCR-3, fol. 34, CCR-4, p. 151–fol. 151. Kin as servants: CCR-2, pp. 13, 65, 399, CCR-3, fol. 15; see also John Mapp's references to his master John Johnson, Sr., who was also his uncle (CCR-4, fol. 98, p. 130, CCR-7, fol. 74). Waters: CCR-3, fol. 30, p. 36; see also the debt owed by John Stringer to his relative William Andrews (CCR-3, fol. 13, p. 25). Livestock: CCR-4, p. 151, CCR-5, p. 83–fol. 83, CCR-7, p. 2. Tobacco: CCR-3, fol. 176, CCR-4, p. 158, fol. 204, CCR-5, fol. 151, CCR-6, fols. 7, 8, and unnumbered fragmentary pages at the end of the volume, CCR-7, p. 57–fol. 57.

14. CCR-3, p. 35–fol. 35, p. 241.

following his marriage to Ann West, who was the widow of Anthony West, Charlton sold a colt to his stepson John West. Having received about a third of the purchase price, Charlton impatiently awaited the rest of the payment. Discussing the problem with Thomas Harmanson, Charlton explained that "hee was constrained to let the payment of the Tobacco alone (for causeinge difference between him and his wife)."[15] Apparently a happy marriage was worth more to him than two-thirds of the price of a young horse. But ties of kinship did not always prevent the institution of legal proceedings. Before Stephen Charlton married Ann West, he had been married to Bridgett (Pott) Severne, the sister of Francis Pott. After concluding a substantial deal for black servants and cattle, the brothers-in-law had disagreed about Charlton's payment. The case came before the county court, which referred it to the quarter court at James City. At the proceedings there, the governor and Council ordered that the case be heard again by the county commissioners, provided that two councillors from the Eastern Shore and Captain Claiborne were present. The county court finally reached a decision.[16]

The foregoing description of the types of contacts that linked relatives, although anecdotal, is suggestive. A clearer idea of the frequency of these links is hindered by the fact that the proceedings of the county court did not usually record sociable visits, gifts, favors, and economic exchanges. References to these actions, by their very nature, must be considered as random rather than systematic. Nevertheless, a more complete understanding of the kin network and its functioning is not entirely inaccessible. The official record, although not comprehensive in its references to the types of action discussed thus far, is far more complete in documenting death and its effects, for two reasons. First, the need to probate the estate of the deceased, in combination with the effort to settle debts and credits, usually involved the court actively. Second, the need to care for the interests of the surviving children frequently resulted in recorded actions. In addition to these two main categories of evidence, there exists a large residual category of random references to deaths and the actions that followed. Viewed together, the evidence relating to mortality and its consequences is voluminous and reveals many facets of the kin network.

A rigorous statistical analysis of mortality on the Eastern Shore cannot be squeezed from existing documents, but some information is available.

15. CCR-5, fol. 108.
16. CCR-4, p. 28–fol. 28, p. 81–fol. 81; Whitelaw, *Virginia's Eastern Shore*, I, 397.

Table 10. Age at Death of Resident Landholders

Age	No. of Dead, Higher Bracket	Proportion of Total Deaths	No. of Dead Lower Bracket	Proportion of Total Deaths
25–29	1		2	
30–34	6		8	
35–39	14	77%	14	74%
40–44	10		7	
45–49	3		3	
50–54	4		4	
55–59	1		1	

Note: Because of uncertain death dates and contradictory ages given in the county court record, ages at death have been entered in two columns, one reflecting the higher age, the other reflecting the lower.

Of the 315 adult resident landholders who had appeared before the mid-1650s, at least a third (109) died before 1655. This loss of population was supplemented by another fifth of the total adult resident landholders, who either moved or disappeared from the court record, presumably because of death or mobility. Therefore, slightly fewer than one-half of the 315 adult resident landholders before 1655 were alive on the Eastern Shore after that date. It is clear that the Eastern Shore was not immune to the high mortality characteristic of other English settlements in the Chesapeake region during the seventeenth century.

More important for the argument here is the age breakdown of those who died. Such information is available for slightly more than a third of the dead, and there is no reason to think that it is unrepresentative. About three-quarters of those who died did so between the ages of thirty and forty-four; at least a third of those who died did so between thirty-five and thirty-nine. Again, this experience fits the pattern noted for other populations in the Chesapeake during this century.[17] This age dis-

17. Ages are scattered at random throughout the county court record, usually in connection with depositions. There are two problems associated with an effort to compile them for analysis. First, there is an occasional variation of age given for the same person; the difference, however, is rarely more than a year or two. Second, sometimes the date of death can be determined only within one or two years. Nevertheless, these uncertainties do not change the generalizations made here.

Walsh and Menard note a similarly high mortality in the age bracket 30–50, in "Death in the Chesapeake," *MHM*, LXIX (1974), 217. Although their figures are not strictly comparable to those presented here because of a different base population, the

tribution for decedents guaranteed that a large proportion of them would be survived by spouses or children or both. About 16 percent of adult resident landholders died with neither surviving spouse nor orphan referred to in the court record. One-half, however, left behind both spouse and offspring; a quarter left a spouse only; and about one-twelfth left offspring and no spouse. How the survivors responded to this traumatic event, what happened to them, and how other Eastern Shore relatives were involved in the adjustment all reveal a great deal, not only about the impact of mortality on the nuclear family but also about the functioning of the kin network.

In nearly every instance of death's claiming the landholding head of a family, the widow, or relict, played an important role in the settlement of the estate. This role was legitimated in one of two ways. First, the husband could have designated his wife as executrix of his will. In virtually all recorded wills, the widow was so named, occasionally with supervisors or overseers designated as well. Moreover, there are many references to widows as executrices even in the absence of a will on record.[18] But there must have been a will in these cases as well, because the legal definition of an executor / executrix is "a person appointed by a testator to carry out the directions and requests in his will, and to dispose of the property according to his testamentary provisions after his decease."[19] It is clear that the county officials knew the legal definition and used the term scrupulously. In January 1653 Christopher Kirke made his last will and testament, in which he gave his wife Alice his whole estate, with the exception of specific items for his children. Furthermore, to provide for

---

evidence of a very high death rate for those in their fourth or fifth decade is irrefutable.

18. Only two landholding wives seem to have left a husband to cope with their estates. Examples of widows appointed as executrices can be found in the wills of Thomas Wyatt, Garrett Andrews, John Wilkins, John Harlow, and William Cornish (CCR-2, p. 161, CCR-3, fol. 147–p. 148, p. 238–fol. 238, CCR-4, fol. 73, CCR-5, p. 103). Examples of widows appointed as executrices with overseers named as well can be found in the wills of John Waltham, George Traveller, John Holloway, William Cotton, John Major, and Stephen Charlton (CCR-2, pp. 46–49, 246–248, 302–304, CCR-3, p. 55, fol. 133–p. 134, CCR-5, fol. 56–p. 58). On executrices not named in will on record, see references for Elizabeth Carsley, Elizabeth Beamond, Elizabeth Weed, Elizabeth Walton, and Ann Littleton (CCR-1, p. 63, CCR-2, pp. 201–202, 432–433, CCR-4, p. 75, CCR-7, fol. 22–p. 25).

19. *Black's Law Dictionary*, 4th ed., rev. (St. Paul, Minn., 1968), s.v. "executor." See also Henry Swinburne, *A Treatise of Testaments and Last Wills*, 2 vols. (1590; reprint ed., London, 1803).

the raising of his children, he granted certain cattle "unto there mother Towards bringeinge them upp with Learneinge and in the feare of god." But he did not officially declare his wife executrix. By the next month he had died and left the county court commissioners in a quandary over his intentions. After deliberating the proper legal course, they declared:

> Its the unanimous oppinion of the Court that it was the intent and meaneinge of Christopher Kirke decd, by the sense of his last will, that his wife Alice Kirke should bee Executrix of his said will dated the 18th of January 1652 [1653]. And therefore doe adjudge Alice Kirke widdowe capable to perform all things concerneinge the said will (as an Executrix).[20]

The precision with which the commissioners and clerks of the court used the term "executrix" suggests that those wills that were not recorded also sanctioned the authority of the relict to handle the disposition of the estate; hence the references to executrices even with no will extant.

The other way by which a widow could assume this power was through a letter of administration granted by the commissioners of the county court. The need for such a grant arose in the absence of a will made by the husband. Inasmuch as almost all testators waited until they were on their deathbed before they made their wills, there was always a strong possibility that they would not live to sign them. Although the commissioners accepted nuncupative, or oral, wills on the testimony of two individuals, only three such wills are recorded for landholders.[21] In those instances where a husband died intestate, however, the relict had to appeal to the county court to be declared administratrix. Letters of administration and references to the widow as administratrix appear in about the same number of cases as do examples of the widow as executrix. In sum, except for the few instances where a widow died a short time after her husband or where the demands of creditors strained the assets at hand, a relict's control over the settlement of the estate of her deceased spouse was uncontested.[22]

20. CCR-4, p. 134, fol. 169.
21. Nearly all wills mentioned that the testator was ill. For examples, see CCR-1, pp. 161–162, CCR-2, pp. 46–49, 246–248, 293–295, 302–304, 402, 415–418, CCR-3, pp. 55, 115, fol. 133–p. 134, CCR-4, fol. 64–p. 65, fols. 65, 73, fol. 131–p. 132, p. 134, CCR-5, fol. 56–p. 58, p. 85–fol. 85, fol. 90–fol. 91, p. 103.
Nuncupative wills: CCR-2, p. 161, CCR-3, p. 224, CCR-5, fol. 73–p. 74.
22. The only example of a widow's dying before settlement of the estate is Hannah Savage-Cugley, who apparently had been sick at the same time as her husband just before his death (CCR-2, pp. 86, 117). Examples of creditors' acting as administrators are John Stringer and William Taylor (CCR-3, p. 243, CCR-4, p. 71).

The widow's next concern had to be the long-term support not only of herself but of her children as well. Moreover, the presence of stepchildren or servants, or both, frequently compounded the responsibility. Inasmuch as the widow's future security and that of her dependents usually rested on the continuing productivity of land and livestock as well as on myriad transactions involving marketing and labor supply, the task at hand must have appeared formidable. She would now have to do the work of her deceased husband as well as her own. This choice was open to her. Women frequently acted on their own or in behalf of their husbands in and out of the county court.[23] Hannah Mountney, after the death of her husband Alexander early in 1644, remained a widow at least through 1655 and maintained an extensive business that is chronicled throughout the county court record. But she was already forty-two at the time her spouse died, does not seem to have had to care for young children, and appears to have been wealthy enough not to have to worry about her future financial security.[24]

Hannah Mountney was the exception that proves the rule; and the rule for the vast majority of widows faced with the responsibilities following the death of a spouse was remarriage. Other factors undoubtedly played a part in the decision to remarry. Left alone or with dependents, some widows may have wanted the comfort and affection of a new partner. In addition, the demographic makeup of the population—with a ratio of men to women heavily weighted toward males—also may have had some influence: widows had a large field from which to choose a new husband.

Remarriage on the Eastern Shore, as well as elsewhere in the Chesapeake, usually took place within a year and almost never more than two years after the death of a spouse. For example, William Burwell died between June and September 1647. By October of the same year, his widow, who acted as administratrix of the estate, married William Denham, who took over as administrator. Likewise, the widow of John Studson, alive at least through February 1649, had a new husband by July of the same year.[25] This haste prevented any deterioration of the estate.

23. For examples, see the wives of Randall Revell, Stephen Charlton, Nathaniel Littleton, John Wilkins, Roger Moye, Richard Vaughan, Thomas Moore, Edmund Scarburgh, and David Dale (CCR-1, p. 117, CCR-2, pp. 262–263, 315, 325–326, CCR-3, fols. 8, 10, p. 129, CCR-5, fol. 92).

24. CCR-2, pp. 319, 326, CCR-5, fol. 87–p. 88.

25. Burwell: CCR-3, pp. 115, 122, fol. 158. Studson: CCR-3, pp. 166, 176. Lorena Seebach Walsh found that two-thirds of surviving marriage partners remarried within

A most important factor affecting the continuing administration and care of the estate was direct oversight. This could be achieved in one of two ways that together account for almost all instances of remarriage. First, the widow could marry someone with no land, who then lived with her on the acreage left by her deceased husband. Thus Frances, the widow of John Blower, married Roger Sanders, who owned no land, and he took up residence on the acreage of the deceased Blower. When Sanders died, his relict Frances Blower-Sanders next married William Burdett, also without land of his own. In his marriage contract with his wife-to-be, Burdett bound himself

> not to take or meddle with any of the goodes of Frances Sanders which shee now enjoyeth, or with any of her Childrens portions which they now have . . . Provided that hee the said William doth promise to manage the Cropps and other Affaires belonging unto the said Frances, or her Children.

Burdett and his wife continued to live on the land inherited by Burdett's stepson, William Blower. While there, Burdett accumulated a large acreage on adjacent tracts that allowed him to oversee his stepson's interests as well as his own. His predecessor Roger Sanders had done the same.[26]

The other way that a widow could ensure direct oversight of the estate was through marriage with someone who owned land nearby, a pattern that the Eastern Shore shared with other areas in the Chesapeake.[27] An example of this is Alice, the relict of George Traveller. The same year that her husband died, Alice married William Burdett, whose wife Frances had been dead for about two years. Both Burdett and Traveller lived on Old Plantation Creek and possibly on the same tract. When her new husband died almost immediately, Alice Traveller-Burdett next married Peter Walker, a merchant who had earlier claimed land near the tip of the peninsula about six miles away. Immediately after his marriage, however, he patented land on the same tract as his new wife's.[28] Whether the new

---

twelve months: "Charles County, Maryland, 1658–1705: A Study of Chesapeake Social and Political Structure" (Ph.D. diss., Michigan State University, 1977), 67.

26. CCR-2, pp. 126–127; Nugent, ed., *Cavaliers and Pioneers*, I, 13–15, 20, 111, 121, 129–130, 550; Whitelaw, *Virginia's Eastern Shore*, I, 138.

27. Darrett B. Rutman and Anita H. Rutman note the prevalence of widows' marrying men living nearby: *A Place in Time: Middlesex County*, 121.

28. CCR-2, pp. 126–127, 239–241, 246–248, 293–295; for Burdett's landholdings, see n. 26, above. Walker: CCR-1, pp. 130–131, CCR-2, pp. 22–26, 293–295, 387; Whitelaw, *Virginia's Eastern Shore*, I, 140.

husband moved to the home of his new wife or whether he already lived nearby, the family of the deceased was disrupted as little as possible. The estate was protected without uprooting the widow and children. Familiar surroundings and continued contact with the same local network of friends and neighbors may have helped ease the survivors' adjustment.

Moreover, when mortality removed the head of household, the survivors could count on the support of whatever kin there were on the Eastern Shore. Of the 109 adult resident landholders who are known to have died by 1655, 40 left kin on the Eastern Shore. For 16 of these decedents, a member of the kin network is known to have been involved in some aspect of the survivors' adjustment. Focusing on those 37 decedents who left wills on record, 14 had kin on the Eastern Shore.[29] For 11 of these decedents, these kin were mentioned in the wills; and for 5, some member of the kin network helped the widow and children in some way. The varied functions performed by relatives are revealed in wills, marriage contracts, and deeds of gift.

William Cotton is an example of a dying individual's seeking the help of kin to oversee the disposition of his estate. He appointed two brothers-in-law to oversee his will. Similarly, John Waltham, having included detailed instructions for the education of his son, sought the services of his brother-in-law Stephen Charlton and a friend William Roper to supervise

> this my last will and testament and of the due performance and right execution of the same in each particulaer Earnestlie intreatinge [them] to have a tender Care and respect unto my child John Waltum aswell in his Infancy as when he shall atayne his riper age and more especiallie in the particuler choyce of his education and breeding in the rudimentes of good learninge. . . . As also my desire is that my welbeloved Brother Stephen Challeton will take the paines and care of takeing up land for my said Child according to certen Indentures in my wifes possession.[30]

The county court record reveals other examples of relatives involved in the settlement of an estate and the care of children left behind. After the recently widowed Agatha Stubbings married Ralph Wormeley of

29. The number 37 includes 3 nuncupative wills; it excludes, however, 3 wills that were merely mentioned and whose contents are unknown.
30. CCR-2, pp. 46–49, CCR-3, p. 55. See also the wills of Ann Pettit and Ralph Barlow (CCR-3, fol. 221–fol. 222, CCR-4, fol. 131–p. 132).

York County, Virginia, her brother-in-law Edwin Conaway acted as attorney for her new husband, who became the administrator for the estate. On several occasions, Richard Vaughan acted as feoffee-in-trust to protect the inheritance of his niece Bridgett Charlton. When the widow of Henry Carsley died shortly after he did, she appointed her stepfather Henry Wilson to oversee her bequest to her two daughters Frances and Agnes Carsley.[31]

A statement recorded in the mid-1650s probably captures the sentiments of most individuals on the death of an Eastern Shore relative:

> This daye Capt. Jno Stringer declared (in open Court) That he hath heard some reports that hee intendeth to clayme parte of the Estate of his deceased Brother (Mr Steph: Stringer) As next heyre thereunto; Whereupon . . . Jno . . . made this answer That hee did love his Brother soe well; That hee had rather add to the Estate of his said deceased brother than take anythinge from the widdow.

Such feelings also were reflected in deeds of gift.

> John Pott of Northampton County in Virginia geneleman doe for and in consideration of the love and affection I have and beare towards my Nephew Peter Severne the younger sonne John Severne Chirurgion deceased give bequeath and deliver unto his Mother Bridgett Severne Widdow For the use of the said Peter Severne one Cowe Calfe.

Similarly, Ralph Benoni Barlow, born after the death of his father, received gifts from a grandmother and two uncles.[32]

This concern for kin was very rarely violated, but there were examples of abuse. According to the terms of the will left by his brother-in-law John Waltham, Stephen Charlton took up land for his nephew John Waltham, Jr. The acreage was adjacent to Charlton's land, and this fact may have facilitated a more effective supervision of the estate. By 1643 the widow Grace Waltham had married Richard Vaughan, and they lived on the land of her son. When Grace and Richard moved north to a large

31. For the relevant citations concerning Agatha Stubbings, see CCR-2, pp. 412, 430, 433, 449–450, CCR-3, pp. 69, 99, fol. 100, p. 133; Whitelaw, *Virginia's Eastern Shore*, I, 154; *WMQ*, 1st Ser., XII (1903–1904), 265. Vaughan's actions can be found in CCR-5, fol. 125–fol. 126, p. 135. For the appointment of Wilson, see CCR-1, p. 63.

32. For the Stringer statement, see CCR-5, p. 128; the Pott deed of gift is in CCR-2, p. 293; the gifts to Barlow are recorded in CCR-4, p. 136–fol. 136, fol. 191–p. 192, CCR-5, p. 36.

tract on Occohannock Creek, John Waltham, Jr., received title to more land, this time adjacent to that of his stepfather. Throughout this period, Stephen Charlton continued to look after the interests of his nephew. For example, in 1646 he gave an account of the cattle belonging to the estate. Eight years later Charlton defended the land of his nephew against the pretensions of another claimant. Finally, in his last will he bequeathed clothing and cattle to John. After Charlton's death, however, certain irregularities were uncovered in his supervision of the estate entrusted to him. Several individuals testified that, after Richard and Grace Vaughan had moved north, Charlton had rented the land of his nephew to tenants and had not provided an accounting of the proceeds. When the matter was adjudicated, the commissioners of the county court ordered Charlton's widow to provide restitution.[33]

A brief statement filed in connection with the litigation between John Waltham, Jr., and the heirs of Stephen Charlton reveals a great deal about the normal relations between stepparents and stepchildren. "I Richard Vaughan doe acknowledge that I received . . . a pattent for the plantation of John Waltome in Nuswattocks, and seated it, And when I left it (with sufficient howseinge and fenceinge) I gave it [to] his mother for the use of Jno. Waltome it beinge his fathers right." This concern for the interests of stepchildren is evidenced throughout the county court records. Thus, Richard Baily reported the increase of cattle belonging to his stepchildren Stephen, John, and Philip Fisher. Bequests to stepchildren were not uncommon. Stepparents also had the county court clerk record their deeds of gift to their stepchildren. Examples of continuing trust and support also appear in the court record. When William Waters became sheriff of Northampton County in 1652, his stepfather Obedience Robins stood security for Waters's performance of the duties of that office. Similarly, three years later, when William Andrews, Jr., became sheriff, the stepfather of his wife was one of those who stood security.[34]

Most revealing is the fact that remarkably few conflicts between step-

33. CCR-2, pp. 320–321, CCR-3, fol. 45, p. 135a, CCR-4, p. 217, CCR-5, p. 124–fol. 124, CCR-7, pp. 3, 49; Nugent, ed., *Cavaliers and Pioneers*, I, 131, 183–184.

34. Waltham: CCR-5, p. 124–fol. 124. Baily: CCR-3, fol. 45, p. 107. Bequests to stepchildren: CCR-3, fol. 147–p. 148, CCR-5, fol. 56–p. 58. Deeds of gift to stepchildren: CCR-3, p. 226, records one from John Rutter to Jonathan Newton; CCR-4, p. 4, records one from John Robinson to John and Mary Studson (CCR-3, pp. 176, 237); CCR-2, pp. 437–438, records one from Henry Bagwell to Mary Buckland (CCR-1, p. 67). Robins: CCR-4, fol. 63. Andrews: CCR-7, fol. 18; his wife was Elizabeth Traveller.

parent and stepchild appear in the official record. Again, one of the problems involved Stephen Charlton. Following his marriage to the widow of John Severne, Charlton became the guardian of John Severne, Jr. This relationship was amicable until John's mother died in the early 1650s. By that time John was almost of age, and friction developed when he sought a measure of freedom from the dictates of his stepfather. The commissioners of the county court ordered an end to the dispute with a detailed agreement recorded as settlement. But coexistence could not be reestablished, and the court specified that Charlton only had to provide his stepson's "dyett (if the said John Severne cometh for it)."[35]

The interests of children who lost one or both parents generally were protected and nurtured. Resident kin, aware that they too might die at an early age, knew that their families might need such help someday.[36] As previously noted, the will of a deceased parent sometimes called on the aid of relatives to supervise the estate for the benefit of the survivors. Yet even in the absence of a will, there is evidence of such help. In 1647 John Savage, about twenty-three years old and parentless, petitioned the county court to have the "tuition and guardianship" of his stepsister Margery Cugley, who also was an orphan. Nine years later Margery reached majority and requested that her stepbrother continue as guardian with the aid of James Bruce, "that [she] maye bee provided for her fitt and necessary accommodation; And her Estate taken care of." John Hinman provided protection of another sort to his stepdaughter Ann Smith. In an effort to clear Ann's reputation of several slanders directed toward her, Hinman proceeded on an action of defamation against the accused parties.[37]

In addition to the care provided children by widows and relatives (if any) in the event of mortality, the county court also acted responsibly to protect the interests of minors. It did so even in the absence of any

35. CCR-5, p. 2, records the court's order. CCR-3, p. 232–fol. 232, CCR-4, fol. 130–p. 131, p. 161, CCR-5, fol. 112.

36. Darrett B. Rutman and Anita H. Rutman note that "given the extensiveness of parental loss and the number of children whose estates were vulnerable, the number of assaults upon the estates of orphans seems relatively few" (" 'Now-Wives and Sons-in-Law,' " in Tate and Ammerman, eds., *Chesapeake in the Seventeenth Century*, 159–168 [quote on p. 166]). See also Smith, "Mortality and Family in the Colonial Chesapeake," *JIH*, VIII (1977–1978), 426.

37. Savage: CCR-3, p. 112, CCR-7, fol. 32–p. 33. In a touching gesture, John Savage accepted the tuition of one of the orphans of John Webster, who had served as his guardian years before (CCR-2, p. 86, CCR-3, fol. 223). Hinman: CCR-3, p. 62, fol. 62–p. 63, p. 65–fol. 65, fol. 100–p. 101.

surviving relatives. Studies of seventeenth-century Maryland have also found the same care taken by the local courts there.[38] The local court's authority on the Eastern Shore derived first from the fact that it held jurisdiction over the enforcement of legal instruments relating to the welfare of children. Wills specified bequests to minors as well as their education and care. Widows signed deeds of gift detailing what was due to their children. Marriage contracts between widows and their prospective husbands were drafted to prevent the embezzlement of their estates.[39]

The commissioners of the county court also were responsible for the enforcement of legislation respecting orphans' estates. In March 1643 the General Assembly of Virginia passed an act stating that "no land belonging to any orphant . . . be alienated, sold estranged or taken up as deserted by any person or persons during their minoritie, until three years after their full age." The act further prohibited any lease of an orphan's land if the terms of agreement allowed possession beyond the time when the child became an adult before the law.[40] One case involving such an issue came before the commissioners of Northampton County. On November 21, 1644, Phillip Chapman signed his last will and testament, in which he appointed William Roper to "have the tuition and Keepeing of my . . . child John Chapman with his dew share of Estate suddaynely after my decease to bee improved untill he shall come to the Age [of 21]." Having reconsidered this point and fearing that "the howse might bee ruinated and the Land worne out before the child came to age," Chapman

about one day or two before hee dyed . . . desired . . . Reginald Hawis and Hannah Mountney . . . to beare Witnes that notwith-

38. For Maryland, see Carr, "The Development of the Maryland Orphans' Court, 1654–1715," in Land *et al.*, eds., *Law, Society, and Politics in Early Maryland*, 41–62; and Walsh, " 'Till Death Us Do Part,' " in Tate and Ammerman, eds., *Chesapeake in the Seventeenth Century*, 151.

39. For examples of deeds of gift, see those signed by Anna Taylor, Elizabeth Walton, Anne Ward, Ann Wilkins, Ann Cozier-Harlow, Sarah Williams, and Sarah Dorman (CCR-2, p. 120, CCR-3, p. 202–fol. 202, p. 218–fol. 218, fol. 241, CCR-4, pp. 96, 193, CCR-5, p. 95–p. 96). For examples of marriage contracts, see those between Frances Blower-Sanders and William Burdett, Anne Ward and George Smith, and Sarah Williams and Stephen Horsey (CCR-2, pp. 126–127, CCR-3, p. 218–fol. 218, CCR-4, p. 193). For Maryland, see Walsh, " 'Till Death Us Do Part,' " in Tate and Ammerman, eds., *Chesapeake in the Seventeenth Century*, 137.

40. William Waller Hening, ed., *The Statutes at Large; Being a Collection of All the Laws of Virginia . . .* , I (New York, 1823), 260.

standing any thinge in his will by writeing to the contrary hee the said Chappman gave full power and Authority unto Capt. William Roper to sell or dispose of his Land and Plantation for the good of his Children.[41]

Accordingly, Roper sold the land. After Roper's death, however, the feoffee-in-trust for Elizabeth Chapman, the sister and heir of John, who died in his minority, raised the question "whether it were Lawfull for Capt: Roper to sell the Land devised by will to Jno. Chapman . . . (or not) It beinge pleaded by the Feoffe in trust for the next heyre that the will had not Tollerated any Executor to sell the Land." Keeping in mind the strictures of the act of the General Assembly, the commissioners still decided in favor of the purchaser of the land. They justified their decision on the basis that Phillip Chapman's oral revision of his will, which was heard by Hawis and Mountney, qualified it as a nuncupative will. They also argued that the sale had benefited the estate.[42]

The same attention to the letter and spirit of the law marked other actions of the commissioners in relation to orphans. At the same General Assembly that passed the aforementioned act, another law was enacted to protect orphans. Noting that some orphans' estates had been neglected by overseers and guardians, the Assembly ordered

> that the guardians and overseers of all orphants shall carefully keep and preserve such estates as shall be comitted to their trust either by order of court or otherwise, And shall likewise deliver an exact accompt once everie year to the commissioners of the severall county courts respectively of the said estates and of the increase and improvement, who are hereby required to keep an exact register thereof.[43]

Apparently the commissioners of Northampton County took this charge seriously. On June 30, 1646, they "ordered . . . that those men that have Orphants estates in their hands shall bring in a just Accompt of all the said estates at the next Court being on the 28th of July next." While several individuals complied with the order, the commissioners found it necessary to repeat it. At the July court they

41. CCR-2, pp. 410–411, 415–418, CCR-5, fol. 87–p. 88.
42. CCR-3, p. 241, p. 242–fol. 242.
43. Hening, ed., *Statutes at Large*, I, 260–261. Both acts were renewed in 1653. Warren M. Billings, ed., "Some Acts Not in Hening's *Statutes*: The Acts of Assembly, April 1652, November 1652, and July 1653," *VMHB*, LXXXIII (1975), 42–43.

ordered . . . that all men that have any interest in thestates of Orphants within this Countye of Northampton shall bring in their Accompt unto the next County Court . . . and shall hereafter give a yearely Accompt of all Orphants estates that are or hereafter shalbe on the 28th day of July yearely.[44]

In conformity with the first part of this order, a few additional individuals reported the estates entrusted to them when the court next met on August 28. But contrary to the second part of the order, the commissioners do not seem to have enforced strict observance of a July date for reporting orphans' estates.[45] A rigorous enforcement probably was not really necessary. The overseers of orphans' estates knew that actions against them could be brought before the commissioners. Such actions were facilitated by the fact that certain courts were designated especially for the hearing of orphans' causes.[46]

Undoubtedly, high mortality on the Eastern Shore and elsewhere in the seventeenth-century Chesapeake created a very fluid social setting. And yet even such a baneful influence as a high death rate could have a socially unifying function. It led to the rapid proliferation of kin ties as widows and widowers remarried and linked themselves to other kin networks. Relatives provided help in time of need, and they supported their kin on a daily basis by providing sociability, favors, and economic exchanges. Individuals were less isolated to the extent that they were a part of these kin networks. Through time, landholders increasingly formed bonds with their fellow settlers. The network of kinship provided support as well as exacting responsibilities.[47] It was an important part of the developing societal web.

44. CCR-3, fol. 37, p. 40–p. 41.

45. CCR-3, fol. 45, pp. 107, 146, fol. 151, p. 167, fol. 205, CCR-4, fol. 132.

46. CCR-3, p. 154, fol. 156, CCR-6, p. 8, fol. 20, CCR-7, fols. 27, 28. Nora Miller Turman and Mark C. Lewis note in the introduction to their edition of "The Will of Ann Littleton of Northampton County, Virginia, 1656" that a 1658 reference to an orphans' court was the only one they knew of for Northampton County in the 17th century; the information provided here extends such references to an earlier period (*VMHB*, LXXV [1967], 14). Turman and Lewis err by stating that Hening's *Statutes at Large* does not mention these courts until after 1700.

47. Rutman and Rutman, " 'Now-Wives and Sons-in-Law,' " in Tate and Ammerman, eds., *The Chesapeake in the Seventeenth Century*, 168; Rutman and Rutman, *A Place in Time: Middlesex County*, 59–60.

4 *Friends and Neighbors*

NOT ALL LANDHOLDERS on the Eastern Shore had relatives there. And even those who did could not safely assume that their kin would continue to be supporting. Arguments might estrange relatives, although they appear to have done so infrequently. Occasionally one or more relatives moved off the peninsula. Mortality frequently attenuated and sometimes obliterated the kin network of a landholder. Such attenuation was a threat to social cohesion on the Eastern Shore, which, like the rest of Virginia, lacked the well-articulated communal goals that linked individuals to one another in New England.

But the danger was averted and social cohesion fostered by other interpersonal networks that bound the population together. Most important was the pattern of contacts encouraged by the spatial proximity of residents. In early seventeenth-century Virginia, the totally self-reliant individual operating in relative isolation was a rarity. People turned to their neighbors for an exchange of sociability and favors as well as responsibilities. Individually and collectively, neighbors also exercised a degree of social control. This skein of interactions helped to bind landholders together on the Eastern Shore.

There is no way to reconstruct spatially the total network of contacts that linked propertyholders, but the official county court record reveals a suggestive outline. The innumerable depositions that were entered as evidence in cases frequently include explicit references to the location of face-to-face contacts between landholders. Combining this evidence with that on residency creates a sketch, albeit incomplete and faint, of the local web of interactions.[1]

The pattern that emerges is striking. The overwhelming majority of face-to-face meetings occurred between landholders whose residences were nearby. In 53 percent of the cases, the witnesses to any given incident lived on the same or adjacent tracts, across, or at least on, the same creek. Another 27 percent lived on tracts separated by fewer than three miles, 12 percent on tracts four to six miles apart, and 8 percent at a

1. The following analysis focuses on those contacts that can be identified as to locale and for which the residences of both parties could be determined.

greater distance. A similar pattern has been demonstrated throughout the Chesapeake.[2]

A few examples serve to illustrate the systematic proximity of these random contacts. In August 1643, when John Holloway was on his deathbed, he made certain oral provisions not included in his will. William Jones, who lived on an adjacent tract, was present and testified three years later concerning these unwritten statements. In October 1651, Ann, wife of William Ward, recounted a visit that summer by Ann, wife of Walter Williams, during which the latter spoke about Mary Adkinson. At that time, Ann Ward and Ann Williams lived on adjacent tracts on Hungars Creek. James Adkinson, the husband of Mary, had been living and planting on Williams's plantation the year before and probably still lived there in the summer of 1651. Finally, John Savage mentioned in a 1655 deposition that he had been at the house of Henry Boston, who lived across the creek.[3]

These incidents and those cited hereafter exemplify the spatially restricted interactional networks of Eastern Shore landholders. For the

2. Lorena Seebach Walsh, "Charles County, Maryland, 1658–1705: A Study of Chesapeake Social and Political Structure" (Ph.D. diss., Michigan State University, 1977), 294–296; Darrett B. Rutman and Anita H. Rutman, *A Place in Time: Middlesex County, Virginia, 1650–1750* (New York, 1984), 120–121; Lois Green Carr, "Sources of Political Stability and Upheaval in Seventeenth-Century Maryland," *MHM*, LXXIX (1984), 45–46; James Horn, "Adapting to a New World: A Comparative Study of Local Society in England and Maryland, 1650–1700," 165–174, and Lorena S. Walsh, "Community Networks in the Early Chesapeake," 218–219, 222, in Lois Green Carr, Philip D. Morgan, and Jean B. Russo, eds., *Colonial Chesapeake Society* (Chapel Hill, N.C., 1988).

3. Holloway and Jones: CCR-3, p. 46; Nell Marion Nugent, ed., *Cavaliers and Pioneers: Abstracts of Virginia Land Patents and Grants, I, 1623–1666, II, 1666–1695* (Richmond, Va., 1934, 1977), I, 123, 135.

For the incident of October 1651, see CCR-4, p. 79. William Ward and his wife lived on the land of her prior husband, Edward Stockdell. There was a great deal of litigation about this acreage, but the Wards were still in possession in the summer of 1651 (CCR-4, fol. 110–fol. 111, fol. 179; Nugent, ed., *Cavaliers and Pioneers*, I, 74). Walter Williams had bought the land next to Stockdell in 1649 and was definitely living there in the summer of 1651 (CCR-3, p. 206–fol. 206, CCR-4, fol. 91). For the information about James Adkinson, see CCR-3, fol. 196. There is no evidence that Adkinson and Williams had a formal leasing agreement.

Savage and Boston: CCR-5, fol. 146. Although Savage inherited an enormous tract from his father, his house has been placed on Cherrystone Creek by Ralph T. Whitelaw, *Virginia's Eastern Shore: A History of Northampton and Accomack Counties*, 2 vols. (Richmond, Va., 1951), I, 220–221. Boston leased land from Obedience Robins, all of whose tracts were contiguous with a boundary on Cherrystone Creek (CCR-7, p. 12; see Chapter 3, n. 8, above, for Robins's land).

most part, residents tended to associate with others who lived nearby. Unfortunately, few of the depositions reveal what prompted them to get together. Most depositions were recollections of occurrences incidental to the contact between landholders. In the course of a visit, individuals happened to witness events about which they were asked to testify at a later date. But not all depositions were so cryptic. Some included details that are glimpses into the nature or content of these contacts.

First, there is evidence of social gatherings. During testimony William Gowers disclosed that Richard Hill and Jonathan Hudson had been "playeing with a Maule all night att Jenkin Price his howse." Hill and Price lived on adjacent tracts just north of Occohannock Creek. In 1643 William Roper deposed

> That whereas there is a Rumor that there was a health druncke Att the house of Mrs. Alice Burdett Widdow To the damnation of Pymms God and the Confusion of the Parliament There was not any such health drunck in this deponents heareing and to the best of his Knowledge by any of them whoe were there in his Company.

In addition to demonstrating the colonists' active and potentially controversial interest in English political developments, this deposition records an occasion of sociability between residents on the same creek. Another example is afforded by John Severne's account of a conversation with Levin Denwood when they were at prayer together; at that time they lived quite near to each another. Obedience Robins, a resident on Cherrystone Creek, mentioned a trip to "Mr. Edward Drews to visit him in his sicknes"; Drew's house was on a tract adjacent to land belonging to Robins. John Hammond's *Leah and Rachel* noted the practice of neighbors who took care of a sick man's crop so that it would not be lost. A visit, whether to see the sick man or to help in his fields, might be the occasion for making a will when the illness worsened. Thus Phillip Chapman, on his deathbed, asked William Roper, who lived nearby and was at Chapman's house, to write his will.[4]

The last example illustrates how proximity could foster contacts not

4. Hill and Price: CCR-5, fol. 131. For their locations, see CCR-7, p. 51, and Nugent, ed., *Cavaliers and Pioneers*, I, 261–262, 276, 285.

Roper and Burdett: CCR-2, p. 297. For Roper's residence, see Nugent, ed., *Cavaliers and Pioneers*, I, 46, 482. Alice Burdett also lived on Old Plantation Creek. She had lived there with her prior husband George Traveller, and she continued to reside there with William Burdett (CCR-2, pp. 246–248; Nugent, ed., *Cavaliers and Pioneers*, I, 43; see Chapter 3, n. 26, above, for Burdett's lands).

Severne and Denwood: CCR-2, pp. 59–60. They probably lived on the same tract strictly social. Neighbors also exchanged favors, including loans. In the mid-1630s Daniel Cugley lent a hog house to Edward Drew. Ten years later Edmund Scarburgh asked John Pott whether he might borrow a mare, and the latter agreed. John Savage, in an attempt to salvage a sloop that had been "cast away," borrowed a length of rope from William Munns, who lived nearby. Finally, there are references to loans of tobacco.[5] Such loans between neighbors were measures of trust, and they also served as social bonds between those involved.

The record of deeds of gift and bequests provides another clear indication of the close bonds between neighbors. An example is Edward Drew's gift of a cow to Hannah, daughter of Joan and David Windley. Drew lived on Cherrystone Creek. In 1634 David Windley applied to the county court for one hundred acres abutting Drew's holding and subsequently received a patent. There are numerous references to contact between the Drews and Windleys: Edward and David were two of the appraisers for the estate of Henry Bagwell, their wives searched together for a cow, and David witnessed a conversation at Edward's house.[6] After 1639 the county court record contains no reference to Windley's being

---

(CCR-1, p. 102, CCR-2, pp. 16, 60–61; Nugent, ed., *Cavaliers and Pioneers*, I, 43, 71).

Robins and Drew: CCR-3, p. 241. All of Robins's land bordered on Cherrystone Creek. For Drew's house, see CCR-3, fol. 239–p. 240; Nugent, ed., *Cavaliers and Pioneers*, I, 46; Whitelaw, *Virginia's Eastern Shore*, I, 188.

John Hammond: *Leah and Rachel; or, The Two Fruitfull Sisters Virginia, and Maryland* . . . , 19, in Peter Force, ed., *Tracts and Other Papers, Relating Principally to the Origins, Settlement, and Progress of the Colonies in North America from the Discovery of the Country to the Year 1776*, 4 vols. (Washington, D.C., 1836–1847), III.

Chapman and Roper: CCR-5, fol. 87–p. 88. For Chapman's residence, see CCR-6, p. 4; for Roper's, see above.

5. Cugley and Drew: CCR-1, pp. 99–100. The Cugleys lived on Cherrystone Creek, where Daniel Cugley's stepson John Savage had inherited a huge acreage from his father, next to which Cugley had patented (Nugent, ed., *Cavaliers and Pioneers*, I, 23, 75). See n. 4, above, for Drew's land. Scarburgh and Pott: CCR-3, p. 111, fol. 112–p. 113. Scarburgh's residence was at Magatty Bay, as was Pott's (CCR-2, pp. 22–26, CCR-3, fol. 75). Savage and Munns: CCR-5, fol. 146–fol. 147. William Munns leased land from Hannah Savage-Cugley on Cherrystone Creek (CCR-2, p. 128). See above for Savage's land.

Loans of tobacco: the first loan involved John Dixon and John Smothers (CCR-3, p. 237); for their residences, see CCR-3, fol. 4, CCR-4, p. 13, fol. 25. The second loan involved Gideon Tillisson and Richard Hudson (CCR-4, fol. 106–p. 107); for their residences, see CCR-3, p. 171.

6. CCR-1, pp. 16, 27, 37–38, CCR-4, p. 48–fol. 48. For Drew's land, see n. 4, above. For Windley's, see CCR-1, p. 21; and Nugent, ed., *Cavaliers and Pioneers*, I, 77.

on the Eastern Shore; but whether he died or moved away, his wife Joan remained. The Windley land was repatented in the name of Pharaoh Young, Joan's son by an earlier marriage, and in 1649 Young sold to Christopher Jarvis this land "nowe in the tenure and occupation of . . . Jarvis and Joane the wife of David Winleye."[7] Joan Windley was still living there a year later, when Edward Drew died; they had been neighbors for more than fifteen years. Before his death, Drew gave a cow to Joan Windley's daughter.[8]

Individuals also made bequests to their neighbors. In 1636 William Smith left a sow to Elizabeth Harlow, daughter of John Harlow, who lived across Old Plantation Creek.[9] A decade after this, Ann Hookings signed her will. In it she left bequests to several neighbors. She gave to Richard Smith "for his paynes in my sickness" a flock bed and pillow; to Thomas Stratton, a runlet, frying pan, kettle, and "my plantation for foure yeares betwixt the said Smyth and Stratton." Hookings also made bequests to other neighbors: two barrels of corn with a carpet to Goodman Harlow; several items of apparel to Margery, the wife of Henry Williams; and miscellaneous items to Alice, Rebecca, John, Thomas, and Henry Bagwell (whom she appointed as her executor).[10] Walter Irby

7. The last reference to David Windley was CCR-1, p. 137. There were several claims made on Windley's estate in 1639, which might indicate his death (CCR-1, pp. 153, 155). But Joan Windley was never referred to as a widow and in fact was called the wife of David Windley as late as 1649 (CCR-3, fol. 161–p. 162). The wording of the Young patent suggests that Windley had claimed this land in the name of his stepson rather than for himself (Nugent, ed., *Cavaliers and Pioneers*, I, 77, 107). For Young's sale, see CCR-3, fol. 161–p. 162.

8. CCR-3, p. 134, fol. 172, p. 191, fol. 239–p. 240, CCR-4, fol. 18–fol. 19, p. 48–fol. 48.

Another illustration here is John Vaughan's gift to Kathryne, daughter of Thomas and Welthiana Evans (CCR-4, p. 68). For the land of Vaughan, see CCR-1, p. 104, and Nugent, ed., *Cavaliers and Pioneers*, I, 114; for Evans's residence, see CCR-5, p. 138. John Vaughan and his neighbor, Goodwife Evans, seem to have engaged in an affair that scandalized the court (CCR-4, fols. 89, 90).

9. For the land of Smith, see CCR-1, pp. 31, 61–62, and Nugent, ed., *Cavaliers and Pioneers*, I, 14; for that of Harlow, see CCR-1, p. 37, and Nugent, ed., *Cavaliers and Pioneers*, I, 46.

10. CCR-3, p. 134a. The will reveals that Hookings, Smith, and Stratton all lived near one another on Old Plantation Creek. For Stratton's subsequent land deals here, see CCR-5, fol. 87–p. 88; and Nugent, ed., *Cavaliers and Pioneers*, I, 295. For Harlow's land, see n. 9, above. For Williams's land, see CCR-1, p. 35; CCR-3, p. 39; Nugent, ed., *Cavaliers and Pioneers*, I, 46, 101. For Bagwell's land, see Nugent, ed., *Cavaliers and Pioneers*, I, 112. There were also bequests to Mary Buckland, who was the stepdaughter of Henry Bagwell and the wife of Richard Buckland (location unknown), and to John and Charles Russell, who may have been related to Mary

provides a final example of such bequests. Apparently planning a trip off the Eastern Shore when he made his will in 1651, he left his entire estate to Ann Johnson. She was the wife of John Johnson, Sr., the "trusty and welbeloved freind," whom Irby at the same time appointed to act as his attorney. Irby and the Johnsons lived near each other on land leased from Argoll Yardley.[11]

The variety of contacts among residents living in proximity resembled in many ways the pattern found among relatives. The comparison is a reminder that, to a large extent, the kin network itself was spatially restricted. Relatives generally lived near one another and, as with all landholders who lived close together, exchanged visits, favors, and support. On the Eastern Shore and elsewhere in the Chesapeake region, the interaction among landholders sometimes encouraged the formation of kin ties.[12] As noted already, widows often sought a new spouse living in the immediate area. Thus the widow Elizabeth Neale married David Dale, who had acquired land from her prior husband, John Neale. But the contact between Dale and the Neale family was not limited to an exchange of land. Seven years before this transaction, Dale had deposed in a case concerning a debt due to John Neale. Coincidentally, this is also the year in which Elizabeth appeared in the record as the wife of John Neale; Dale and she must have known each other at least by that date. Three years after this, Dale and John Neale were jurors together. Most significantly, Dale served Neale just before the latter assigned him land.[13] When the widowed Elizabeth Neale and David Dale married, they were not strangers.

Marriage alliances between people living near each other by no means involved only widows. The marriage of John Tilney and Ann Smith illustrates another possibility. In 1639 John Tilney first appeared in the official record as a headright claimed by John Holloway, a chirurgeon probably located at the head of Hungars Creek. Apparently Tilney lived with Holloway, possibly to learn the latter's medical skills, as suggested by the fact that, when Holloway died in August 1643, he bequeathed to

Russell, cousin of Mary Buckland (CCR-1, p. 67, CCR-2, pp. 437–438, CCR-3, fol. 160).

11. CCR-4, p. 172–p. 173. For Irby's and Johnson's leases, see CCR-2, pp. 278–279, CCR-4, p. 103–fol. 103, p. 172–p. 173.

12. Darrett B. Rutman and Anita H. Rutman also note the interweaving of kin and friendship ties (*A Place in Time: Middlesex County*, 102–103).

13. CCR-1, pp. 74–75, 86–87, CCR-2, pp. 22–26, 389, 390, CCR-4, p. 194.

Tilney all of his "Phisicall and Chirurgicall" books and tools. In addition he desired "that the sayde John Tilney shall possesse and enjoye that hundred Acres of land hee made Choice of by the Bridge; untill such tyme as the lawfull heyres thereof come to Age." This land was Tilney's first holding. Living near Holloway and Tilney throughout this period, Thomas Smith knew them both, and the county court record shows them exchanging favors on several occasions. When Smith died about six months after Holloway, he left behind a widow, Sarah, and three children: Ann, William, and Argoll. Ann was probably the oldest of the three; in 1636 her father had claimed a headright for her transportation into Virginia. He claimed no headright for either of his sons, both of whom may have been born on the Eastern Shore, inasmuch as they were still minors in 1652. Three or four years after her father's death, Ann Smith married John Tilney, who must have been twenty-seven or twenty-eight years old at that time.[14] Although Tilney was no longer a boy, his proximity entitles him to be considered the man next door.

An even more interesting example of such a marriage involved Elizabeth Chapman and John Severne, Jr. Phillip Chapman, Elizabeth's father, owned land on King's Creek from the early 1630s until 1644, when he died. John Severne, Sr., had arrived a few years later and located on the adjacent tract. Coincidentally, Severne died just a few months before Chapman. Up to this point, Elizabeth Chapman and John Severne, Jr., lived near each other. Within a few months after the death of her husband, Bridgett Severne married Stephen Charlton and moved to Nuswattocks Creek, where he lived. Elizabeth Chapman, on the other hand, was orphaned when her father died. In regard to his "fatherless and motherless" daughter, Phillip Chapman wrote in his will that Elias Hartry was to "have the Education and Tuition of . . . Elizabeth Chapman with her due share of estate suddaynely after my decease to bee improved to her best Advantage untill shee shall come to her age . . . or till her day of Marriage." Hartry, who had acquired title to acreage on the same tract as the elder Severne, may have been living there at the time Chapman entrusted the care of his daughter to him. But all evidence points to the

14. For Holloway's will, see CCR-2, pp. 302–304. See also CCR-1, pp. 40, 149–150, CCR-3, fol. 63–p. 64; Nugent, ed., *Cavaliers and Pioneers*, I, 135. Thomas Smith: CCR-2, pp. 190–191, 203, 206, 318, 321, 362; Nugent, ed., *Cavaliers and Pioneers*, I, 115. Ann Smith: CCR-2, p. 327, CCR-4, p. 119–fol. 119; Nugent, ed., *Cavaliers and Pioneers*, I, 43. Smith and Tilney: CCR-3, fol. 100–p. 101, fol. 142; Whitelaw, *Virginia's Eastern Shore*, I, 444.

conclusion that Hartry already had moved or shortly did move to a tract only one-half mile from that where Stephen Charlton lived. Thus the children, John Severne, Jr., and Elizabeth Chapman, continued to live close together. As John reached majority and friction increased between him and his stepfather, he took up residence on the land patented for him after his father had died. Significantly, this acreage was wedged between the tracts where lived, on the one side, Stephen Charlton, and, on the other, Elias Hartry (and his ward Elizabeth Chapman). In October 1654 John Severne, Jr., "in consideration of the Love, and affection" he felt toward Elizabeth Chapman and "especially in consideration of matrimony intended (by gods permission) presently to bee solempnized" between them gave to her ten cows and one bull as a free jointure. "And I . . . Request, appoynt and make my Loveinge freind Elias Hartrey . . . Agent and Feoffee in trust for . . . Elisabeth (my intended wife)." After living close to each other since childhood, John and Elizabeth were married, and Elias Hartry had fulfilled the last wishes of the bride's father.[15]

Living near one another also fostered the formation of another type of kin tie among landholders. Parents frequently chose neighbors as godparents for their children. In fact, they did so with almost no exceptions. They probably would have preferred to appoint a relative, but kin networks were not sufficiently dense to allow the choice to be restricted to relatives, so instances of neighbors as godparents abound. For example, William Burdett owned extensive acreage on both sides of Old Plantation Creek.[16] When he died in 1643, he bequeathed to each of his god-

15. Phillip Chapman: CCR-1, p. 21, CCR-2, pp. 396, 410–411, 415–418, CCR-3, p. 241, CCR-4, fol. 181–p. 182, CCR-6, fol. 3, p. 4, fol. 4; Nugent, ed., *Cavaliers and Pioneers*, I, 7. Severne Senior: CCR-1, p. 117, CCR-2, pp. 16, 60–61, 371–373, 393–394, CCR-3, p. 241; Nugent, ed., *Cavaliers and Pioneers*, I, 20. Bridgett Severne: Nugent, ed., *Cavaliers and Pioneers*, I, 82, 129, 157–158. Elizabeth Chapman: CCR-2, pp. 415–418.

Hartry: Nugent, ed., *Cavaliers and Pioneers*, I, 103. There is no record of Hartry's disposition of his first land. There are, however, numerous references to his land transactions on Nuswattocks Creek from 1642 through 1655 (CCR-3, fol. 20–p. 21, fols. 61, 143; Nugent, ed., *Cavaliers and Pioneers*, I, 233, 286, 414, 482, 520). In 1656 he was identified as an inhabitant of Nuswattocks Parish (CCR-5, p. 105–fol. 105).

Severne Junior: see Chapter 3 for an account of the dispute with stepfather. For Severne's land and his residency, see CCR-5, pp. 2, 70; and Nugent, ed., *Cavaliers and Pioneers*, I, 157–158. For the jointure, see CCR-5, fol. 47–p. 48. The first reference to John and Elizabeth as married appears about a year after the signing of the jointure (CCR-6, fol. 3).

16. See Chapter 3, n. 26, for citations concerning his land.

children—William Roper, Jane Williams, and William Smith—a year-old cow. At the time of this bequest, the Roper and Williams families lived on Old Plantation Creek. The Smiths lived to the north but formerly had lived on Old Plantation Creek as well. Burdett probably had been named godfather to William Smith when his parents lived nearby.[17]

Another case illustrating this point is that of Ann Littleton, the god-mother of Sarah, Edward, and Elizabeth Douglas. Ann's first husband had been Charles Harmar, an early resident on the Eastern Shore and, at one time, an overseer for the estate of Lady Elizabeth Dale. When he finally claimed his own land, it was adjacent to that of Lady Elizabeth. After Harmar's death, Ann next married Nathaniel Littleton. They continued to live on her first husband's land, which Littleton eventually bought from the heirs and expanded by additional grants.[18] Meanwhile, Edward Douglas, a cousin of Lady Elizabeth, arrived on the Eastern Shore and acted as one of the overseers of the Dale estate after her death. As part of the redistribution of the Dale landholdings, Douglas patented acreage adjacent to the Littletons. Sometime in late 1654 or early 1655, Nathaniel Littleton died; Ann referred to herself as the executrix of his will (that document is no longer extant). In about a year and a half, Ann too was dead. Her will provided for the distribution of the Littleton estate. And it is her will that lists bequests to her three godchildren, "the children of my Loveinge Neighbor Lt. Collonll Edward Douglas."[19]

17. For Burdett's will, see CCR-2, pp. 293–295. For the location of the elder William Roper, see Nugent, ed., *Cavaliers and Pioneers*, I, 46, 482; for that of Henry Williams, father of Jane, see CCR-1, p. 35, CCR-3, p. 39, and Nugent, ed., *Cavaliers and Pioneers*, I, 46, 101. Although he had probably moved north by 1643, Thomas Smith, the father of William Smith, had lived across Old Plantation Creek from William Burdett (CCR-1, p. 87, and Nugent, ed., *Cavaliers and Pioneers*, I, 43).

18. For a brief biography of Ann Littleton, including information about Charles Harmar and Nathaniel Littleton, see the introduction to Nora Miller Turman and Mark C. Lewis, eds., "The Will of Ann Littleton of Northampton County, Virginia, 1656," *VMHB*, LXXV (1967), 11–16. On Littleton's land purchases, see CCR-2, pp. 4, 42–43, 148–151; Nugent, ed., *Cavaliers and Pioneers*, I, 331; Whitelaw, *Virginia's Eastern Shore*, I, 79.

19. Douglas: Nugent, ed., *Cavaliers and Pioneers*, I, 414; Whitelaw, *Virginia's Eastern Shore*, I, 97–98. Ann Littleton: Turman and Lewis, eds., "The Will of Ann Littleton," *VMHB*, LXXV (1967), 17–19. For the death of Nathaniel Littleton, see CCR-5, fol. 27, p. 80. It is worth noting here another example of neighbors who married. Edward Littleton, son of Nathaniel and Ann Littleton, inherited the home plantation adjacent to the Douglas's. In 1657 the will of Edward Douglas mentioned a marriage contract between his daughter Sarah and Edward Littleton (Turman and Lewis, eds., "The Will of Ann Littleton," *VMHB*, LXXV [1967], 20; CCR-7, fol. 76–p. 78).

For other examples of godparents' giving presents to godchildren resident nearby,

The significance of this godparent / godchild relationship and its manifestation in bequests and deeds of gift should not be underestimated. The first generation of immigrants that settled in the Chesapeake region included a significant proportion of unrelated individuals. Although a network of interactions consisting of sociability, favors, and economic exchange linked landholders residing nearby, the presents given by godparents to their godchildren demonstrate the affective aspects of this network.[20]

But this is not the only evidence suggesting the strength of the bonds that developed among neighbors. As with the study of the family and kin network, probably the best indicator of the nature of neighborhood ties was the response of individuals to the crisis of death. Landholders in the Chesapeake area frequently sought the aid of residents nearby to help in the settlement of the estate and care of orphans.[21] Their reliance was not misplaced. When called upon to act, whether by a dying colonist or the commissioners of the county court, neighbors rarely failed to mobilize effectively.

When Hannah Savage-Cugley died in 1641 within a few months of her husband Daniel, two orphans survived. John Savage, her son by a previous marriage, was seventeen years old, and, with his consent, Hannah had appointed John Webster to be his guardian. But no provisions were recorded for the care of Margery Cugley, an infant at the time. Therefore, the commissioners of the county court "ordered that Mrs. Grace Robins Jane Munns and Jone Windley shall agree with whome they cann finde most Fitt to nurse the said child And the nurse shall have satisfaction from the inhabitants resideing within this parish." The naming of these three women was not arbitrary; they all lived near the Cugley home. Likewise their choice of a nurse was well considered. They se-

---

see CCR-3, fol. 94, CCR-4, p. 37, p. 119–fol. 119, CCR-5, fol. 52, fol. 101–fol. 102, fol. 137.

20. Sidney W. Mintz and Eric R. Wolf relate the institution of godparentage in Roman Catholic societies to larger social, economic, political, and legal structures, but the evidence on the Eastern Shore is too thin to support such an analysis ("An Analysis of Ritual Co-Parenthood [Compadrazgo]," *Southwestern Journal of Anthropology*, VI [1950], 341–368).

See also Darrett B. Rutman and Anita H. Rutman, " 'Now-Wives and Sons-in-Law': Parental Death in Seventeenth-Century Virginia," in Thad W. Tate and David L. Ammerman, eds., *The Chesapeake in the Seventeenth Century: Essays on Anglo-American Society* (Chapel Hill, N.C., 1979), 168.

21. Daniel Blake Smith, "Mortality and Family in the Colonial Chesapeake," *Journal of Interdisciplinary History*, VIII (1977–1978), 426.

lected Kathryne White, wife of Lewis White, a former employee of Daniel Cugley. Apparently Margery stayed with the Whites until her step-brother John Savage petitioned for, and was granted, her guardianship in 1647.[22]

Not all orphans were so lucky as to have an elder sibling to take the place of parents who had died. In the absence of kin, nearby residents took over. The case of the Bibby family is illustrative. William Bibby, who lived on King's Creek with his wife and two children, died in 1636 or 1637 around the age of thirty-seven.[23] Although Bibby's will is not extant, a deposition in 1637 revealed that he had made one. Some of the stipulations of that document were revealed in a long passage recorded in the county court book after Mary Bibby's death a year later left her children without parents:

> Whereas Mary Bibby Widdow lately deceased lefte behind her a small estate in goodes and chattells and whereas her husband a yeare since deceased upon his death bedd made Capt. William Roper and George Traveller his overseers, Nowe Forasmuch as hee Beinge dead and leaveinge her said estate dispersed and undisposed of the said overseers formerly appoynted out of charity to her children tooke upon them to be Guardyans of the said estate and procured the same to be sould by the advise of some of the most judiciall neighbours adjacent and neere inhabitinge for the best behoofe of the said children And the said Overseers performeinge the same this Courte doth approve thereof and allsoe conceave them to bee the fittest administrators of the said estate and the same to be a just and legall proceedinge All which is hereby humbly certified.[24]

Traveller, who became Elizabeth Bibby's guardian, lived on a tract adjacent to that owned by William Bibby. At the time that Elizabeth became

22. Daniel Cugley died between November 1640 and February 1641. Hannah Savage-Cugley died after he did, but by May 1641, at which time the commissioners of the county court recognized John Webster as guardian (CCR-1, p. 160, CCR-2, pp. 46, 86). On court order, see CCR-2, p. 160. Margery was of age in 1656. Because 16 was usually the age of majority designated for females in wills and deeds of gift, she was probably only about a year old at the time her mother died (CCR-7, fol. 32–p. 33). See n. 5, above, for the residences of Cugley and of Munns and n. 6 for that of Windley; see Chapter 3, n. 8, for Robins's land. On nurse and guardianship, see CCR-1, p. 73, CCR-3, pp. 112, 114.
23. CCR-1, pp. 6, 28, CCR-2, pp. 271, 383; Nugent, ed., *Cavaliers and Pioneers*, I, 43–44.
24. CCR-1, pp. 85, 104–105.

Traveller's responsibility, she was only ten months old. It was unfortunate for this totally dependent orphan that Alice Traveller, George's wife, was strict to the point of brutality. Although her husband tried to stop her ill treatment of Elizabeth, Alice continued her abusive behavior. When George Traveller died in early 1643, there was no mention of Elizabeth Bibby in his will; ominously, there was no further reference to her as alive.[25]

Alice Traveller's behavior was not typical.[26] The concern of her husband and the help of "neighbours adjacent and neere inhabitinge" were far more characteristic of the response to parental mortality. Compare the story of Edmund Bibby, Elizabeth's brother, who was seven years old at the time both of his parents died. William Roper, who became his guardian, lived less than half a mile from the home tracts of both William Bibby and George Traveller. The county court record over the next thirteen years reveals extensive evidence of Roper's concern for the orphaned Edmund and the improvement of his estate. In 1650 William Roper died, and Thomas Hunt took over as the guardian of Edmund, who was almost of age.[27] Hunt lived on a tract about a mile away from Roper's; he had been a resident there even before Bibby's parents had died. The bonds built up over the years must have made it easier for Edmund Bibby to adjust to Hunt's guardianship. In a few years there was an even stronger bond between them—Edmund Bibby married Frances Hunt, daughter of Thomas.[28]

Another example of neighborly concern for the fate of a child left

25. Nugent, ed., *Cavaliers and Pioneers*, I, 43; CCR-2, pp. 239–241, 246–248, 271–272, 280. Besides an absence of any mention of Elizabeth Bibby, the only evidence suggesting her death is a 1644 court case involving Peter Walker and William Roper (CCR-2, p. 383). Walker was married to Alice Traveller-Burdett (she had been married briefly to William Burdett after George Traveller's death) (CCR-2, pp. 293–295, 387). In the case mentioned above, the court ordered Walker to deliver to William Roper a heifer and bull calf belonging to Edmund Bibby. These may have been part of Elizabeth Bibby's estate that descended to her brother Edmund (CCR-2, pp. 280, 381–382).
26. Alice Traveller was a rather controversial person (CCR-1, pp. 116–117, CCR-2, pp. 235–236, 238).
27. For Roper's land, see n. 17, above, and CCR-4, p. 69. For his concern for estate, see CCR-2, pp. 383, 435, CCR-3, pp. 40, 146. For his death and Hunt's guardianship, see CCR-3, pp. 223, 236, fol. 242–p. 243, CCR-4, p. 69.
28. CCR-2, pp. 306–307; Nugent, ed., *Cavaliers and Pioneers*, I, 46. The marriage must have taken place sometime between December 1651 and August 1653. See will of Thomas Hunt for his bequests to his daughter Frances and her daughter Elizabeth Bibby (CCR-4, p. 195, CCR-5, fol. 90–fol. 91).

parentless involved William Roper again. When Phillip Chapman died in 1644, he was survived by two children, Elizabeth and John. Elizabeth's story has been related already in connection with her marriage to John Severne, Jr. Her brother John, an infant at the time of his father's death, was taken in by William Roper, who owned land about a mile distant from Chapman's. Roper had helped Phillip Chapman when the latter was sick, and he had a hand in the settlement of Chapman's affairs. Most important, all indications reveal Roper's careful management of the estate of his ward, who died as a minor.[29]

Parents frequently appointed neighbors to act as feoffees-in-trust for their children's estates. Consider the example of Alice Kirke, whose husband, Christopher, died in early 1653 and left her to care for three children. Immediately after Christopher's death, Alice arranged for a deed of gift to her young offspring. In it she nominated three friends to be the feoffees-in-trust. The land of two of these friends—James Jones and Alexander Maddocks—can be identified. Jones had bought acreage adjacent to Christopher Kirke, who had sold it to him; Maddocks and Jones then patented land adjacent to this purchase. Therefore, Kirke, Jones, and Maddocks were neighbors as well as friends. Another example of this was Stephen Charlton's appointment of his "Trusty and welbeloved friends" John Cornelius and Sampson Robins as feoffees-in-trust for a deed of gift to his daughter Elizabeth. Both Cornelius and Robins lived near Charlton.[30]

Individuals also asked neighbors to serve as executors and overseers of estates. In 1636 William Smith died, leaving a will to be executed by Nicholas Harwood and Walter Scott, who were to share what remained of the estate after they had distributed bequests and settled debts. Although Scott's residence cannot be identified, Harwood lived on the same tract as Smith. When John Waltham died in 1640, he nominated as estate overseers his brother-in-law Stephen Charlton and his friend William Roper, both of whom lived on the same creek. Similarly, Edward

29. CCR-2, pp. 410–411, CCR-3, pp. 146, 241, p. 242–fol. 242 (see also for the costs of the coffin, winding sheet, and funeral charges for the burial of John Chapman), CCR-5, fol. 87–p. 88, fol. 89. For information on Chapman's land, see n. 15, above; for Roper's, n. 17; see also CCR-2, pp. 415–418, 426–427.

30. Kirke: CCR-4, fol. 133, p. 134; Nugent, ed., *Cavaliers and Pioneers*, I, 233; Whitelaw, *Virginia's Eastern Shore*, I, 495, 498–499. For other contacts among Kirke, Maddocks, and Jones, see CCR-3, fols. 142, 170, CCR-4, p. 30–fol. 30, fol. 114.

Charlton: CCR-5, fol. 17–p. 18. For Cornelius's land, see CCR-4, fol. 110–p. 112; for Robins's land, see Chapter 3, n. 8. Questions later arose as to Cornelius's handling of the estate (CCR-5, p. 101, fol. 141, CCR-7, pp. 5, 51).

Drew in his 1649 will made bequests to his wife Mary and to the children of John Dolby; in addition, he appointed Mary and John as joint executors of his estate. At that time the Drews lived on the same creek as the Dolbys. Finally, Richard Vaughan chose three overseers to see that his will was carried out. Thomas Johnson and John Ellis, the two whose residence is known, lived directly across the creek from Vaughan.[31]

These examples provide additional evidence for the development of a societal network based on spatial proximity. An active sociability, the exchange of a wide range of favors, the formation of ties of kinship and fictive kinship (the godparent-godchild relationship)—these contacts and others bound the first-generation colonists to those residing nearby. Each individual was at the center of a spatially limited, if flexibly bounded, web of interactions. Of course, the limits and boundaries of a landholder's personal network varied according to individual motivation as well as conditions for contact—that is, the geographical situation and the possibilities for transportation. But within the area so defined was the primary social world of the Eastern Shore landholder. There, each resident formed interpersonal bonds that provided support not only during life but also after death.

Moreover, these bonds had significance beyond their linking individuals together. They were, in addition, an affirmation of ties to a group, the whole of which represented more than the sum of its parts. Thus, although interpersonal bonds focused on the sorts of exchange and support discussed already, the patterns formed by the interweaving of these individual networks of contact assumed a meaning quite beyond the actual content of the interactions. As each landholder established a personal web of contacts and as these webs overlapped those of other residents in touch with many of the same people, a sense of group responsibility developed. The expressions of this social obligation—of what was proper behavior in the Chesapeake's nascent societies—can be glimpsed in the actions prescribed as well as those proscribed for neighbors.[32]

31. Smith and Harwood: CCR-1, pp. 21, 31, 61–63; Nugent, ed., *Cavaliers and Pioneers*, I, 14, 20. Waltham, Charlton, and Roper: CCR-1, p. 43, CCR-2, pp. 46–49; see n. 17, above, for Roper's land. Drew and Dolby: CCR-3, p. 36, fol. 239–p. 240, fol. 241; Nugent, ed., *Cavaliers and Pioneers*, I, 46, 434. Mary Drew and John Dolby later disagreed over the settlement of the estate of Edward Drew (CCR-3, fol. 243, CCR-4, p. 13, fol. 18, p. 39, fol. 62). Vaughan, Johnson, and Ellis: CCR-3, p. 135a, CCR-4, p. 35, CCR-5, fol. 101–fol. 102; Nugent, ed., *Cavaliers and Pioneers*, I, 164, 171, 184, 217; Whitelaw, *Virginia's Eastern Shore*, I, 528–529.

32. Walsh, "Charles County, Maryland, 1658–1705," 298–299.

The first example here lends an interesting perspective to the previous discussion of the favors exchanged among residents. The occasion was a 1635 case in which interrogatories were administered to several witnesses. The issue involved the identification and ownership of a particular cow, one belonging to a herd driven from one area of the Eastern Shore to another. John Ashcome responded to the interrogatories as follows:

> Did [he] healpe fetch the cattell from mr. Stonnes? . . . He sayeth that he was one of them that holp dryved the cattell from the kings creecke. . . . Did [he] knowe what number they received how many steeres? . . . *As a neighbour* he holp drove them but tooke now notice of the number.[33]

The first three words of Ashcome's answer to the second question reveal the motivation prompting his behavior, the same sort of favor that can be found throughout the county court record. But they also tell us something about the social norm, the behavior prescribed for a neighbor in response to a request for help from a resident nearby.

The social obligations of neighbors found expression elsewhere as well. In 1638 the county court ordered that nine persons who had given public service and thereby neglected their own work were to receive compensation. In this case each of them was to receive the equivalent of sixteen days of work "from theire next adjacent and inhabitinge neighbours."[34] In this way the residents nearby would repay the social debt owed to their neighbors who had given active service.

The story of William and Alice Clawson illustrates support of another kind. The first time William appeared in the court record, he stood accused not only of murdering Pattricke Cudgley, "a trader amongst the Indians," but also of inciting the Indians against the English. Although there is no further record in this case, Clawson cleared himself of the charge. The next reference to him involved his wife Alice as well. According to the presentment of a jury of inquest in 1654, Alice had borne a child shortly before: "And her husband doth disclayme the said child." Whether true or false, William's accusation indicated that their marriage was on shaky ground. Within a year Alice petitioned the court for a separation and justified her plea by showing that her husband was

33. CCR-1, pp. 38–39, emphasis added.
34. CCR-1, p. 109.

a very Extravigant unworthy person in his life and Conversation, spendinge his tyme amongst the Indyans, and demeaneinge himselfe in a most Lettigious, Leawd, dishonest manner ... whereby the poor petitioner his wife hath much suffered and is probable to continue in extreamity of povertye (if not totallye ruianed).

After reviewing the situation, the commissioners ordered that Alice was free to live wherever she wanted without "the disturbance, mollestation, or claime" of William. They also stipulated, if her husband tried to bother her, "that then she take the Assistance of the Sherriff (or Neighbors) to rescue her."[35] The commissioners felt free to rely on Alice's neighbors to protect her in case of any trouble from her husband. They were aware of the sense of social responsibility that grew out of, and fostered in turn, the network of local contacts; they knew that Alice's neighbors would respond to her appeal for help.

One of the most interesting aspects of the social responsibility generated in the neighborhood context was that it served as the basis for a system of social control, a self-policing mechanism to contain intraneighborhood conflicts. Sometimes this control was implicit, as when accepted neighborhood behavior was cited in juxtaposition to its opposite. For example, when Thomas Savage complained to his cousin John Savage that "I heare you will have mee to keepe upp my hoggs in a ppen all the yeare ... John Savage answered you shall keepe upp your hoggs as the rest of your neighbours doth, if they doth you shall."[36] Inasmuch as wandering livestock frequently destroyed crops, a local consensus on how to control this problem was particularly important. In the foregoing example, John Savage voiced the norm of neighborhood behavior in order to coerce his cousin into compliance.

Supplementing this coercion by example was that arising from the oversight of neighbors. The number and variety of illustrations of the

35. For accusations, see CCR-3, fol. 174–p. 175, p. 179; for disclaimer, see CCR-5, p. 13; for separation, see CCR-4, fol. 226–p. 227, CCR-7, p. 11. Two months later, the commissioners granted Alice Clawson a divorce. They cited (CCR-5, p. 135) as a justification that

William Clawson her husband ... (as the Court hath sufficiently bine informed) hath lived in an Adulterous life amongst the Indyans, the greatest part of the tyme hee hath bine marryed And is nowe soe Naturalized to the pagans That hee is knowne by the name of the Emperor of the Nanticoke Indyans (sonne in lawe to Cockasimmon the Kinge of Nanticoke).

36. CCR-3, p. 35–fol. 35.

latter include the whole range of testimony given by neighbors in cases involving residents nearby. One instance of this sort of oversight occurred when the neighbors of Armstrong Foster attested to his expenses in trying to recover three runaway servants. In other instances, James Bruce, Mark Hammon, and John Harlow each received a certificate for acreage on the basis of specific headrights "as appears by indenture and the testimony of his neighbors." In addition, the testimony of neighbors in cases involving abuse of orphans was important on the Eastern Shore and elsewhere in the Chesapeake.[37]

Such testimony represented only one sort of oversight, which was characterized by the passive witnessing of an act and a subsequent statement about it. Another sort of oversight involved neighbors more actively. Consider the evidence revealed during an investigation of suspected murder in 1647. The case involved the unusual circumstances surrounding the death of Jonathan Sneere, a Dutch boy who served John Nuthall. When Sneere disappeared on the morning of Thursday, August 11, Nuthall voiced his suspicions that the youth had overindulged in a feast of "watermillyons" and had gone to sleep somewhere in the fields. In an effort to find Sneere, Nuthall went to the house of Simon Foscutt to inquire whether the latter had seen the lad. Foscutt later testified that he had answered no and that Nuthall had returned home. However,

> in the afternoone the same daye hee came againe and asked this examinant whether he sawe Sneere, this examinant then said Mr. Nuthall, I wonder that you should come here to looke for your servants And told him that hee would harbor none of them: This examinant said that hee was told that Mr. Nuthall beate his servants, and so made them run away.

Stung by the criticism of his neighbor, whose statement later was supported by several witnesses, Nuthall left. On the same day, he also stopped briefly at the house of James Barnaby and told him of the missing servant. The next morning Barnaby received a message from Nuthall that the body of the dead boy had been found. After Barnaby arrived to view the corpse, certain suspicious marks prompted him to tell Nuthall "that hee could not bury him untill hee had sent for some of his Neigh-

---

37. Foster: CCR-4, p. 52. Bruce, Hammon, and Harlow: CCR-2, pp. 82, 117–118. On orphans, see Lois Green Carr, "The Development of the Maryland Orphans' Court, 1654–1715," in Aubrey C. Land *et al.*, eds., *Law, Society, and Politics in Early Maryland* (Baltimore, 1977), 54–55.

bors (vizt) Mr. Andrews or Capt Stone." The advice of Barnaby was echoed by that of Robert Berry, who said that Sneere "must not bee buried untill some of your Neighbors see him." Given the unusual situation and Nuthall's reputation of being harsh to his servants, his neighbors apparently felt that a formal hearing was appropriate. The commissioners, in turn having examined the business, ordered that Nuthall and his black servant Peter were to appear before the governor and Council at James City.³⁸

Another example of a master's abuse of his servant brought a quick and personal response from residents nearby. The deposition of John Williams provides most of the salient details of the incident. According to Williams's statement, sometime in mid-August 1653 he and his wife

> were att the howse of Mr. Jno. Browne and comeinge over the Creecke, in a Canowe, wee heard a loud crye, Then this deponent said, sure Rich: Jacob is beateinge of his boye for runinge awaye, my wife answered noe, it is att Jno. Toulson his howse, sure hee is beateinge of his mayde, Then landeinge I heard one crye out, in a most lamentable manner (Mu[r]ther) I run upp to the poynt over against Jno. Toulsons, And the crye ceased; there this deponent meete with Rich: Jacobs wife and younge Phill: Taylor and another younge man; ... Then this deponent stripped off his cloathes with a purpose to gett over the Creecke to see and understand the meaneinge of that strange crye; then Mr. Jno. Browne his Canowe came upp the Creecke; and this deponent went over with them to Toulson his howse.

When Brown and Williams reached the scene of the cries, Susanna Dowdridge, the servant of Towlson, was in a "deplorable state"—on the ground, with her clothes in tatters, and stained with mud and blood. Towlson refused to take care of her, so she was brought to Jacob's house. The depositions of Mary, wife of John Williams, and Mary, wife of Richard Jacob, corroborated this account and added further evidence as to the serious nature of Susanna's injuries, "as will bee further Testified by women." What aroused the concern of all involved was, as the court clerk phrased it, the "most viollent, Inhumane, immoderate manner [in which Towlson has] beatten and abused Susanna Dowdridge (contrarye

38. CCR-3, fols. 114, 115, p. 116–fol. 118. Apparently Nuthall and his black servant Peter both were acquitted; see the reference to them in CCR-4, p. 42–fol. 45.

to reason and conscience)." As Mary Jacob later recounted, her fear for Susanna's life had led her to intervene: "This Deponent went down to the Creecke side, and said Jno. Towlson, doe you murther your Mayde." Of central interest is that all of the individuals mentioned in conjunction with this incident were neighbors. Towlson, Jacob, and Brown all lived near one another on a branch of Nuswattocks Creek; and Williams's tract, about one mile distant, was on the next branch to the north.[39] As with the neighbors of John Nuthall, those of John Towlson were alert to occurrences nearby. Aware of their public obligations, these individuals responded quickly and responsibly.[40]

Other examples of oversight reveal another aspect of local affairs that came under the scrutiny of residents nearby—that is, births out of wedlock. Thus, when Frances Smith, a servant of Thomas Powell, named Clawse Johnson of Amsterdam as the father of her baby, Johnson asked Powell's neighbors Grace Robins and Dorothy (Robins) Eveling to look into the accusation for him. This sort of oversight was not unusual. The primary interest of the local inhabitants as well as of the authorities was that the illegitimate child should not become a burden on the public revenues, that the parish not be "charged or molested therewith."[41] Therefore, establishing paternity was a paramount concern. In 1654 the commissioners heard evidence presented in an odder case, where neither the father nor the mother of a newborn child could be identified. Again the role of neighbors was instrumental in revealing this situation. "Robert Baily . . . hath received into his howse a young child permittinge his wife to Nurse the same, which seeameinge a thinge both newe and strange To Neighbors there resideinge . . . presentment [has been] made thereof to the Court by the Church officer."[42]

Some breaches of the local norm were so serious as to warrant more than coercion by example or the implicit pressure of neighborly oversight. In these cases, residents as a group turned to the county court for redress. Thus,

Upon the Complaynts of Capt William Whittington, Urmstronge Foster, Nicholas Grandger, Rich: Nottingham and Elder Aldridge

39. For residences, see CCR-4, fol. 114, fol. 204–fol. 205, CCR-5, p. 86–fol. 87; Nugent, ed., *Cavaliers and Pioneers*, I, 129, 130, 164–165, 194, 199, 203. For quotations, see CCR-4, p. 206, fol. 206.

40. The commissioners ordered that Susanna Dowdridge be released from her one-year contract with Towlson. The latter was to pay any wages due as well as all charges and damages. CCR-4, p. 206–fol. 206.

41. CCR-3, p. 225–fol. 225, p. 235.

42. CCR-5, fol. 26–p. 27.

this daye declared to the Court . . . it manifestly appeareth that Mr.
Ben: Cowdery is a very turbulent man towards his Neighbors. And
in his personall Actions much offencive unto them, severall tymes
exciteinge and provoaking his said Neighbors with deffamatorye
speeches.

Ordered that . . . Cowdery shall . . . enter into bond with sufficient security for his good behavior otherwise to stand comitted in
the custodye of the sherriffe And that hee . . . forthwith make payment of all costs and charges in the perticular suits.

Clearly, the commissioners hoped that Cowdery's bond would ensure his
good behavior in the future. Moreover, in two related suits Cowdery's
punishment can be viewed both as payment for damage inflicted on
particular individuals and as payment due for a violation of the social
order. In the first case, he had to pay William Whittington for the destruction of personal property. In the second, convicted of stealing
peaches from Armstrong Foster, Cowdery (and a servant who had helped
him in the deed) were fined a total of five hundred pounds of tobacco
to be disposed for public use "as a deserved merritt of the fact, and for
example to others that maye hereafter presume to committ the like
offence."[43]

Another example of a neighborhood effort to control the destructive
behavior of an individual involved William Stephens, Sr. Again the commissioners granted an award for damages to the complainants as well as
a general fine. The court's rationale was stated clearly in the record. .

Forasmuch as many Complaynts have bine made and some of them
proved That William Stephens Senior hath frequently shoote att his
Neighbors horses mares and colts . . . Ordered that . . . Stephens be
fyned the summe of four hundred pounds of tobacco . . . to bee paid
for the use of the County.

In addition, "for prevention of the like Actions (de future) and example
to others that they maye bee deterred from such practizes," they ordered
Stephens to pay three hundred pounds of tobacco to each of the two
neighbors who had proved their accusations.[44]

This was not the only example of neighborhood friction caused by the
destruction of livestock. The potential for trouble was exacerbated by
the fact that many settlers allowed their animals to wander freely in

43. CCR-5, fol. 61, p. 71–fol. 72.
44. CCR-6, p. 6.

search of forage. Because one possible source of food could be found
growing in neighbors' fields, the court record contains evidence of local
conflict caused by the depredations of roaming beasts. That the damage
could be considerable is attested to by the fact that eight of William
Stone's servants were kept busy a full day in order to replant corn up-
rooted by hogs in the spring of 1642.[45]

Inasmuch as landholders were responsible for protecting their crops
with fences, it sometimes became an issue whether the owner of the
errant livestock was liable to pay damages.[46] Thus, according to a deposition made in 1647 by George Smith, "Thomas Peake aboute August
last haveinge hoggs in his corne desyred this deponent to come and veiwe
his fence to see if it were sufficient or not: And upon veiw this deponent
found the fence very good and sufficient Except three places which were
broaken downe by hoggs." Smith's assessment of the situation agreed
with that given by another witness, Anthony Raboone. Another example
sums up the potential for friction because of wandering livestock. In
1651 Benjamin Mathews shot one of Stephen Charlton's oxen, which
had destroyed part of Mathews's corn crop. The ox was so seriously
wounded that Charlton had to kill it. Angered by the loss, he told
Mathews to "take a Couple of men and let them veiwe thy fence and if
thy Fence bee sufficient I will [give] thee satisfaction for the dammages."
The two fence viewers reported that the fence around Mathews's corn
field was "Four foote and an Inch (or thereabouts) in some places more
and in some less." This was not enough. The court ordered Mathews to
enter into bond for his good behavior (he had threatened further damage
to Charlton's livestock), to pay for the ox he had shot, and to give "as a
deserved fine" a hogshead of tobacco toward the building of a bridge at
Hungars Creek.[47]

Of further significance in this last case was that, at one point, Charlton
told Mathews, "I have lost many Hoggs and For ought I knowe thou
hast made them awaye."[48] This magnification of the accusation demon-

45. CCR-2, pp. 166–167. For examples of livestock roaming freely, see CCR-1, pp.
29–30, 158, 159, CCR-2, pp. 213–214, 386–387, CCR-3, fol. 18, CCR-4, fol. 52–p.
53, fol. 119–p. 120, CCR-5, p. 7–fol. 7.

46. William Waller Hening, ed., *The Statutes at Large; Being a Collection of All the
Laws of Virginia*, I (New York, 1823), 244; Warren M. Billings, ed., "Some Acts Not
in Hening's *Statutes*: The Acts of Assembly, April 1652, November 1652, and July
1653," *VMHB*, LXXXIII (1975), 58–59.

47. Peake: CCR-3, fol. 126, p. 127. Mathews: CCR-4, p. 50–fol. 50, fol. 54–p. 55,
fol. 56.

48. CCR-4, p. 50–fol. 50.

strates how a vague suspicion of wrongdoing could sever neighborly bonds. A long deposition given by Robert Berry in 1652 reveals the same problem in greater detail. Berry described how he had been walking in the woods, when he heard a gunshot and the cry of a hog. Hastening to the scene, he saw a man carry the hog away. After a brief search of the area, Berry found the hog's ears, which were mutilated but still bore the identifiable mark of John Tilney's livestock. He then pursued the poacher and stopped his flight. Having accused the thief, Berry threatened to expose him. The man cried and begged for mercy, claiming that this was the first and last time he would ever kill another's hog. "This deponent told him that hee heard many of his Neighbors (in this case) mistrust him But nowe hee did knowe and see it was true; And said plainly that hee would not Conceale it, for honest men were mistrusted for such knaves as he is."[49] In addition to revealing the active oversight and social control of neighbors, this passage testifies to the potentially poisonous consequences that such suspicions could generate. Neighborhood ties were not indestructible.

A final example of discord relating to livestock is recorded in the particularly long petition of Thomas Gascoyne, who sought to maintain local harmony at the same time that he recovered a stray hog. Explaining how the beast had been taken up by John Wilkins, Gascoyne explained that he

> no wayes aymeth att the subversion or dissuasion of the said Wilkins or his estate, neither is your petitioners affected with or addicted to, anie malignancy or malevolenc in his proceedings But altogether desireth aswell the tranquillity and peace of himselfe, as also of his neighbors.

Nevertheless, he argued, it was only fair and just that he be reimbursed for his loss. The commissioners agreed, but, in assigning damages, they ascribed Wilkins's action to "a mistake . . . concerninge the markeing of the said hogg."[50] Gascoyne was satisfied, Wilkins's reputation intact, and neighborly bonds not irrevocably damaged.

Inasmuch as nearby fields provided the attraction for most wandering livestock, the suits that resulted generally involved neighbors. Such was also the case for disputes about the boundaries and ownership of land-

49. CCR-4, fol. 109. For legislation designed to control hog poaching, see Hening, ed., *Statutes at Large*, I, 244; Billings, ed., "Some Acts Not in Hening's *Statutes*," *VMHB*, LXXXIII (1975), 62.
50. CCR-2, pp. 51–52.

holdings. The vast majority of such litigation represented conflicts between individuals who believed they had a legitimate title to the disputed
acreage. Several explanations account for the conflicting claims. An individual might patent acreage but fail to seat it; a conflicting claim resulted
when another person, assuming that the land was available, filed for a
second patent. Other sources of trouble included failure to have the land
surveyed, faulty surveying, or following an improper patent procedure.[51]
An increase in the number of surveyors made it more difficult to keep
track of where land was and was not available. From the mid-1630s to
the early 1650s, Edmund Scarburgh served as surveyor on the Eastern
Shore. In 1653, however, three more men began to act in that capacity,
and from then on it became essential for all practicing surveyors to check
with one another to prevent a duplication of land measurements.[52]

Much of the litigation generated by conflicting claims for land would
have been prevented if the county had kept a central record of which
land was available and which claimed. John James took a step in that
direction in 1653 when he petitioned the commissioners of the Northampton County court.[53] Beginning with a statement of the problem,
James showed that

> there bee many and great controversyes amongst the Inhabitants
> Concerneinge the bounds of their Lands, cheeifly occasioned, by

51. For conflicting patents, see William Andrews v. Francis Stockley, in CCR-1, p.
116; John Lock and John Little v. Levin Denwood, CCR-1, p. 102. For other sources
of troubles, see Thomas Powell v. Obedience Robins, CCR-2, p. 220; William Melling
v. Hannah Mountney, CCR-4, fol. 83; George Parker v. John West, CCR-4, p. 207;
William Johnson v. Anthony Hodgskins, CCR-4, fol. 210; and Edmund Bibby's claim
for land, CCR-5, fol. 24.

52. On Scarburgh, see CCR-1, pp. 91, 116, CCR-2, pp. 34, 234, 306, 311–312,
387, CCR-4, fol. 78, pp. 144, 214, fol. 219, CCR-5, fol. 106–p. 107, p. 108.
For new surveyors, see CCR-4, p. 142, fol. 212–p. 213, p. 216. For William
Melling's checking with Scarburgh, see CCR-5, p. 125, p. 134–fol. 134. Scarburgh
became primus inter pares when the commissioners ordered that he examine the
qualifications of all surveyors (CCR-5, p. 134–fol. 134).

53. CCR-4, fol. 212–p. 213. It also would have helped if the county had maintained a record of all land sales, mortgages, and conveyances. In 1652 an act was
passed ordering the counties to keep such a record, but there is no evidence of
compliance. Billings, ed., "Some Acts Not in Hening's *Statutes*," VMHB, LXXXIII
(1975), 35.
For examples of disputed ownership, see William Berriman v. Thomas Smith, CCR-
1, p. 87; Roger Sanders v. Thomas Savage, CCR-1, p. 102; Thomas Savage v. William
Whittington, CCR-3, p. 159; Henry Armitrading v. John Williams, CCR-5, fol. 143.
For the General Assembly's efforts to set up guidelines for fair judgments and to
control the amount of litigation, see Hening, ed., *Statutes at Large*, I, 260, 331.

reason that many have taken surveys and pattents alsoe have a longe tyme seatted their land, haveinge never measured nor knowne the just bounds and limmits thereof; whereby they often intrench upon their Neighbors. And doe cause great confusion and disturbance in this place.

James continued to explain that he already had chosen William Melling to assist him

that they might goe together through the County to survey and doe their Indevors to compose all Cases (in that behalfe) And that a Booke maye bee kept for the whole County of Entrys for Land; And of the surveys granted; That heereafter all men maye knowe the Antiquitye thereof; the scituation; marks, Bounds and Lymmits of their lands and possessions.

Following James's petition and his signature, the court clerk recorded an epigram indicating an awareness of the threat of land controversies to local bonds: "Cursed is the man that removeth the marks of his Neighbors Land." The commissioners, recognizing James's qualifications as a surveyor and the prior approval of the governor and Council, granted his petition. The worthy project had everyone's blessing. But it failed. The partnership was dissolved at the request of Melling a year after the grant of James's petition.[54] The failure may have been due to a personality conflict. Or the project may have faltered because of their effort "to compose all Cases" of discord, a difficult task that would have required great tact and skill in arbitration. In any event, lack of success probably was inevitable. As with certain problems arising from roaming livestock, most disputes about land ownership involved economic considerations that weakened the force of neighborhood control.

For slightly different, if no less compelling, reasons, local control frequently failed to contain serious interpersonal conflict arising from slander, assault, and accusations of wrongdoing. Of eighty-four such incidents that involved at least one landholder, the residences of both parties can be determined in twenty-one cases.[55] In 86 percent of the twenty-one

54. CCR-4, fol. 212–p. 213, CCR-5, p. 71. James's petition may have been prompted by passage of the act mentioned in n. 53, above.

55. Omitted from the total number of incidents are those involving slander or assault directed toward a commissioner in his official capacity. These cases, which usually occurred in court, were different in quality from those that arose out of daily intercourse and will be discussed in Chapter 8.

cases, plaintiff and defendant were neighbors. The nature of these disputes, which involved accusations of sexual misconduct, theft, abuse of servants, dishonesty, and so forth, made unlikely their resolution at the local level. The arbitration of the county court was necessary.

Interestingly, many of these cases of slander naturally grew out of social control based on neighborhood ties. Incidents of sexual misconduct, theft, abuse of servants, and such were brought to the attention of the county court through the efforts of neighbors. Inevitably, some of these accusations were buttressed by insufficient evidence, whether because of overzealousness, drink-loosened lips, or malice on the part of the accuser. Whatever prompted the accusation, failure to prove it left the accuser open to a charge of slander. The commissioners, probably intent on maintaining neighborhood social control, punished those who violated their role as guardians of the public welfare. The nature of the punishment served to emphasize this violation. Those convicted of slander usually were ordered by the commissioners to ask forgiveness in public, sometimes in church, sometimes in court. Occasionally other punishments were prescribed. Convicted slanderers were towed over creeks, ducked, placed in stocks, whipped, or commanded either to pay a fine for the public use or to perform a public service.[56] Whatever the punishment meted out, its public nature served as an example and a warning of the consequences of disturbing the local peace.

The spatially restricted interactional networks and neighborhood orientation sketched here were shaped by the conditions of settlement on the Eastern Shore. Overland travel was difficult for long distances. In addition, not everyone had immediate and constant access to a water carrier. Given these limitations of transportation, settlers turned to their neighbors for sociability, favors, support, and the formation of kin ties. This local orientation was buttressed by the fact that, for the most part, relatives lived nearby. Describing Virginia in 1656, John Hammond commented on "the many delightfull rivers, on which the inhabitants are settled (every man almost living in sight of a lovely river)," and he

56. For orders to ask forgiveness, see CCR-1, pp. 116–117, 142, 145, CCR-2, pp. 201, 208, 235–236, 238, CCR-3, p. 229, CCR-4, p. 7–fol. 7, pp. 8, 90, fols. 105, 142, fol. 143–p. 144, p. 168, CCR-5, pp. 3, 14, fol. 135–p. 136. For towing, see CCR-1, pp. 20, 22–23, 38, CCR-4, fol. 90. For ducking, see CCR-1, p. 88. For the use of stocks, see CCR-1, pp. 134, 150. For whipping, see CCR-1, pp. 49, 86, 118, CCR-2, pp. 351, 395, CCR-3, fols. 2, 196, CCR-4, p. 42–fol. 45, p. 90. For fines and public service, see CCR-1, pp. 15, 23, 117, CCR-2, pp. 59–60, CCR-4, p. 89, CCR-5, fol. 20, CCR-6, p. 6.

extolled "the extraordinary good neighbour-hood and loving conversation they have one with the other." Despite Hammond's pro-Virginia bias, this account seems accurate in the light of the available evidence.[57]

Gideon Tillisson's brief residency on the Eastern Shore serves to illustrate Hammond's depiction. Tillisson arrived on the Eastern Shore in late 1648 or early 1649. He immediately leased land and tobacco housing from Richard Hudson, and he purchased two heifers. Tillisson was either married when he arrived or found a wife very quickly, because in September 1649 Eleanor Tillisson appeared in court and accused Barbara Winbery of slander. Gideon Tillisson and John Winbery each entered into bond to prevent any such disturbance in the future. Richard Hudson, Tillisson's landlord and neighbor, witnessed the bond. The closeness of Tillisson's relationship to Hudson was revealed when Tillisson died in early 1652. At that time Hudson owed him 1,586 pounds of tobacco; Tillisson in turn owed Hudson a hogshead of tobacco and some milk that Hudson had lent to him. More important was a strong emotional tie. Tillisson, apparently a widower by this time and concerned about the future of his son Gideon Junior, arranged to "bequeath" him "into the hands of Richard Hudson (as his Guardyan) to see and provide that hee maie bee brought upp in the feare of god. And as his owne Children And to have a fatherly care over him and not to lett him bee abused." Finally, he appointed Hudson his executor and ultimate heir in case Gideon Junior died. Such could be the strength and reliance on neighborly ties.[58]

57. Hammond, *Leah and Rachel*, 18, in Force, ed., *Tracts and Other Papers*, III. See also Rutman and Rutman, *A Place in Time: Middlesex County*, 59–60. For Maryland, see Carr, "Sources of Political Stability and Upheaval," *MHM*, LXXIX (1984), 45–47.
58. For Tillisson's will, see CCR-4, fol. 65; see also CCR-3, p. 171–fol. 171, CCR-4, p. 92, fol. 106–p. 107.

5 The Local Economic Network

TO A LARGE EXTENT, the familial and familiar world of landholders on the Eastern Shore extended only a very few miles from their residences. Conditions for transportation in a dispersed settlement made inevitable this constricted range of daily contacts. Economic transactions occurred within equally narrow confines. This conclusion arises from an examination of where the creditors and debtors of recently deceased landholders lived. It is reinforced by a broad sampling of all economic exchanges and by a study of the role of stores and ordinaries in shaping the local economic network.

Toward the end of 1645 or the beginning of 1646, Richard Lemon died. He had lived on the Eastern Shore for about five years. A year or two before his death, he had married Jane Jackson, widowed mother of Jonas Jackson, and established his family on Cherrystone Creek. Immediately after Richard Lemon died, Jane Jackson-Lemon, widowed again, received a letter of administration from the commissioners of the county court, and for the next year and a half she paid debts and collected amounts due to the estate. Among the estate's creditors and debtors were eight landholders whose residences at the time of Lemon's death can be located. Five of the eight lived on the same creek as Lemon, two lived about three miles away, and one lived eight miles away.[1]

By itself this pattern merely fleshes out the details of Lemon's brief residency on the Eastern Shore. But its significance is actually much greater. The pattern formed by the geographic dispersion of Lemon's debtors and creditors is representative of the patterns of other Eastern Shore residents that died before the end of 1655. For the entire period

1. See CCR-2, pp. 172–174, for the first reference to Richard Lemon; CCR-2, pp. 450–451, CCR-3, p. 6, for his death; CCR-2, p. 266, for the last reference to the widow Jane Jackson; CCR-3, fol. 55, for their residence; CCR-3, pp. 7, 113, for Jane Jackson-Lemon as administratrix. Richard Lemon had probably married Jane Jackson by July 1644, when he acted as attorney for her brother, William Berriman (CCR-2, p. 374; Ralph T. Whitelaw, *Virginia's Eastern Shore: A History of Northampton and Accomack Counties*, 2 vols. [Richmond, Va., 1951], I, 444).

The eight landholders were Obedience Robins, Stephen Charlton, William Stephens, John Savage, Edward Drew, William Berriman, Phillip Taylor, and John Harlow. CCR-3, fol. 7, p. 12, fols. 19, 20, p. 44, p. 90–p. 91.

under consideration, more than half the accounts outstanding at the time of death were with landholders living on the same or an adjacent tract, across or on the same creek, or less than three miles from the decedent's home tract. The period before 1640 had the highest proportion (82 percent) of contacts in this category. This is not very surprising: settlement on the peninsula was not very spread out before 1640, and contacts took place within a smaller spatial setting than was later the case. After 1640 this five-year proportion of nearby contacts fluctuated from 64 percent to 77 percent to a low of 57 percent. The last and lowest percentage belongs to the period 1651–1655, when settlement expanded dramatically on the Eastern Shore and the possibility for long-range contacts increased.

But not all landholders took advantage of the possibility. Significant differences are revealed by separating landholders into groups according to factors that might be expected to influence the range of the economic network. The first group includes commissioners, who had a better opportunity to deal with people in different parts of the county because of the peripatetic nature of the county court. This first group also includes merchants, who had the same opportunity because of the demands of their occupation. The second group consists of ministers, storekeepers, and ordinarykeepers. Ministers have been included in a separate group, because, until 1652, there was only one officiating on the Eastern Shore at any one time; as the area of settlement spread, the minister would travel in rotation to preside at services in different parts of the county. Therefore, ministers had the same chance for broader contacts as had commissioners. Storekeepers and ordinarykeepers, because of the nature of their work, were similar to merchants in the possibility for extensive networks.[2] The third and last group includes all individuals who do not fit into either of the first two groups.

It is evident that a systematic relationship exists between these different groups and the distances involved in economic transactions. Thus, before 1640, when 82 percent of all contacts were between people living not more than three miles apart, a slightly lower 79 percent of the contacts involving commissioners and merchants were in that range. Throughout the period under consideration, this relationship was invari-

2. Although this second group includes very few contacts, it was separated from the first group of commissioners and merchants because it made less clear the distinctiveness of the latter's pattern. For the same reason, the second group was separated from the third.

Table 11. Range of Economic Network at Death

	Date of Death			
Contacts by Landholders	Before 1640 (N = 5)	1641– 1645 (N = 14)	1646– 1650 (N = 12)	1651– 1655 (N = 11)
1–3 Miles, Same or Adjacent Tract, on or across Same Creek				
Commissioner or merchant				
No. of contacts	11	29	18	25
Proportion in same role	79%	55%	72%	53%
Minister, store-keeper, ordinarykeeper				
No. of contacts	1	2	1	2
Proportion in same role	50%	67%	100%	33%
Other				
No. of contacts	7	19	7	9
Proportion in same role	100%	83%	88%	90%
Proportion of all contacts	82%	64%	77%	57%
4–6 Miles				
Commissioner or merchant				
No. of contacts	2	9	3	8
Proportion in same role	14%	17%	12%	17%
Minister, store-keeper, ordinarykeeper				
No. of contacts	0	0	0	4
Proportion in same role				67%
Other				
No. of contacts	0	1	0	1
Proportion in same role		4%		10%
Proportion of all contacts	9%	12%	9%	21%

Table 11. *Continued*

Contacts by Landholders	Before 1640 (N=5)	1641– 1645 (N=14)	1646– 1650 (N=12)	1651– 1655 (N=11)
			Date of Death	
7 + Miles				
Commissioner or merchant				
No. of contacts	1	15	4	14
Proportion in same role	7%	28%	16%	30%
Minister, store-keeper, ordinarykeeper				
No. of contacts	1	1	0	0
Proportion in same role	50%	33%		
Other				
No. of contacts	0	3	1	0
Proportion in same role		13%	13%	
Proportion of all contacts	8%	24%	15%	22%

Note: An effort was made to identify residences of as many deceased landholders as possible. Because the residences of prominent individuals can be identified more often than others, a bias toward the broader networks of this group would result if they were not segregated. Thus, decedents are placed in one of three groups. The first includes merchants and commissioners of the county court; the second, ministers, storekeepers, and ordinarykeepers; the third, everyone else. Next, the names of creditors and debtors were recovered from inventories and from individual claims made at meetings of the county court, and the residences of these individuals identified where possible. Finally, the debts arising from settlement of an estate—minister's fee for a funeral sermon, payment to a carpenter for a coffin, clerk's charge for official duties—are, whenever identifiable, not included as part of the economic network of the deceased.

able: at a distance of three miles or less, the proportion of contacts involving this group of landholders was consistently lower than the overall proportion of contacts at that distance. On the other hand, in the same mileage range, the individuals in the third group just as consistently accounted for a proportion of contacts higher than the overall proportion. Thus, although 82 percent of all pre-1640 contacts were at a distance of three miles or less, 100 percent of the contacts between individuals in the third group fell into that range. While the overall proportion of contacts at this distance fluctuated between 77 percent and 57 percent from 1641 to 1655, the proportion between individuals in the third group never fell below 83 percent.

At the other end of the scale, where contacts spanned seven miles or more, the above situation was reversed. In the years from 1641 to 1645, when 24 percent of all contacts were at a distance of seven miles or more, a disproportionately low 13 percent of contacts between individuals in the third group fell into this range, compared to a disproportionately high 28 percent of contacts involving merchants and commissioners. More dramatically, from 1651 to 1655, when 22 percent of all contacts extended seven miles or more, 30 percent of contacts involving commissioners or merchants were in this category, but the percentage between landholders in the third group was zero.

In sum, the unusually high proportion of contacts involving merchants and commissioners at a distance of seven miles or more indicates the extent to which they dominated the long-range economic network. By occupation and official position, they possessed an opportunity to form ties with individuals at a distance far greater than that possible for others not so fortunately situated. The relative lack of opportunity for individuals who were not commissioners, merchants, ministers, storekeepers, and ordinarykeepers is obvious from the extraordinarily high proportion of their contacts that fall in the range of three miles or less. This does not mean that these landholders never formed ties at a distance greater than three miles; it means that, if they did so, the contacts were with commissioners or merchants. And inasmuch as landholders in the third group infrequently formed long-range economic contacts among themselves, it is most likely that the mobility of the commissioners and merchants made long-distance ties possible. Very tentatively, a sketch of the economic network on the Eastern Shore would depict each landholder's residence as a point surrounded by a circle with a three-mile radius, representing the range of contact for most landholders. From the residences of commissioners and merchants would extend lines at a much greater distance, corresponding to their wider range of ties. Studies of the range of economic contacts in other areas of the Chesapeake replicate this pattern.[3]

3. Lorena Seebach Walsh, "Charles County, Maryland, 1658–1705: A Study of Chesapeake Social and Political Structure" (Ph.D. diss., Michigan State University, 1977), 294–296; Darrett B. Rutman and Anita H. Rutman, *A Place in Time: Middle-*

A few examples illustrate the position of commissioners and merchants in the economic network of the peninsula. In this connection, it is interesting to consider again the case of Richard Lemon, who was a "third group" landholder. As noted earlier, of the eight landholders mentioned in conjunction with the settlement of his estate and whose residences can be located, seven lived on the same creek as Lemon or less than three miles away from him. The eighth, Stephen Charlton, lived on a tract eight miles distant. The significance of Charlton as an exception lay in the fact that he was a commissioner and merchant. The greater distance between his residence and that of Lemon is explicable in terms of the broader economic networks of individuals in Charlton's official or occupational category. The sketch of the geographic dispersion of Richard Lemon's debts and credits at the time of his death thus also demonstrates how contacts with commissioners and merchants tied other landholders into a broader economic network than otherwise would have been the case. It exemplifies the economic view from the perspective of a modest landholder.

For the perspective of a commissioner, Argoll Yardley provides a good case study. Yardley was the eldest son of a former governor of Virginia and lived on a large tract of land that he had inherited from his father. When Argoll Yardley died sometime in September or October 1655, he had been a commissioner for fifteen years. His wife, Ann, immediately received from Yardley's fellow commissioners a letter of administration to settle the accounts of the estate. In November 1655 she petitioned the county court to grant her a *quietus est*, signifying a conclusion to her role as administratrix of her deceased husband's estate.[4] Of the many debtors and creditors whose accounts had been brought forward and ranked according to precedence by this time, there were nine landholders whose residences can be identified. The geographic dispersion of Yardley's economic network, as represented by a plotting of these nine individuals, is characteristic of the pattern for contacts involving commissioners. Thus, five of the nine landholders lived on tracts within three miles of Yardley's

---

sex County, Virginia, 1650–1750 (New York, 1984), 120–121, 206; Lorena S. Walsh, "Community Networks in the Early Chesapeake," in Lois Green Carr, Philip D. Morgan, and Jean B. Russo, eds., *Colonial Chesapeake Society* (Chapel Hill, N.C., 1988), 226–227.

4. CCR-2, pp. 34, 53, 278–279, CCR-3, p. 44, p. 90–p. 91, CCR-5, fol. 117–fol. 119, CCR-6, p. 7, fols. 16, 27; Nell Marion Nugent, ed., *Cavaliers and Pioneers: Abstracts of Virginia Land Patents and Grants*, I, 1623–1666, II, 1666–1695 (Richmond, Va., 1934, 1977), I, 96; Whitelaw, *Virginia's Eastern Shore*, I, 408.

Table 12. Range of Economic Networks for Fifty-six Landholders

Contacts by Landholders	Date of Interaction			
	Before 1640	1641–1645	1646–1650	1651–1655
1–3 Miles, Same or Adjacent Tract, on or across Same Creek				
Commissioner or merchant				
No. of contacts	8	12	8	16
Proportion in same role	80%	63%	38%	49%
Minister, storekeeper, ordinarykeeper				
No. of contacts	3	0	5	7
Proportion in same role	100%		56%	50%
Other				
No. of contacts	12	13	18	8
Proportion in same role	71%	81%	90%	89%
Proportion of all contacts	77%	70%	62%	55%
4–6 Miles				
Commissioner or merchant				
No. of contacts	0	4	4	5
Proportion in same role		21%	19%	15%
Minister, storekeeper, ordinarykeeper				
No. of contacts	0	0	1	2
Proportion in same role			11%	14%
Other				
No. of contacts	4	1	1	0
Proportion in same role	24%	6%	5%	
Proportion of all contacts	13%	14%	12%	13%

Table 12. *Continued*

	Date of Interaction			
Contacts by Landholders	Before 1640	1641– 1645	1646– 1650	1651– 1655
7 + Miles				
Commissioner or merchant				
No. of contacts	2	3	9	12
Proportion in same role	20%	16%	43%	36%
Minister, storekeeper, ordinarykeeper				
No. of contacts	0	1	3	5
Proportion in same role		100%	33%	36%
Other				
No. of contacts	1	2	1	1
Proportion in same role	6%	13%	5%	11%
Proportion of all contacts	10%	17%	26%	32%

Note: Landholders are divided into the same three groups as in Table 11. To simplify a potentially endless compilation, only landholders with identifiable occupations are chosen. To reduce the enormous number of economic links involving commissioners and merchants, the myriad contacts of landholders in this first group are omitted unless the contacts turned up among the economic links of other landholders of identifiable occupation. Also, because contacts before 1640 were between settlers in a relatively smaller settlement than was later the case, landholders who died before that date are eliminated from consideration; pre-1640 contacts of those who lived after are included.

home tract, one was at a distance of four miles, and three lived on tracts more than six miles away.[5]

In the same way that Argoll Yardley's economic network was representative of that for commissioners, Luke Stubbings's was typical for merchants. Stubbings, a resident for at least six years, died in the spring of 1645, and his wife became the administratrix of his estate. Residences can be found for nine of his creditors and debtors.[6] Four of the nine lived

5. CCR-6, p. 7, fols. 7, 8, pp. 13, 14, fol. 15.
6. CCR-2, pp. 171, 412, 430; "Viewers of Tobacco Crop, 1639," *VMHB*, V (1897–1898), 122. Residences: CCR-2, pp. 10, 430, 449–450, CCR-3, p. 8, fols. 9, 10, p. 11–fol. 11, p. 12.

on tracts less than three miles away, one was six miles distant, and four more lived at a greater distance.

The estate debts and credits of Yardley and Stubbings demonstrate how widespread were the economic networks of commissioners and merchants. As with the accounts for deceased landholders in the third group, they provide a snapshot of the economic links binding the population together. Unfortunately, the total number of such links identifiable for deceased landholders is low; therefore, the patterns formed by these links are sketchier than desirable.

An alternative approach to the issue of the geographic dispersion of economic networks is based on an effort to map a comprehensive range of economic contacts between landholders. These contacts are documented in contracts recorded in the county court records, suits instituted to collect debts, and random references in depositions and elsewhere. Most striking about such a compilation is the consistency of the trends over time in each of the mileage classifications. Thus the proportion of all economic contacts at a distance of three miles or less fell steadily from 77 percent before 1640 to 55 percent in the period 1651–1655. This decline corresponded to the spread of population over a wider and wider area and the consequent increase in the chances for contact at a greater distance. The latter development is dramatically illustrated by focusing on the links at a distance of seven miles and more. At this distance, the trend was the reverse of that for contacts under three miles. The proportion of all contacts increased from 10 percent in the years before 1640 to 32 percent in the five years 1651–1655.

Within these broad trends appeared the same sorts of variation, based on office and occupation, seen in the examination of economic networks at time of death. For the most part, the proportion of contacts involving a commissioner or merchant fell below the average at a distance of three miles or less; on the other end of the scale, at a distance of seven miles or more, the proportion of contacts for this group generally was above the average. For contacts between landholders in the third group (those not commissioners, merchants, ministers, storekeepers, or ordinarykeepers), the proportion was almost invariably above average in the lowest mileage category and below the average in the highest.

Thus the "moving picture" of all litigated debts, contracts, and random references to economic links over time repeats and helps to confirm the same patterns seen by examining the cumulative snapshots of economic networks at the time of death. The similarity of patterns produced by these two different approaches strengthens the image sketched earlier.

The economic networks of most individuals were circumscribed within a very few miles of their home tracts. Contacts outside these fairly narrow bounds were to a large extent contacts with commissioners or merchants; and, given the broader economic networks characteristic of commissioners and merchants, they were probably responsible for the formation of these ties. Increasingly, as the area of settlement expanded, commissioners and merchants dominated to an ever greater extent the economic network reaching beyond the distance of three miles.

It should be noted that, while the official and occupational activities of commissioners and merchants were contributing to the breadth of their economic networks, so too was their disproportionately high ownership, at one time or another, of either a vessel or a horse or both. Excluding four individuals who died in the mid-1630s (when settlement was still concentrated and who left no record of owning any means of transportation) yields a figure of 64 percent of commissioners and merchants in possession of either a vessel or a horse or both. As noted earlier, evidence of such ownership is by no means complete, so 64 percent is very likely a low figure. By way of contrast, this proportion is very high relative to that for individuals belonging to group 3 (tables 11, 12); only 19 percent of them are known to have owned a vessel, and only one owned a horse. This contrast helps explain the more narrowly bounded economic networks of landholders in the latter category.

In fact, economic networks were probably somewhat more restricted than the evidence above suggests, because two factors contributed to inflating the number of long-range contacts. One factor was mobility. Certain economic links appear to extend over a much greater distance because one of the parties involved moved away from the other. For example, when Elias Taylor died in late 1640 or early 1641, he owed tobacco to Stephen Charlton, who lived on a tract twelve miles distant. Shortly before, however, Charlton had resided on a tract across the creek from Taylor's. Another example also involves Charlton. When he died, one of his creditors was Jeffrey Minshall, who lived on a tract about six miles from that of Charlton. But Minshall had just moved to this tract; before that he had lived on a tract adjacent to Charlton's residence. It seems likely that the debt Charlton owed to Minshall at the time of the former's death was incurred at a time when they were neighbors.[7]

---

7. Taylor: CCR-2, pp. 15, 51, 70–71; Nugent, ed., *Cavaliers and Pioneers*, I, 82. Minshall: CCR-5, fol. 17–p. 18, p. 124–fol. 124, p. 141, CCR-7, p. 3.

Family and kin ties also contributed to an inflation of long-distance economic links. Thus when Jane Jackson-Lemon died, she owed tobacco to her relative Thomas Johnson, who lived about fifteen miles away.[8] The nature of the evidence available in the county court records makes it very difficult to quantify the impact of mobility and kin relations on the shape of economic networks. But the examples above as well as others suggest the part they played in contributing to the number of contacts at a distance greater than normal.

Illustrative of the distances people normally traveled to conduct their economic affairs is a mapping of the location of residences of people who attended an auction of goods from the estate of Daniel Cugley. When Cugley died, sometime between the end of November 1640 and the beginning of February 1641, he left behind him a complicated skein of debts and credits. In the normal course of events, his widow would have taken charge of the estate. But Hannah Savage-Cugley, sick at the same time as Daniel just before his death, died before she could begin to settle the estate's accounts. Therefore, at a meeting of the county court of May 17, 1641, the commissioners ordered that

> an outcry be made of all the Estate whatsoever belonging unto Daniell Cugley deceased at his house . . . upon the Last day of this instant May, and that in the mean tyme the Sheriff of Ackowmacke together with the Overseers of the sayd Estate give notice to all the Inhabitantes of the County.

The court officials also ordered that an account of the estate sold at the outcry, or auction, be presented to them at the court.[9]

The county court record occasionally mentions such outcries, but the outcry of goods belonging to the estate of Daniel Cugley was the only one recorded in detail. The account of the Cugley auction fills five pages in the county court volume and includes information on the goods sold, their prices, and the purchasers.[10] Of the thirty-eight people who bought

---

8. For Jane Jackson-Lemon's death, see CCR-3, fol. 135a, p. 141. She was related to Thomas Johnson through a Carsley connection (CCR-3, fols. 102, 177). Nugent, ed., *Cavaliers and Pioneers*, I, 164.

9. For court orders, see CCR-2, p. 86. For Hannah Savage-Cugley's death, see CCR-2, pp. 86, 117. For Daniel Cugley's death, see CCR-1, p. 160, CCR-2, p. 46. Most of Cugley's accounts were settled in the year following his death; see CCR-2, pp. 63, 66, 83, 85, 88–89, 90–91, 117, 129, 130, 142. See also the inventory of debts due to the estate: CCR-2, pp. 78–81.

10. For other references to outcries, see CCR-2, p. 236, CCR-3, fol. 31, fol. 228–p. 229, CCR-6, p. 10, CCR-7, p. 17, p. 67–fol. 67. For the account of the auction of Cugley's goods, see CCR-2, pp. 109–114.

items, fourteen can be identified residentially; eleven (79 percent) lived on tracts at a distance of three miles or less from that of Cugley on Cherrystone Creek; three (21 percent) lived on tracts from four to six miles away. Including in the computation four individuals whose residences can be tentatively identified yields virtually the same results: fourteen (78 percent) three miles away or less, four (22 percent) in the range of four to six miles. Despite the dearth of purchasers among landholders living seven or more miles away, these figures are broadly comparable with those for 1641 in the "moving picture" of economic links.

Focusing on the group of landholders who were not commissioners, merchants, ministers, storekeepers, or ordinarykeepers reveals some further variation in scope of network (table 13). In particular, tradesmen, although roughly similar to physicians and planters, exhibited slightly broader networks. This finding is not surprising, given the widespread demand for their scarce talents for wood- and metal-working, bricklaying, tanning, shoemaking, and tailoring.[11]

Data from the limited number of landholders whose occupations and residences both are known are better viewed in relation to the occupational distribution of all residents at five-year intervals (table 14). Landholders of unknown occupation ranged between 35 percent and 41 percent of all landholders in any given year. Two considerations argue for their inclusion in the category of planters. First, in an economy devoted to planting, the designation of "planter" might be assumed unless some other were specified. Those who practiced a nonplanting profession were far more likely to distinguish themselves occupationally from their fellow residents. Second, except for 1635, individuals in nonplanting pursuits formed a fairly constant one-third of the total number of occupationally identified residents and landholders of unknown occupation.[12] The constancy of this figure suggests a balance of nonplanting and planting occupations in the Eastern Shore economy.

Although the ratio of those in nonplanting occupations to those who were planters and landholders of unknown occupation remained constant from 1640 to 1655, the composition of the nonplanting occupations underwent several changes. First, an expanding number of mer-

11. For similar observations about the relationship of occupation to extent of network, see Walsh, "Community Networks in the Early Chesapeake," in Carr, Morgan, and Russo, eds., *Colonial Chesapeake Society*, 226–227.

12. The anomalous position of 1635, when only one-quarter of occupationally identified residents and landholders of unknown occupation held nonplanting occupations, results from a lack of primary sources. The county court record, begun in 1633, does not allow a sufficient tracing of individuals to identify their occupations.

Table 13. Range of Economic Networks by Occupation

	Occupation		
Object of Contact	Planters (N = 23)	Physicians (N = 4)	Tradesmen[a] (N = 19)
1–3 Miles, Same or Adjacent Tract, on or across Same Creek			
Commissioner or merchant			
No. of contacts	19	6	10
Proportion in same role	70%	75%	53%
Minister, storekeeper, ordinarykeeper			
No. of contacts	5	0	3
Proportion in same role	83%		75%
Other			
No. of contacts	30	4	17
Proportion in same role	81%	80%	85%
Proportion of all contacts	77%	77%	70%
4–6 Miles			
Commissioner or merchant			
No. of contacts	2	1	4
Proportion in same role	7%	13%	21%
Minister, storekeeper, ordinarykeeper			
No. of contacts	0	0	0
Proportion in same role			
Other			
No. of contacts	4	1	1
Proportion in same role	11%	20%	5%
Proportion of all contacts	9%	15%	12%

Table 13. *Continued*

	Occupation		
Object of Contact	Planters (*N*=23)	Physicians (*N*=4)	Tradesmen[a] (*N*=19)
	7+ Miles		
Commissioner or merchant			
No. of contacts	6	1	5
Proportion in same role	22%	13%	26%
Minister, storekeeper, ordinarykeeper			
No. of contacts	1	0	1
Proportion in same role	17%		25%
Other			
No. of contacts	3	0	2
Proportion in same role	8%		10%
Proportion of all contacts	14%	8%	19%

Note: Landholders are divided into the same three groups as in Table 11.
[a]Carpenters, joiners, coopers, shipbuilders, blacksmiths, bricklayers, tailors, tanners, shoemakers.

Table 14. Occupational Distribution of Residents

	No.				
Occupation	1635	1640	1645	1650	1655
Planter					
Landholder	17	27	39	43	49
Nonlandholder					
Holding land before 1656	1	1	3	6	
Not holding land before 1656	0	0	6	13	25
Merchant/mariner					
Landholder	3	9	9	10	12
Nonlandholder					

Table 14. *Continued*

Occupation	No.				
	1635	1640	1645	1650	1655
Holding land					
before 1656	2	0	0	2	
Not holding					
land before					
1656	0	0	3	4	6
Minister					
Landholder	0	1	1	1	1
Nonlandholder					
Holding land					
before 1656	1	0	0	0	
Not holding					
land before					
1656	0	0	0	0	0
Doctor					
Landholder	1	3	3	3	5
Nonlandholder					
Holding land					
before 1656	1	1	0	0	
Not holding					
land before					
1656	0	1	0	3	1
Woodworker[a]					
Landholder	2	5	10	12	19
Nonlandholder					
Holding land					
before 1656	1	0	3	4	
Not holding					
land before					
1656	0	0	3	6	5
Ordinarykeeper/					
storekeeper					
Landholder		1	2	3	3
Nonlandholder					
Holding land					
before 1656		0	0	0	
Not holding					
land before					
1656		0	0	0	0
Blacksmith					
Landholder		2	1	1	1
Nonlandholder					
Holding land					
before 1656		0	0	1	

Table 14. *Continued*

Occupation	No.				
	1635	1640	1645	1650	1655
Not holding land before 1656		0	0	0	0
Brewer					
Landholder		1	1	1	1
Nonlandholder					
Holding land before 1656		0	0	0	
Not holding land before 1656		0	0	0	0
Butcher					
Landholder			1	1	0
Nonlandholder					
Holding land before 1656			0	0	
Not holding land before 1656			0	0	0
Tailor					
Landholder			1	0	5
Nonlandholder					
Holding land before 1656			1	2	
Not holding land before 1656			0	3	4
Bricklayer					
Landholder			0	0	1
Nonlandholder					
Holding land before 1656			1	1	
Not holding land before 1656			0	1	0
Tanner					
Landholder				1	2
Nonlandholder					
Holding land before 1656				1	
Not holding land before 1656				1	0

Table 14. *Continued*

Occupation	No.				
	1635	1640	1645	1650	1655
Shoemaker					
Landholder				0	1
Nonlandholder					
Holding land before 1656				0	
Not holding land before 1656				1	1
Miller					
Landholder					0
Nonlandholder					
Holding land before 1656					
Not holding land before 1656					1
Barber					
Landholder					0
Nonlandholder					
Holding land before 1656					
Not holding land before 1656					1
Total					
Landholder	23	49	68	76	100
Nonlandholder					
Holding land before 1656	6	2	8	17	
Not holding land before 1656	0	1	12	32	44
Unknown					
Landholder	14	28	37	45	70

Note: Several decisions influence the above data. (1) If a person is identified by occupation after becoming a landholder, he is classified in that occupation from the time of first landholding; if a peson is identified by occupation before becoming a landholder (or if he never became a landholder), he is classified in that occupation immediately. (2) Certain individuals are identified at different times in the court record as practicing two occupations, such as planter on one occasion and carpenter on another. In such cases, where the former is generic, applying to most everyone owning land, and the latter specific, the latter identification is chosen. (3) When there is doubt whether a nonlandholder was an Eastern Shore resident, it is assumed that he was.

[a]Carpenter, cooper, joiner, sawyer, boatwright.

chants represented the development of active mercantile contact connecting the Eastern Shore to the rest of the world of trade. Second, the woodworking professions also experienced marked growth, based on the settlers' need for housing, vessels, tobacco casks, and other items as well as for their repair. Third, practitioners of other service occupations began to ply their trades to the benefit of the peninsula's growing population. These tradesmen worked to satisfy a strictly local consumption. Inhabitants of the peninsula did produce for an extralocal market, but the commodities were agricultural: most important, tobacco, but also corn and cattle to some extent. People relied on local tradesmen to fulfill basic needs. The peninsula's service trades also were important, because they fostered local contact.

Two questions might be raised about individuals identified as planters but for whom there is no record of holding land. First, who were they? And, second, what role did they play in the expanding societal network?

Do these planters in fact represent a group of previously unidentified landholders? It is possible that some people could hold land without an official record surviving of their acquiring it: the patent record clearly is incomplete, the county court record does not supply information on all sales and purchases, and leases were recorded infrequently. If there has been a random undercounting of landholders, the aggregate life profile of this group of planters without known land should be similar to that of individuals who were first called planters after holding land. A careful comparison of the aggregate life profiles of these two groups reveals sharp distinctions between them. Through 1655, seventy-three individuals were identified as planters with no prior evidence of their holding land. In the same period eighty-five individuals were identified as planters only after becoming landholders. The first difference between these two groups is the amount of time that their members had appeared in the available record before being identified as planters. For the landholding planters, the average was 9 years (median 8); for the nonlandholding planters, the average was 5.4 years (median 4). They differed also in the extent of their kin networks. Of the landholding planters, 60 percent had references to kin before they were called planters; of the nonlandholding planters, the corresponding figure was 27 percent. In addition, 36 percent of landholding planters had held servants before being identified as planters; for nonlandholders, the figure was 14 percent. Landholding planters were, on average, 35.8 years old (median 35) at the time when they first were referred to as planters; nonlandholders were 30.5 (median

28.5). Clearly, the aggregate life profiles of landholding and nonland-holding planters differed significantly. As a group, most nonlandhold-ing planters were not, simply, landholders for whom no evidence of prior land acquisition survives; if they had been, their aggregate life profile would not have diverged so distinctively from that of landholding planters.[13]

Inasmuch as these planters were not landholders, whence the title "planter"? In the early seventeenth century, there were several related meanings attached to the word "planter." A planter could be (1) an early settler who plants (or founds) a colony, (2) a person who places plants in the ground, or (3) the owner or occupier of a cultivated estate.[14] The first meaning had been applied to the early colonists of Virginia, but that use would not have served any purpose in differentiating people in the county court record, because almost all of the people mentioned therein were colonists. Inasmuch as the word "planter" was not used to identify landholders only, it must have been used as a general occupational de-scription; that is, a planter was someone who planted. An indentured servant might also be a planter, but the relationship of servant to master took precedence over that of planter to land, and indentured servants were thus identified accordingly.[15]

If the word "planter" was in fact used as a general occupational de-scription, then what relation did nonlandholding planters have to the land on which they planted? The answer to this question is frustratingly elusive, but bits of evidence suggest some of the possibilities. In 1655 William Moulte, planter, died. The inventory of his estate included a servant, Jonathan Savage, and the crop that they had made together on the plantation of William Jordan. Moulte seems to have had an agree-ment with Jordan allowing him to plant on Jordan's land.

An example of such an agreement appears in the court record in 1642, when William Hensley contracted to plant on the ground of William Stephens. Hensley would get to keep one-half of the crop of corn and tobacco and whatever else he wanted to plant. In exchange he would reimburse Stephens for any provisions he required; he also would work

13. Of course, a few individuals within the group of nonlandholding planters may have held land; the point here is that it is unlikely that this group as a whole repre-sents a large number of landholders for whom there is no record of prior landholding.

14. See *Oxford English Dictionary*, s.v. "planter."

15. I have not found one clear-cut case of an indentured servant's being called a planter in the county court record of the Eastern Shore.

Table 15. Individuals Called Planters before 1655

	Men Holding Land before Being Called Planter (N = 85)	Men Called Planter before Any Record of Landholding (N = 73)
Years in record when first called planter		
Average	9	5.4
Median	8	4
(No. calculated)	(82)	(67)
Men with references to kin on Eastern Shore before being called planter		
Proportion	60%	27%
(No. calculated)	(83)	(71)
Men with reference to having servants before being called planter		
Proportion	36%	14%
(No. calculated)	(84)	(73)
Age in years when first called planter		
Average	35.8	30.5
Median	35	28.5
(No. calculated)	(27)	(12)

the ground with (and presumably supervise) a servant of Stephens. Hensley maintained close ties with William Stephens. When William Hensley, planter, died in January 1655, he named Ann Stephens (the wife of William Stephens) the executrix of his estate and left his entire estate to her and to her two children.[16]

Other agreements specified a particular reimbursement rather than the sharing of crops. In 1650 James Adkinson agreed to plant on Walter Wil-

16. For William Moulte, see CCR-7, fols. 4, 7, p. 8. For William Hensley, see CCR-2, pp. 188–189, CCR-5, p. 81, fol. 107.

liams's land (where Adkinson lived that year) and to pay Williams 2,177 pounds of tobacco. In late 1650 Richard Smith, planter, agreed to serve William Whittington for one year; Whittington in turn agreed to provide Smith with food, housing, and laundry service and to pay him tobacco, corn, and clothing. The next year Smith and Whittington reached a similar agreement.[17]

Simon Foscutt and Robert Berry show how individuals might drift from one such agreement to another. In 1642 Foscutt agreed to serve John Holloway for one year in exchange for clothes and a cow and calf. Two years later the court record reveals that Foscutt had performed work for Sarah Smith the preceding winter and that he agreed to serve her during the next crop. In 1651 Simon Foscutt, planter, was identified as the overseer of William Whittington.[18]

Robert Berry provides a case history of how someone might be a landholder and then engage in a series of yearly agreements. In 1645 Berry and Thomas Bell bought one hundred acres of land on a branch of Nuswattocks Creek. Within a year Berry sold his share to Bell. In 1647 Berry testified in a case involving John Nuthall; it is clear from Berry's testimony that he was overseer for Nuthall's field work force. Two years later Berry was called a planter. In 1650 he was working in the fields of John Dixon. And, finally, in 1654 Berry was in court in a suit involving John Tilney, with whom Berry had signed articles of agreement. Berry was ordered to pay 1,082 pounds of tobacco in casks out of his crop at Tilney's house, and two men were appointed to investigate further differences between Berry and Tilney.[19]

Some individuals identified as planters were married to women seated on land of their deceased spouses. When Richard Baily was called a planter the first time, he probably was already married to Elizabeth, the widow of Henry Weed. John Hinman, planter, was married to Sarah, formerly the wife of Thomas Smith.[20]

If many of the nonlandholding planters were in fact planting on the land of others, a further question arises. Is it possible that, given time, these planters might have acquired land? The answer is yes. Some pre-

17. For James Atkinson, see CCR-3, fol. 196. For Richard Smith, see CCR-3, fol. 233, CCR-4, fol. 30–p. 31.

18. CCR-2, pp. 220, 361, CCR-4, fol. 149, CCR-5, p. 71–fol. 72.

19. CCR-3, p. 61–fol. 61, p. 116–fol. 118, fol. 196, CCR-4, p. 158, fol. 215.

20. For Baily, see CCR-2, pp. 402–403, 432–433, CCR-3, fol. 57–p. 58. For Hinman, see CCR-3, fol. 35, p. 41, CCR-2, p. 327.

Table 16. Comparison of Nonlandholding Planters before 1655

	Became Landholders before 1655 (N = 22)	Remained Nonlandholders before 1655 (N = 27)
Years in record when first called planter		
Average	5.7	5.0
Median	5.5	3.0
(No. calculated)	(22)	(24)
Men with references to kin on Eastern Shore before being called planter		
Proportion	32%	22%
(No. calculated)	(22)	(27)
Men with references to having servants before being called planter		
Proportion	23%	15%
(No. calculated)	(22)	(27)

Note: Insufficient data exist to determine meaningful statistics on age when first called planter.

1655 landholders were called planters before they are known to have held land. For this group of twenty-two individuals, the time between first reference as planter and first evidence of landholding averaged four years (median three).[21] Compare this to the twenty-seven nonlandholding planters who died, moved, or disappeared from the court record before 1655. On average, the individuals in this group died, moved, or disappeared within slightly more than a year of being called planters for the first time; the median was less than a year.[22] Overall, planters who

21. The vast majority of landholders (85 in all) were referred to as planters after, rather than before, the first indication of their holding land (average 4.8 years after; median 3). It is important to note that the moment when a settler was called a planter was not the historical moment when he became one. This is why landholding and nonlandholding planters are compared as aggregates, so that any such inherent flaw in the record is balanced between the two groups.

22. Of those 24 nonlandholding planters who are known to have lived after 1655, some are known to have acquired land eventually.

then became landholders before 1655 were quite similar to those planters who did not; the one major difference was that those who became landholders did not die, move, or disappear from the available record.

In other words, a man who planted on someone else's land might someday acquire land himself so long as he remained alive and resident. In 1654 Richard Hill testified that fourteen years before, at age eighteen, he had been a servant to John Neale. In 1641 Hill was a servant of Aaron Cursonstam; the following year, of Samuel Lucas. By 1650 Hill was called a planter and overseer of Edmund Scarburgh. Two years later he patented three hundred acres land on the basis of six headrights, including three assigned to him by Scarburgh.[23]

This information on nonlandholding planters helps to fill in the lifecycle portrait of an early Virginia settler. For those that did not acquire land immediately or move in with relatives already resident, a period of indentured servitude was likely. Completing their often lengthy terms of service, many would not have the resources to acquire and cultivate land of their own. In order to accumulate capital toward this goal, a former servant could sharecrop the land of another; or, on a yearly basis, he could plant the land and possibly supervise the servants of a landholder in exchange for part of the crop, housing, and any other return previously agreed to (for example, use of a cow). During this phase, he might acquire a servant or servants of his own. He might even be lucky enough to marry the widow of a landholder and thereby gain access to land. Finally, if he lived long enough, he might go on to patent or purchase his own land or lease a tract for a long term.[24] Some immigrants were able to skip indentured servitude and immediately make agreements for labor, sharecropping, or leasing.

The phenomenon of nonlandholding freemen in the Chesapeake has been noted by other historians. It has been estimated that between one-quarter and one-third of the free adult male population at any one time

23. CCR-5, p. 10–p. 11, CCR-2, pp. 149–151, CCR-3, p. 212, CCR-4, fol. 34–p. 35, fol. 74; Nugent, ed., *Cavaliers and Pioneers*, I, 261–262.

24. I have distinguished between long-term leases (generally running from 3 to 99 years) and 1-year leases. Those with long-term leases I have called landholders; those with 1-year leases that are clearly of a sharecropping nature I have not. I have tried not to include as landholders those leasing for 1 year on terms. But it is possible that some sharecroppers or 1-year leasers have been included as landholders in those instances where the record refers only to someone's land, fields, or plantation. Such references constitute the first evidence of landholding for 32 individuals; for 20 of these, there is no other evidence of ever acquiring land before 1655.

was landless. Sharecropping, leasing, or laboring on the land of another settler served several purposes. It introduced those individuals new to the Chesapeake to the cultivation of tobacco. It gave those recently freed from servitude the opportunity to accumulate capital toward the acquisition of their own land. From the landholders' perspective, it provided a way to get land cleared and into cultivation. It was far cheaper to arrange an agreement for labor, sharecropping, or leasing than it was to invest in indentured servants.[25] The role that these landless freemen played in binding the society together also should not be underestimated. By moving from contract to contract, place to place, they served to expand and intensify the network of contacts on the Eastern Shore.

One final concern in the analysis of the range of personal economic networks is the role played by such focal points as stores and ordinaries. To begin, it is necessary to explain that the word "store" was used to designate both a public storage facility for tobacco and a private stock of a variety of goods. A store in the latter sense was nothing more than the accumulation of goods in the possession of a single individual. People occasionally sold or traded goods out of their personal stores.[26] Economic contacts did not focus on one or two nodal trade centers. This

25. Wesley Frank Craven, *The Southern Colonies in the Seventeenth Century, 1607–1689* (1949; reprint ed., Baton Rouge, La., 1970), 210; Carville V. Earle, *The Evolution of a Tidewater Settlement System: All Hallow's Parish, Maryland, 1650–1783* (Chicago, 1975), 207; Edmund S. Morgan, *American Slavery, American Freedom: The Ordeal of Colonial Virginia* (New York, 1975), 220–223; Russell Robert Menard, "Economy and Society in Early Colonial Maryland" (Ph.D. diss., University of Iowa, 1975), 94–97, 257; Walsh, "Charles County, Maryland, 1658–1705," 167–169, 327; Lois Green Carr and Russell R. Menard, "Immigration and Opportunity: The Freedman in Early Colonial Maryland," in Thad W. Tate and David L. Ammerman, eds., *The Chesapeake in the Seventeenth Century: Essays on Anglo-American Society* (Chapel Hill, N.C., 1979), 209–210, 212; Rutman and Rutman, *A Place in Time: Middlesex County,* 71, 73–75. John Hammond recommended that freemen immigrating to the Chesapeake board or rent for their first year, in *Leah and Rachel; or, The Two Fruitfull Sisters Virginia, and Maryland,* 14–15, in Peter Force, ed., *Tracts and Other Papers, Relating Principally to the Origin, Settlement, and Progress of the Colonies in North America, from the Discovery of the Country to the Year 1776,* 4 vols. (Washington, D.C., 1836–1847), III. A more recent examination of tenancy in the early Chesapeake is Lorena S. Walsh's "Land, Landlord, and Leaseholder: Estate Management and Tenant Fortunes in Southern Maryland, 1642–1820," *Agricultural History,* LIX (1985), 373–396. See also Walsh, "Community Networks in the Early Chesapeake," in Carr, Morgan, and Russo, eds., *Colonial Chesapeake Society,* 206, 214–215.

26. CCR-1, pp. 110–111, CCR-2, pp. 51, 388, CCR-4, p. 169, CCR-5, p. 12–p. 13.

dispersion was probably inevitable because of the ready access to water transportation that allowed landholders to deal directly and at no great distance with merchants, either resident or nonresident, importing goods and exporting tobacco.

In addition to private stores, there were references to public stores as well. In 1633 the Virginia Assembly ordered the colonists to send all of their tobacco to one of seven stores, where it would be inspected for quality. The colony's leadership hoped that this action, in conjunction with others, would help to maintain the price of tobacco. The store for inhabitants on the Eastern Shore was across the bay on the Southampton River.[27] The inconvenience of such long-distance transport and the fact that no reference to that store appears in the county court record suggest that residents on the peninsula simply ignored the statute.

In 1641 the Assembly abolished the system of central storage facilities and tried a more local approach. As part of a program to control the production of tobacco, the burgesses ordered that stores be established in each county and that all tobacco be shipped from these points. In accordance with this act, two "common stores" were designated for the Eastern Shore: one on King's Creek with Alexander Mountney as store-keeper and one on Old Plantation Creek with Anthony Hodgskins in charge.[28]

But this attempt to control the tobacco trade was short lived. Only two references to these stores appear in the county court record. Both references were in bonds signed by Hendrick Litehart, who promised to make payment of a debt at the common store at King's Creek; significantly, Litehart entered into these bonds before, and in anticipation of, the founding of the warehouse. It is unlikely that either store was ever established. As part of a revision of the legal code in March 1643, the Virginia Assembly repealed all laws and then selectively reenacted some of them and added others; no statutes relating to stores were reenacted.[29]

These county warehouses were destined to fail. Besides imposing an uncomfortably close supervision of tobacco marketing, their functioning would have required the imposition of fees to support them as well as

27. William Waller Hening, ed., *The Statutes at Large; Being a Collection of All the Laws of Virginia*, I (New York, 1823), 203–207, 209–212.
28. "The Virginia Assembly of 1641: A List of Members and Some of the Acts," *VMHB*, IX (1901–1902), 57. Two proclamations recorded in the Eastern Shore county court books note the actions of the burgesses; see CCR-2, pp. 100–102, 125–126. For the appointment of Mountney and Hodgskins, see CCR-2, p. 121.
29. CCR-2, pp. 115–116; Hening, ed., *Statutes at Large*, I, 238–282.

extra time and labor to pack, transport, unpack, inspect, repack, and reship the tobacco. Given the ready access of most planters to water transport and the relative shortage of labor, it made more sense to pack and ship directly. If the effort to centralize storage facilities had succeeded, it would have provided a focal point for the economic networks of all residents in the county. But the realities of the transportation network, labor shortage, and planter self-interest dictated a more dispersed trade pattern, and the provincial government—lacking persistence, coordination, and a detailed, workable program—failed to overcome these obstacles.

The failure of this effort was a prelude to the failure of town development in the last half of the seventeenth century. In 1652, ten years after the repeal of the store act, the Assembly passed its first town act, and for another fifty years it continued to try to legislate towns into existence. The same factors involved in the failure of the effort to establish stores also defeated the legislative attempts to develop towns. In addition, the conflicting goals of provincial and imperial authorities further compounded the problem of implementing this legislation.[30]

With the exception of the integrative potential of gatherings at the county court, church, and militia practice (all of which will be discussed subsequently), the only other continuing focal points of interaction with implications for the economic network were ordinaries. The first reference to an ordinary on the Eastern Shore occurred in 1640, when Anthony Hodgskins received a license to keep "an ordinary or Victuallinge howse." The license stipulated that Hodgskins take care that the laws be obeyed and peace maintained in his establishment. It also explicitly forbade "anie uncivill or unlawfull Games" and "anie riotous or unlawfull person." Hodgskins opened his ordinary on Old Plantation Creek, for which creek he also received an appointment as storekeeper in 1641, as already noted. His business was augmented by the fact that the commissioners of the county court took advantage of his accommodations by holding court there.[31] By 1645 Hodgskins had transferred management of his ordinary, known as the Point House, to John Dixon and John

30. Warren M. Billings, ed., "Some Acts Not in Hening's *Statutes*: The Acts of Assembly, April 1652, November 1652, and July 1653," *VMHB*, LXXXIII (1975), 70; John C. Rainbolt, "The Absence of Towns in Seventeenth-Century Virginia," *Journal of Southern History*, XXXV (1969), 343–360. For the failure of market legislation in Lancaster County in the early 1650s, see Rutman and Rutman, *A Place in Time: Middlesex County*, 210.

31. CCR-2, pp. 30–32; Whitelaw, *Virginia's Eastern Shore*, I, 122–123. See Chapter 7 for a discussion of the location of the county court meetings.

Badham, and these partners continued to run the ordinary until around 1650.³² Throughout this period the commissioners held meetings there. The business of the county court probably accounted for the longevity of the ordinary on Old Plantation Creek.

The only other ordinary to remain in operation for more than a short period of time also benefited from its designation as the location of sittings of the county court. In 1647 Walter Williams received a license to operate an ordinary on the neck of land between Hungars and Nuswat-tocks creeks. Two years later the commissioners scheduled regular meet-ings of the county court at Williams's ordinary. This arrangement was altered in 1652, when the commissioners ordered that the court convene exclusively at Williams's.³³ Subsequently, when they decided to sit in several different locations, Williams, alarmed by the potential loss of business, petitioned the commissioners. His petition is important for understanding the viability of ordinaries on the Eastern Shore and, in turn, the place of these establishments within the interactional networks of the inhabitants there. In part Williams argued,

> The devideinge of the courts into three places in the County is and hath bine much prejudiciall unto him and greatly disinabled him, either for his owne private subsistance or to provide for the Accom-modation of the people, att his howse (upon publique meeteinges) by reason of his smale profitts.³⁴

This statement demonstrates that, without the business generated by providing accommodations for people attending the county court, Wil-liams could not keep his ordinary open.

Other evidence indicates that Williams was not merely soliciting the sympathy of the commissioners with an exaggerated story. The only other ordinary able to survive, the Point House, had done so with the patronage of the court's meetings.³⁵ The fact is that the population was

32. CCR-3, fol. 4. The last accounts suggesting their maintenance of the ordinary were for 1649; see CCR-3, p. 202, CCR-4, fol. 74. Dixon was referred to as a planter in 1652 (CCR-4, p. 93).

33. CCR-3, pp. 70, 174, CCR-4, fol. 66–p. 67. At the same time, the commission-ers ordered that Williams receive a new license.

34. CCR-5, p. 4.

35. Thomas Wyatt received a license to run an ordinary in 1641 but died shortly thereafter (CCR-2, pp. 121, 161). In 1647 Nicholas Scott, with the support of Obedi-ence Robins, received a license to open an ordinary, but there is no evidence that he did so (CCR-3, fol. 127).

not densely concentrated enough to support such establishments. The two that survived did so by supplementing the income they derived from inhabitants nearby with profits generated by people attending the county court. The value of ordinaries in promoting economic—or any other— contacts at a distance was directly attributable to their role as temporary courthouses.

This investigation of the local economic network documents that the ties linking individuals to one another rarely extended further than the familial and familiar networks examined in earlier chapters. When land-holders did transact business at a greater distance, they usually did so because the transactions involved a merchant or commissioner, whose networks stretched further than those of other landholders. In this way merchants and commissioners acted to widen the focus of other land-holders beyond the spatial limitations of their everyday world. But the role of merchants in expanding the local field of vision did not stop at the peninsula's water boundary. Their business activities involved them in networks that extended across the bay, included other colonies (both English and foreign), and tied them to England and other parts of Europe.

6 Contacts off the Eastern Shore

RESIDENTS ON THE Eastern Shore did not live in isolation from the rest of the world. Mercantile, familial, and other ties linked them with the rest of Virginia as well as with Maryland, settlements on the Delaware Bay, New Amsterdam, New England, the West Indies, England, and Holland. The mercantile network was highly personalized, relying heavily on ties of kinship and friendship for support and information. Merchants, whether or not they resided on the peninsula, formed an essential part of the extralocal network. They established avenues of trade, which in turn became avenues of communication by which individuals maintained contact with relatives and friends off the Eastern Shore. Other factors, including institutional ties, mobility, and travel, also promoted the integration of the Eastern Shore into the larger Atlantic world.

The rhythm of tobacco production dictated the rhythm of trade, predicated primarily on the export of tobacco and the import of necessary supplies and labor not available on the peninsula. The harvest and curing of the tobacco crop lured merchants to Virginia in the fall. Thus, when David Pietersz. de Vries sailed up the James River in mid-September 1635, he saw thirty-six English ships there "for the purpose of loading with tobacco." He reported that "There come here yearly, between thirty and forty ships of various sizes . . . which come here to load tobacco, and carry it to England." Other evidence points to the arrival of the bulk of the Chesapeake tobacco fleet in October and November.[1]

The earliest that tobacco could be fully cured and ready for shipment

---

1. David Peterson de Vries, "Voyages from Holland to America, A.D. 1632 to 1644," trans. Henry C. Murphy, New-York Historical Society, *Collections*, 2d Ser., III (New York, 1857), 37, 77. For references to departures from England and arrivals in Virginia, see Peter Wilson Coldham, ed., *English Adventurers and Emigrants, 1609–1660: Abstracts of Examinations in the High Court of Admiralty with Reference to Colonial America* (Baltimore, 1984). See also Carville V. Earle, *The Evolution of a Tidewater Settlement System: All Hallow's Parish, Maryland, 1650–1783* (Chicago, 1975), 162; David W. Galenson, *White Servitude in Colonial America: An Economic Analysis* (New York, 1981), 89. Russell R. Menard states that ships began to arrive in the colonies in early December, which seems late given the available evidence cited here ("A Note on Chesapeake Tobacco Prices, 1618–1660," *VMHB*, LXXXIV [1976], 401).

was October. De Vries, recounting his travels, noted, on the "1st of October, I began to sail up and down the river . . . in order to collect my debts" and to pick up tobacco. In addition, Henry Fleet's journal of a voyage made in the bark *Warwick* during 1631 and 1632 records his trading tobacco in Virginia in mid-October.[2]

Compared to the schedules of de Vries and Fleet on the Western Shore, the most active time of mercantile activity on the Eastern Shore began one month later. An analysis of the distribution by month of the appearance of nonresident and nonlandholding merchants in the court records for the Eastern Shore reveals a peak period in November, December, and January. The delay probably resulted from geographic and economic realities. If tobacco had been loaded on the Eastern Shore first, it would have traveled in the holds of vessels as they subsequently moved from landing to landing on the Western Shore. Then the merchant ships would have carried the tobacco past the Eastern Shore again as they sailed into the Atlantic Ocean. This extra time in closed storage would have made no economic sense because of the perishability of tobacco. Therefore, the Eastern Shore probably was the last stop made by merchants in their Virginia circuit. Supporting evidence is found in the account of the voyage of the ship *Tristram and Jane* in late 1636 and early 1637. Last on the list of places where the vessel landed to trade is "Accamack," that is, the Eastern Shore.[3] On February 24, 1637, Robert Reeves, on board the *Tristram and Jane*, wrote to his friend Thomas Smith, a landholder on Old Plantation Creek. In his brief letter, Reeves apologized to Smith for not sending a promised hogshead of bread, but that commodity was scarce on the ship and he couldn't afford to part with any.[4] Given the late date and the fact that more bread might have been procured elsewhere in Virginia if needed, the conclusion must be that the Eastern Shore was the last stop in Virginia for the *Tristram and Jane*.

2. De Vries, "Voyages from Holland to America," trans. Murphy, NYHS, *Colls.*, 2d Ser., III (1857), 77; Henry Fleet, "A Brief Journal of a Voyage Made in the Bark Warwick to Virginia [1631/2]," in Edward D. Neill, *The English Colonization of America during the Seventeenth Century* (London, 1871), 221–237. For the cycle of tobacco production, see Kevin Peter Kelly, "Economic and Social Development of Seventeenth-Century Surry County, Virginia" (Ph.D. diss., University of Washington, 1972), 120–122.

3. Martha W. Hiden, ed., "Accompts of the Tristram and Jane [a ship arriving at Virginia, 1637]," *VMHB*, LXII (1954), 433. This account was filed in London in connection with the probate of the will of Daniel Hopkinson, one of the partners in the ship (*ibid.*, 435).

4. CCR-1, pp. 83–84.

After a brief lull, mercantile contact on the peninsula peaked again in March, April, and May. Thus Henry Fleet, having sailed to New England after his trading activities in Virginia, returned to the Chesapeake in April 1632. One reason for this second period of mercantile activity was to pick up tobacco not ready earlier. Another explanation appears in de Vries's account of his voyage in 1635. Arriving in Virginia in the spring, he left his cargo in the colony and sailed away to engage in coastal trade elsewhere. He planned to return to Virginia after the fall tobacco harvest, when he would trade the goods that he had left behind for the new leaf. De Vries gave a second reason for his departure in May. He did not want to be in Virginia during June, July, and August, which were known to be particularly hazardous to the health of newcomers.[5] Reports of summertime mortality and sickness continued through midcentury. Those captains and merchants arriving during the summer months risked their lives. De Vries reported that on his return to Virginia in mid-September 1635, "fifteen of the [36] captains were dead, in consequence of their coming too early in the unhealthy season, and not having been before in the country."[6]

The month-by-month distribution of references to merchants on the Eastern Shore thus registers a pronounced lull during June, July, and August. Actually, because of the pattern of trade described above and the consequent delay in arrival of the tobacco merchants, the lull continued through September and October. Some exceptions to this general avoidance of the dangers of Virginia's summer climate suggest that only a prolonged period of seasoning or an unavoidable emergency would persuade a merchant to linger on the Eastern Shore during Virginia's hottest months. Thus, Samuel Chandler, on the Eastern Shore in July 1642, was a London merchant. But he was not a newcomer to Virginia; he had been trading there at least since 1638. Thomas Bushrod, on the Eastern Shore in the summer of 1647, was a Virginia merchant who had lived in the colony for many years. And, because of a dispute about a contract for

5. Fleet, "A Brief Journal," in Neill, *English Colonization*, 221–237; Galenson, *White Servitude in Colonial America*, 89; de Vries, "Voyages from Holland to America," trans. Murphy, NYHS, *Colls.*, 2d Ser., III (1857), 75. Earlier in his account de Vries had commented on English reports of high mortality during the three summer months (35).

6. Beauchamp Plantagenet, *A Description of the Province of New Albion . . . 1648*, 4–5, in Peter Force, ed., *Tracts and Other Papers, Relating Principally to the Origin, Settlement, and Progress of the Colonies in North America, from the Discovery of the Country to the Year 1776*, 4 vols. (Washington, D.C., 1836–1847), II; de Vries, "Voyages from Holland to America," trans. Murphy, NYHS, *Colls.*, 2d Ser., III (1857), 77.

freight and because of the sizable economic interests involved, litigation delayed a vessel on the Eastern Shore in the summer of 1652.[7]

In accordance with the temporal ebb and flow of mercantile activity, ships arrived at and departed from the Eastern Shore and served to integrate the peninsula into the Atlantic world of trade. Excluding the ubiquitous trade with the Western Shore of Virginia, the most important mercantile connection was with England. The colonists exchanged their tobacco for imported goods and a continuing supply of servants.[8] Credit and bills of exchange provided the mercantile system with necessary flexibility. Similar financial arrangements smoothed the way for trade elsewhere besides with England. Trade with Maryland was limited by the fact that tobacco was the chief item of exchange there too.[9] There was some contact with the Indians and European settlers on the Delaware Bay as well as with settlements in the West Indies.[10] But the most important non-English trade routes connected the Eastern Shore with New England, New Amsterdam, and Holland.

Trade with New England began shortly after the settlement of that area. In a letter to their superiors in England, the governor and Council of Virginia wrote in 1632, "The Planters are carried with a great forwardnes to seeke trade abroad, to which purpose we have now 7 or 8 pinnaces and Barques bound to New-England and the Northward." By the mid-1630s Virginia supplied the young colony on Massachusetts Bay with food. Captain Thomas Young reported that in 1634 Virginia had "bene able to spare their zealous neighbours of New England tenne thousand bushels of corne for their releefe, besides good quantities of beeves, goats and hoggs, whereof this country hath great plentie."[11]

7. Chandler: CCR-1, pp. 128, 129, 163, CCR-2, pp. 341–343. Bushrod: CCR-2, 378–379, CCR-3, fols. 99, 100, pp. 110, 113. Vessel delay: CCR-4, fol. 93, p. 94–p. 96.

8. For a random sample of references to tobacco exports, see CCR-1, pp. 2, 86, CCR-2, pp. 83, 164–165, 204–205, 326, 363–366, 387–388, CCR-3, fol. 11, p. 25, p. 240–fol. 240, CCR-5, p. 43–p. 46, fol. 68, p. 144–fol. 144, fol. 147–p. 149, CCR-6, fol. 22. See also John R. Pagan, "Growth of the Tobacco Trade between London and Virginia, 1614–1640," *Guildhall Studies in London History*, III (1977–1979), 248–262.

9. CCR-2, pp. 9, 329.

10. CCR-1, pp. 151–152, CCR-2, p. 305, CCR-3, fol. 30, CCR-4, p. 41–fol. 41, CCR-5, p. 43–p. 46, p. 127–fol. 127, CCR-6, fol. 22. See also Plantagenet, *A Description of the Province of New Albion*, 5, in Force, ed., *Tracts and Other Papers*, II.

11. "Virginia in 1632," *VMHB*, LXV (1957), 466; "Captain Thomas Yong's Voyage to Virginia and Delaware Bay and River in 1634," in Massachusetts Historical Society, *Collections*, 4th Ser., IX (Boston, 1871), 110 (see also 98–99). De Vries also mentions this trade in "Voyages from Holland to America," trans. Murphy, NYHS,

Table 17. Nonresident Merchants, Mariners, and Captains, 1641–1655

Identified Origin	No.
Virginia or Maryland	7
England	18
New England	15
Holland	10
New Amsterdam	3

Note: An additional 30 appeared so fleetingly in the record that their residence cannot be determined; the paucity of references to them suggests that they were not resident. Thus, a total of 83 nonresident merchants, mariners, and captains are known to have plied their trade on the Eastern Shore sometime between 1641 and 1655. How many more traded on the peninsula without appearing in the county court record is unknown.

The expansion of extralocal trade in the 1640s was an outgrowth of the disruption of established contacts with England as a result of the civil war there. The uncertainty caused by closed ports and severed communications encouraged merchants to look elsewhere for outlets. Trade to England never stopped completely, but the difficulties of engaging in it led merchants to channel some of their trade elsewhere.[12] An active exchange connected the Eastern Shore with New England, which imported tobacco, cattle, and corn and returned miscellaneous goods, services, and, late in the 1640s, horses. In addition, tobacco exports increasingly were directed from Virginia to New Amsterdam and Holland. The importance of the New England and Dutch trade grew dramatically as civil war raged in England.[13]

The home ports of nonresident merchants whose transactions appear

---

Colls., 2d Ser., III (1857), 43, 44, 101. John Hammond noted that both New England and the Indies had been supplied with cattle and hogs from Virginia (*Leah and Rachel; or, The Two Fruitfull Sisters Virginia, and Maryland*, 9, in Force, ed., *Tracts and Other Papers*, III. See also Harold B. Gill, Jr., "Wheat Culture in Colonial Virginia," *Agricultural History*, LII (1978), 380.

12. See Bernard Bailyn, *The New England Merchants in the Seventeenth Century* (1955; reprint ed., New York, 1964), 76–86, for a similar development in New England.

13. On trade with New England, see CCR-1, pp. 151–152, CCR-2, pp. 76, 82–83, 95, 195, 227–233, CCR-3, pp. 33, 97, CCR-4, fol. 124. For more on the Virginia trade with New England in the 1640s, see *A Perfect Description of Virginia . . .*, in Force, ed., *Tracts and Other Papers*, II.

On trade with New Amsterdam and Holland, see CCR-2, pp. 432–433, 435, 440, CCR-3, fol. 7, fol. 180–p. 182, CCR-4, fol. 102–p. 103, fol. 181–p. 182, CCR-5, fol. 82. See also *A Perfect Description of Virginia*, 14, in Force, ed., *Tracts and Other Papers*, II.

in the county court record on the Eastern Shore reflect the gradual broadening of the trade network. Through 1640, merchants based in Virginia and England totally dominated local exchange. After that date, the majority of traders came from ports outside Virginia and England. This preponderance of merchants based at ports other than those of England was reflected also in a 1649 tract that noted that "at last Christmas we had trading [in Virginia] ten ships from *London*, two from *Bristoll*, twelve *Hollanders*, and seven from *New-England*."[14]

Viewed from the perspective of the Eastern Shore, these merchants were more than economic contacts; they also facilitated personal contacts with the outside world. Along with the captains and mariners on their ships, these merchants brought news about England and messages from family and friends. For example, Mr. Phillips wrote a letter from London to his brother on August 16, 1644. In it he instructed his brother to enclose a letter

> in Mr. Stones packett, And gett Mr. Nuthall to doe the like; in his to his father. Mr. Huchinson I have not seene this Twelve moneths and more, hee beinge gon out into the Parlaments service The three Kingdomes beinge nowe upp in Armes I pray god send us an end of this unnaturall warr. That wee maye injoye peace and a free Trade, (as formerlye) Remember my Kinde Respects to Mr. Nuthall and tell him his father, mother and sister are all in good health.

In a postscript, Phillips added, "Enclosed in Mr. Nuthalls letter from his father you shall receive another letter from me."[15] In addition to the news about events in England and the well-being of friends, this letter suggests the ad hoc mode of conveyance for correspondence. Phillips was relying on the communication, on the one hand, between William Stone and John Nuthall, two residents of the Eastern Shore, and, on the other, between their contacts in England. Delivery depended on the reliability of friends and shipping.

The world of commerce in the seventeenth century was highly personalized.[16] The letter from Mr. Phillips includes a lengthy passage detailing

---

For more on the New England and Dutch trade during the civil war, see Wesley Frank Craven, *The Southern Colonies in the Seventeenth Century, 1607–1689* (1949; reprint ed., Baton Rouge, La., 1970). For an excellent account of the Dutch trade with Virginia at this time, see John R. Pagan, "Dutch Maritime and Commercial Activity in Mid-Seventeenth-Century Virginia," *VMHB*, XC (1982), 485–501.

14. *A Perfect Description of Virginia*, 14, in Force, ed., *Tracts and Other Papers*, II.
15. CCR-3, fol. 188.
16. Bailyn, *New England Merchants in the Seventeenth Century*, 79; J. M. Sosin,

a business transaction involving his brother. This sort of connection was very common. Merchants, well informed about the markets of New England, Holland, and England, needed sound information on the market in Virginia. What imports did the colonists need? How was the tobacco crop shaping up? While the merchants may have gleaned some details from other traders, they learned most of what they needed to know from local contacts, whether friends or relatives.

The use of local residents as attorneys to recover debts and handle local litigation reveals the value of these ties. A common practice followed by nonresident merchants was to appoint as their attorneys prominent individuals who sat on the county court. Thus in 1643 Aries Topp, a merchant of Amsterdam, appointed as his attorney his "welbeloved friend" Obedience Robins, a commissioner since 1633. Robins served Topp for more than ten years. In addition Robins was attorney for the London merchant Thomas Crowdie. Stephen Charlton, who became a commissioner in 1640, engaged in trade with New England and served as attorney for Isaac Allerton and John Cogan, both prominent merchants from that area. He also represented a Virginia merchant, Thomas Bushrod.[17] One advantage of this practice was that the merchant was assured of having a representative at court to counter any unanticipated suit that might be instituted. In addition it probably ensured a full hearing of any cause involving the outsider and allowed for prompt claims to be made against the estates of decedents.

In the same way that Stephen Charlton was a focal point for much of the trade with New England, John Michael was one for trade with Holland. The major and important difference was that, in his first years of contact, Michael did not live on the Eastern Shore, but instead was himself a Dutch merchant. The first definite reference to Michael was an April 1649 letter of attorney in which he and Peter Peterson, both identified as merchants from Graft in Holland, appointed two friends on the Eastern Shore as agents in their absence. Five days later Michaels witnessed a letter of attorney from two Dutch merchants to John Stringer.

English America and the Restoration Monarchy of Charles II: Transatlantic Politics, Commerce, and Kinship (Lincoln, Nebr., 1980), chap. 1.

17. Topp and Crowdie: CCR-1, p. 1, CCR-2, pp. 321–322, CCR-3, p. 45, p. 192–fol. 192, CCR-6, p. 18. Allerton and Cogan: CCR-3, p. 48. Bushrod: CCR-1, p. 159, CCR-2, pp. 227–233, 234, CCR-3, pp. 12, 158, p. 192–fol. 192, CCR-5, p. 73–fol. 73, fol. 119–p. 120. Other commissioners who acted as attorneys for nonresident merchants were Argoll Yardley, Edmund Scarburgh, William Stone, William Waters, William Roper, and John Stringer.

Apparently Michael left the Eastern Shore and returned the following winter, a pattern conforming to that of other merchants. He appeared at court in November and December 1649 and January 1650.[18] During the summer of 1652, he and his kinsman John Johnson (also from Graft) became involved in a controversy with Rowland Savery, a merchant from Amsterdam, and John Clawse de Boll, master of the ship *Farewell*. This case involved the refusal of the shipmaster to comply with articles of agreement that bound the ship to a schedule convenient to Johnson in his efforts to load tobacco in Northampton County and ship it to Holland. The commissioners referred the complex case to James City. But before they did, Savery insulted Michael, who petitioned the court that the slander called into "question the reput and credit of you[r] suppliant Not only in Virginnia But alsoe in other parts beyonde the seas, Those which have intrusted your petitioner maye have notice of this aspersion." Protesting that his "Actions and dealings have bine Knowne to bee honest and with fayre Correspondencye," he forced Savery to retract his insult.[19]

Michael's concern for his reputation was not misplaced. Trust formed the foundation for the system of exchange.[20] His reference to the opinion of others "beyonde the seas" demonstrates that contemporaries recognized that the Eastern Shore was integrated into a larger Atlantic trading world. A slur on Michael's reputation there could spread throughout the mercantile network. A 1651 petition of John Nuthall to the local court provides further evidence of a similar concern for the spread of character aspersions. Planning to travel to England with his wife, Nuthall requested a certificate clearing his spouse of all guilt in a recent slander against her. Concerned that the slander might reach England, the court directed that the certificate be directed "unto whome it maye concerne in England or else where."[21]

When John Michael became a full-time resident cannot be determined. He may have been one as early as March 1652, when he signed the engagement to the Commonwealth of England. In May 1653 Governor Richard Bennett, recognizing him as an inhabitant, as a subscriber to the

18. CCR-3, pp. 142, 184, 188, fol. 194, pp. 200, 201, fol. 201.
19. CCR-4, fol. 93–p. 96.
20. That very month, Michael's kinsman Johnson transferred to him two letters of attorney from Jacob and Syvert Derrickson, who were Dutch mariners (CCR-4, p. 121–fol. 122).
21. CCR-4, p. 42–p. 46.

engagement, and as "liable to all Dutyes and services in this Countrye," granted him "equall priviledges and protection here (as well as others)." Now a resident, Michael continued to serve as an attorney to represent the interests of several Dutch merchants as well as of merchants elsewhere.[22] In addition he became actively involved in the affairs of John Cornelius and John Custis, two Dutch merchants who also had taken up residence on the Eastern Shore. Like Michael, Cornelius, who had traded from Amsterdam, had had contacts on the peninsula for several years before he took up residence. Custis became a resident after his sister Ann married Argoll Yardley. As was true with John Michael, Cornelius and Custis maintained mercantile contacts off the Eastern Shore.[23]

Local contacts were of paramount importance to nonresident merchants. Whether they appointed friends, relatives, prominent individuals, or other merchants to act as their agents, traders from England, New England, Holland, and the rest of Virginia relied on trusted personal acquaintances to conduct their business.[24] Local agents facilitated the flow of trade, including the extension of credit, the collection of debts, the assembling of cargoes, and the handling of the minutiae of deals involving temporary and shifting partnerships. By means of these myriad transactions, individuals on the Eastern Shore were drawn into the larger Atlantic circuit of trade.

But the Eastern Shore was not merely a passive recipient of whatever trade came its way through the agency of outside merchants. As with John Michael, John Cornelius, and John Custis, other merchants became resident on the peninsula. This arrangement had many advantages. When the tobacco harvest was ready, local merchants could more easily assemble a cargo for shipment. Time was an important factor in the export trade. Not only was tobacco perishable, but demand and price fluctuated with supply. The first shipments to reach foreign ports stood a

22. CCR-4, fol. 146 (for quotations), p. 165–fol. 165, fol. 188–p. 189, p. 195–fol. 195, CCR-6, p. 13.

23. Michael: CCR-4, fol. 146, p. 147, fol. 148, p. 151–fol. 151, p. 165, fol. 193. Cornelius: CCR-3, pp. 142, 199, fol. 199, p. 239–fol. 239, CCR-4, fol. 23, p. 110–fol. 112. Custis: CCR-4, fol. 188–p. 189; Ralph T. Whitelaw, *Virginia's Eastern Shore: A History of Northampton and Accomack Counties,* 2 vols. (Richmond, Va., 1951), I, 108. Custis's family was English by origin, Dutch by residence.

Cornelius's postresidence transactions included CCR-5, fol. 120–fol. 121, fols. 139, 149, CCR-6, fol. 10, p. 17. For Custis's, see CCR-4, p. 107, fol. 202, CCR-5, p. 8.

24. See also Pagan, "Dutch Maritime and Commercial Activity in Mid-Seventeenth-Century Virginia," *VMHB,* XC (1982), 488–490.

good chance of a greater return than those arriving later. Local merchants were also in an advantageous position to seize tobacco debts owed by small producers who might not have produced enough to cover all of their debts.[25]

The county court record contains references to twelve merchants that took up residence on the Eastern Shore but did not become landholders. A few brief examples show how this arrangement worked. Philip Dodsworth, a merchant who acted as agent for the Dale estate, probably lived on the extensive Dale holdings. Another example was Mathew Stone, whose brother William Stone became governor of Maryland after living on the Eastern Shore for more than twenty years. Mathew had been a partner with his brother before the latter's appointment to the governorship and continued to be involved in transactions involving William. After his brother's move to Maryland, Mathew apparently stayed on William's land, most of which was sold in small parcels.[26]

Two previously nonresident merchants demonstrated another option by marrying widows of landholders on the Eastern Shore. William Smart, a merchant from Bristol, had transacted business on the peninsula for two years before he married Mary Andrews, the widow of William Andrews. The latter, a prominent figure in the county for more than thirty years, had made arrangements in 1654 and 1655 (just before his death) to provide for his wife and children. After William Smart married Andrews's widow, he took up residence on the Andrews estate.[27] The second such marriage involved William Stranguidge, a Boston mariner whose contacts reveal his extensive involvement in the trade between New England and the Eastern Shore. His name appears in connection with this exchange between 1643 and 1652. In the latter year, he became

25. De Vries, "Voyages from Holland to America," NYHS, *Colls.*, 2d Ser., III (1857), 77.

26. Dodsworth: CCR-1, pp. 45–46, 147. Stone: CCR-2, p. 15, CCR-3, fols. 51, 123, CCR-4, p. 31–fol. 31; Nell Marion Nugent, ed., *Cavaliers and Pioneers: Abstracts of Virginia Land Patents and Grants*, I, *1623–1666*, II, *1666–1695* (Richmond, Va., 1934, 1977), I, 27–28. For indications that Mathew Stone continued to live on the peninsula, see CCR-4, fol. 50, p. 84–fol. 84, p. 130, p. 172–p. 173, fol. 188–p. 189, CCR-5, fol. 25, pp. 26, 84, fol. 93. For Mathew's continued involvement in his brother's transactions, see CCR-3, pp. 199, 210, fol. 212–p. 213, fol. 225, CCR-4, fol. 19, p. 20–fol. 20. For the sale of lands, see CCR-3, fol. 166, fol. 212–p. 213, fol. 225, CCR-4, p. 121, p. 145–fol. 145.

27. For William Smart's transactions, see CCR-5, fol. 15, p. 16, fol. 30–p. 31, pp. 55, 69, fol. 140–p. 141, fol. 144, CCR-6, fol. 7, and fragmentary unnumbered pages at the end of the volume. For references to the marriage and estate, see CCR-4, p. 190–fol. 190, CCR-5, p. 85–fol. 85, fol. 99–p. 100, p. 105–fol. 105.

the husband of Mary Drew, widow of Edward Drew, who had died in 1650 after living on the peninsula for more than twenty-five years. Stranguidge became a resident, presumably on the land that Mary Drew-Stranguidge had inherited for life from Edward Drew.[28]

Whereas some merchants established a local base of operations by the means described above, others did so by the acquisition of land. Although the following passage exaggerates somewhat the extent to which merchants became landholders, it does suggest the nature of the phenomenon as noted in 1649:

> Most of the Masters of ships and chief Mariners have also there Plantations, and houses, and servants, etc. in *Virginia*; and so are every way great gainers by Fraight, by Merchandize, and by Plantation and Pipe-staves, Clap-board, choice Walnut-tree-wood, Ceader-tree-timber and the like, is transported by them if Tobacco is not their full lading.[29]

Twelve of the merchants and mariners who acquired land on the Eastern Shore never took up residence there. At least six called London their home port, three were Virginians, and one hailed from New England. In addition to the three Virginians, who owned land on the Western Shore, three of the London merchants owned land elsewhere in Virginia. The three Londoners—Cornelius Lloyd, Maurice Tompson, and Thomas Deacon—all were involved in the same company that bought from the Adventurers and Company of Berkeley Hundred the eight-thousand-acre Berkeley Hundred in Charles City County. Whether these nonresident merchants acquired land in order to provide a base for their operations on the peninsula is unknown. But if they did, they did not stay committed to the long-term development of their plantations. Only one nonresident merchant, Thomas Burbage, held on to his land for more than five years. But Burbage, a prominent landholder on the Western Shore of Virginia, did not use his Eastern Shore holdings as a base of operations. He was

28. For Stranguidge's mercantile activities before marriage, see CCR-2, pp. 227–233, CCR-3, p. 78, fol. 235–p. 236, CCR-5, fol. 36–p. 37, p. 73–fol. 73. For Drew's death and the marriage of his widow to Stranguidge, see CCR-3, fol. 239–p. 240, CCR-4, fol. 18–fol. 19, p. 93, fol. 187, p. 200, CCR-5, fol. 36–p. 37, p. 73–fol. 73. For Stranguidge's trade with New England after his marriage, see CCR-4, fol. 157, p. 162, fol. 197, CCR-5, p. 16, fol. 30–p. 31, fol. 36–p. 37, fol. 97, CCR-7, p. 16.

29. *A Perfect Description of Virginia*, 5, in Force, ed., *Tracts and Other Papers*, II. See also Pagan, "Dutch Maritime and Commercial Activity in Mid-Seventeenth-Century Virginia," *VMHB*, XC (1982), 490.

mentioned very infrequently in the county court books after his initial patent in 1639.[30]

Possibly Burbage and other prospective absentee landholding merchants became disillusioned by the need for unremitting oversight of their holdings. For example, three years after his initial patent, Burbage appeared in court to defend his title against the encroachment of Edward Stockdell. Despite a court decision in his favor, Burbage did not recover his land. Ten years later he was embroiled again in litigation involving Stockdell's claim, prosecuted by William Ward, who had married Stockdell's widow. A year later Burbage wrote to Argoll Yardley to conduct negotiations with several individuals interested in his acreage (the list included William Ward).[31] This continual supervision and defense of landholdings would not have encouraged nonresident merchants to acquire acreage.

The alternative was to become resident landholding merchants. John Michael, John Cornelius, and John Custis did just this. The three of them maintained their mercantile contacts at the same time that they served as a focal point for the interests of nonresident merchants trading on the Eastern Shore. Twelve more landholders were merchants or mariners at the time they became residents. As with Michael, Cornelius, and Custis, these individuals, coming from Virginia's Western Shore, New England, and England, brought with them an acquaintance with ports and individuals off the Eastern Shore.[32] Their continuing mercantile activity, relying on prior connections and new links that developed through contact with other merchants, both resident and nonresident, resulted in a constantly expanding network of interactions.

Although certain individuals came to the Eastern Shore as established merchants, at least five residents became merchants after settling on the peninsula. William Waters belonged to this latter group. His father, Edward Waters, had lived in Bermuda for a short time before moving to

30. Nugent, ed., *Cavaliers and Pioneers*, I, 53, 110. Cornelius Lloyd also owned land on the Elizabeth River and later became a resident of Lower Norfolk County. Nugent, ed., *Cavaliers and Pioneers*, I, 27, 52; "Virginia Gleanings in England," *VMHB*, XI (1903–1904), 312.

31. CCR-2, pp. 213, 260–261, CCR-4, p. 179–fol. 179, p. 181, CCR-5, p. 70.

32. CCR-4, fol. 110–fol. 111, CCR-5, fol. 39–p. 40; Nugent, ed., *Cavaliers and Pioneers*, I, 251; Whitelaw, *Virginia's Eastern Shore*, I, 289. See also Pagan, "Dutch Maritime and Commercial Activity in Mid-Seventeenth-Century Virginia," *VMHB*, XC (1982), 487–488; Darrett B. Rutman and Anita H. Rutman, *A Place in Time: Middlesex County, Virginia, 1650–1750* (New York, 1984), 207–208.

Table 18. Status at Time of First Landholding of Resident Merchants

Status as Merchant or Mariner	No.
Already identified	15
Not yet identified	5
Questionable	5
Total	25

Kicoughtan (later Elizabeth City County) and marrying Grace O'Neill. In Virginia at the time of the Indian attack in 1622, they survived the slaughter only after a harrowing escape. Edward Waters served in several official positions—churchwarden, commissioner, burgess, commander—on the Western Shore during the 1620s. He had contacts throughout the colony, including some with people on the Eastern Shore. When he died in England on a trip in 1630, he left his wife a widow at age twenty-six with two children, Margaret and William. Within a few years, Grace married Obedience Robins, one of the most important men on the Eastern Shore.[33] Although her daughter Margaret lived with her mother and her stepfather on the peninsula, Grace's son William may have lived in England with relatives. The first reference to his being on the Eastern Shore appeared in the county court record under date of 1641. This timing coincides with a letter of October 8, 1641, sent from London by John Pemell to his cousin James Neale in Maryland, who was informed that Neale's cousin William Waters was just leaving for Virginia.[34] Dur-

33. CCR-1, pp. 83, 145, CCR-3, fol. 71; Nugent, ed., *Cavaliers and Pioneers*, I, 4, 12; Whitelaw, *Virginia's Eastern Shore*, I, 147; Annie Lash Jester and Martha Woodruff Hiden, comps., *Adventurers of Purse and Person: Virginia, 1607–1625* ([Richmond, Va.], 1964), 256–257, 346; H. R. McIlwaine, ed., *Minutes of the Council and General Court of Colonial Virginia, 1622–1632, 1670–1676* (Richmond, Va., 1924), 95, 124–125; George Sherwood, *American Colonists in English Records* (Baltimore, 1969), 13.

34. CCR-2, pp. 105, 281–283. Waters was related to James Neale through his mother Grace (O'Neill) Waters-Robins. Her maiden name and the surname of James Neale may have been variations of each other. Grace probably was related as well to John Neale, who patented land adjacent to that inherited by William Waters in Kicoughtan (Nugent, ed., *Cavaliers and Pioneers*, I, 18). John Neale, a merchant by trade, purchased and patented more than 2,000 acres on the Eastern Shore shortly after Grace's marriage to Obedience Robins (Nugent, ed., *Cavaliers and Pioneers*, I, 43, 54, 55, 68, 80). Although the many threads connecting the Robins and Neale families are too numerous to note in detail, two are worth mentioning. First, when Francis Pettit, a relative of Obedience Robins, came to the Eastern Shore, he settled on

ing the next several years, Waters's name appeared sporadically in the county court record. In 1644 Sampson Robins signed a statement that he owed 1,550 pounds of tobacco to "William Waters . . . planter." But Waters did not limit himself to being a planter. The same year that Sampson Robins recorded his debt to Waters, the latter set off on an extended mercantile voyage on which he acted as a factor for his stepfather Obedience Robins as well as for Argoll Yardley and John Wilkins, both of them important Eastern Shore residents. During his "factridge," Waters visited Holland, Hamburg, and the West Indies. He sailed on a Dutch ship, possibly the *Sancta Maria* of Amsterdam, which had been anchored on the Eastern Shore in the fall of 1643, at which time he had witnessed a letter of attorney granted to his stepfather by Aries Topp, a Dutch merchant.[35]

This trip began a business career during which Waters frequently dealt with merchants and mariners. Those not resident were invariably Dutch; those resident were often of Dutch background, such as John Michael and John Cornelius. In addition to these personal contacts, Waters became involved in the trading networks of two other individuals. The first was George Clark, who died in the winter of 1649–1650 and whose widow Margaret married Waters that same year.[36] The settlement of Clark's estate drew Waters into a nexus of contacts with individuals in Maryland, New England, and London. The second such set of ties was generated by Waters's appointment as one of the guardians of the orphans of Stephen Charlton. In the course of his efforts to supply these orphans with goods suitable to their station, Waters traded with England

---

land formerly in John Neale's possession. Second, 10 years after Neale died, the county commissioners in 1654 appointed William Waters as guardian to Neale's daughter Margaret, whose mother had died just recently. For the purposes of confirming a kin relationship, it is notable that John Neale's daughter shared the same given name as that of Grace (O'Neill) Waters's daughter Margaret (CCR-1, pp. 105, 113, CCR-4, p. 194). For naming patterns in 17th-century Virginia, see Darrett B. Rutman and Anita H. Rutman, *A Place in Time: Explicatus* (New York, 1984), chap. 7.

35. CCR-2, pp. 321–322, 390–391, 440, CCR-3, p. 23, fol. 30, pp. 31, 36, fol. 36. Other references to Waters include CCR-2, pp. 105, 187–188, 198, 209, 215–216, 270, 281–283.

36. For John Michael and John Cornelius, see CCR-3, fol. 208, CCR-6, p. 8, fol. 17. See also Abraham Johnson (CCR-3, p. 36, CCR-4, fol. 121–p. 122), Tobias Norton (CCR-3, fol. 63–p. 64, p. 71, CCR-4, p. 221), Barnes Johnson (CCR-4, p. 165–fol. 165), Hugh Yeo (CCR-3, fol. 73–p. 74, CCR-4, fol. 209), and Christopher Major (CCR-4, pp. 175, 221). For Clark, see CCR-3, p. 193–fol. 193, p. 208, fol. 224. William Waters had earlier been married to Katherine Waters, for whom he had claimed a headright. She must have died shortly after her immigration (CCR-3, p. 71).

and New Amsterdam. Concomitant with his elaborating web of mercantile contacts, he served as attorney for merchants from England, Holland, and New England. In addition he served as an arbiter in several cases involving merchants from off the Eastern Shore. Finally, although the county court record reveals his impressive array of contacts with merchants, both resident and nonresident, Waters's familiarity with traders frequenting the Eastern Shore was enhanced by his appointment as one of the commissioners of Northampton County.[37]

As impressive as Waters's range of contacts was, his experience was not unique. Other resident landholders developed networks far more extended and complex. These webs were all characterized by a combination of travel abroad, deals with nonresident merchants, indirect ties to mercantile interests scattered throughout the Atlantic world of trade, and random assignments of trust by business contacts. Stephen Charlton's letters of attorney from New England have been mentioned already. What has not been pointed out is that the first reference to Charlton's representing the interests of a New England trader came after more than a decade of trade with that area. As early as 1634, he had been involved in the trade as a partner of Captain John Stone.[38] After Stone's death, Charlton traveled to New England to trade personally. The county court books record his ownership of a series of pinnaces, shallops, and barques. He carried on a considerable coastal trade, not only on his own but also in partnership with several New England merchants, including John Cogan, Edward Gibbons, William Stranguidge (before he moved to the Eastern Shore), John Holland, and John Thorndike. Compared to the extent of his New England trade, Charlton's recorded contacts with Dutch and English merchants were far fewer.[39]

37. Waters's contacts concerning the Clark estate included John Steerman of Maryland, a Mr. Kellohill, Thomas Crowdie of London, John Cogan and Mr. Taynter of New England (CCR-3, fol. 223, CCR-4, p. 38–fol. 38, p. 52, p. 60–p. 61, fol. 70). As guardian: CCR-7, fol. 28–fol. 32. As attorney: CCR-3, p. 145, fol. 152, p. 159, fol. 208, CCR-5, p. 125, CCR-7, p. 27. As arbiter: CCR-3, fol. 137, CCR-4, p. 85, CCR-7, fol. 62–p. 63. Appointed commissioner in 1652, Waters does not seem actually to have sat on the county court until 1654 (CCR-4, p. 117–p. 118, CCR-5, fol. 4).

38. CCR-1, pp. 23–24. De Vries mentions Stone's trade with New England in "Voyages from Holland to America," trans. Murphy, NYHS, *Colls.,* 2d Ser., III (1857), 43–44.

39. On ownership of boats, see CCR-1, p. 141, CCR-2, pp. 217, 227–233, 234, 363, CCR-4, fol. 102, CCR-5, p. 73–fol. 73. Coastal trade: CCR-3, p. 128, fols. 128, 137, p. 140, fol. 140, CCR-4, fol. 102, p. 107, CCR-5, p. 73–fol. 73, fol. 119–p. 120. Dutch and English contacts: CCR-2, pp. 142–143, 435, CCR-3, p. 188, p. 192–fol. 192, p. 240–fol. 240.

The trade network of Edmund Scarburgh, another resident landholder who became a merchant, encompassed a far wider geographical area. His earliest contacts were with English merchants, one of whom remained a partner for many years. Later he traded with the Dutch in Holland and New Amsterdam.[40] He also regularly conducted mercantile relations with the Western Shore, Palmer's Island (in the upper Chesapeake), Maryland, and the Delaware Bay.[41] But as with Charlton, Scarburgh's most frequent recorded ties linked him with New England's mercantile interests. Many of the merchants trading with Charlton traded with Scarburgh as well: John Cogan, William Stranguidge, and Edward Gibbons, for example. Scarburgh also dealt with William Payne of Ipswich and William Brenton of Boston. Edward Gibbons, the most important of his New England contacts, appeared over the course of many years as his partner and agent in trade with England, Ireland, and the Madeiras. Moreover, as the owner or part owner of several vessels, Scarburgh carried on some of his trade either in person or by hired agents. His travels took him to many ports, including those in old and New England.[42]

Thus, landholding residents became merchants. The reverse also held true. But whichever was the case, these resident merchants were a crucial group for the formation and maintenance of links to the larger Atlantic world. Avenues of trade fostered and were fostered in turn by a variety of contacts between the Eastern Shore and other ports. Familial contacts

40. English contacts: CCR-1, p. 95, CCR-3, fol. 101–p. 102. Dutch contacts: CCR-4, p. 24–fol. 24, CCR-5, fol. 62–fol. 66, CCR-7, p. 13; Berthold Fernow, ed., *Documents Relative to the Colonial History of the State of New-York; Procured in Holland, England, and France, by John Romeyn Brodhead*, XII, *Documents Relating to the History of the Dutch and Swedish Settlements on the Delaware River* (Albany, N.Y., 1877), 93–94.

41. CCR-4, p. 22–fol. 22, p. 41–fol. 41, fol. 75; Lancaster County, *Deeds, Etc., No. 2, 1654–1702*, 139; Westmoreland County, *Deeds, Wills, Patents, 1653–1659*, 34. In 1651 Cecilius Calvert, Lord Baltimore, instructed William Stone, governor of Maryland, and the two houses of the General Assembly that all Marylanders were to resist Scarburgh's encroachment on Palmer's Island and in the Indian trade in Maryland. William Hand Browne, ed., *Archives of Maryland*, I, *Proceedings and Acts of the General Assembly of Maryland, January 1637/8–September 1664* (Baltimore, 1883), 328–329.

42. Cogan, Stranguidge, and Gibbons: CCR-3, p. 97, fol. 199, p. 203, CCR-4, fol. 115–p. 116, p. 185, p. 199–fol. 199, fol. 217–p. 218, p. 227, CCR-5, fols. 33, 50, pp. 56, 73, 117, CCR-7, pp. 11, 16, 70. Payne and Brenton: CCR-4, p. 153–fol. 153, fol. 197, CCR-5, fol. 24, fol. 135–p. 136, CCR-7, p. 15, fol. 15–p. 16, fol. 79. Gibbons as partner: CCR-4, p. 185, CCR-5, fols. 21, 50. Travels: CCR-4, p. 41–fol. 41, p. 153–fol. 153, fol. 192–p. 193, CCR-5, fol. 21, CCR-7, p. 15, fol. 78–p. 79.

are an example. Evidence of communications from relatives passing along news, sending instructions, and forwarding gifts and supplies appears frequently in the county court record.[43] The letter quoted earlier from Mr. Phillips was not unique. And these contacts were not limited to relatives in England. At least 9 percent of adult resident landholders on the Eastern Shore are known to have had kin elsewhere in the English colonies in America. This figure must be considered an absolute minimum. (The extraordinary difficulty of tracing individuals and establishing their identities in the fragmentary existing records limits the results of such a search to being suggestive, albeit persuasive, rather than definitive.)

There is also evidence of continuing contact with friends off the Eastern Shore. At least 12 percent of adult resident landholders served as attorneys to represent nonresidents in cases before the local court. Almost without exception, the letters of attorney that survive appoint "respected and loving," "loveing," "welbeloved," "trusty and welbeloved," "very loveinge," and "kind" friends as legal representatives. The county court record also includes many references to friends off the Eastern Shore and a wide variety of favors performed, gifts exchanged, and news reported. These friends were located in other parts of Virginia, Maryland, and old and New England.[44]

To some extent the ties of friendship reflected longtime personal contact with close acquaintances from earlier days. This was true not only for those ties with the mother country but also for those with sister colonies. At least 8 percent of the adult resident landholders came from other parts of Virginia, Maryland, or New England. Moving from these areas to the Eastern Shore, the settlers brought with them a knowledge of other places and the people who lived there. Besides making the outside world a little less unknown, the ties formed the basis of future contacts based on trust and favors.

In addition to acquaintances from earlier places of residence, Eastern Shore landholders met new people and expanded their networks of interaction through travel. About one-quarter of resident landholders on the peninsula are known to have traveled across the Chesapeake Bay or to

43. CCR-2, pp. 69–70, 281–283, CCR-3, p. 6, fol. 95, p. 172, CCR-4, p. 15–fol. 16, fol. 164.

44. Letters of attorney: CCR-2, pp. 324–325, 347–348, CCR-3, fol. 5, p. 28, fol. 63–p. 64. Friends: CCR-2, pp. 69–70, 273–274, 323, 437, CCR-3, fols. 44, 108, 173, CCR-4, p. 15–fol. 16, pp. 67, 185, CCR-5, fol. 36–p. 37, fol. 88–fol. 89, CCR-6, fol. 25, CCR-7, fol. 26, p. 36–p. 37.

Maryland at least once before 1655. Given the fragmentary nature of the extant record and the consequent underreporting of such movements, this figure is surprisingly high. Inasmuch as the county court books are an official register, a predictably high proportion of these contacts related to official business. Slightly more than one-half the residents traveling over the bay were headed to James City to appear at the quarter court, to serve as burgesses, or to pursue some other official mission. In 1644 a company of men from the peninsula joined in a campaign against the Indians on the Western Shore, which had suffered a heavy loss from a surprise attack by the natives.[45]

The reasons behind other trips across the bay are often obscure, because they were extraneous to the substance of the depositions in which the trips were mentioned. Thus, in the mid-1630s, when John Howe was on the other side of the bay, Robert Partine spoke to him about a business matter involving another resident of the Eastern Shore. Howe mentioned the location of the conversation in the course of a deposition about the debt involved. But why he had traveled over the bay is not revealed.[46] In addition to these contacts with the rest of Virginia and Maryland, at least 7 percent of resident landholders traveled greater distances. Generally these trips were for the purpose of trade, as for William Waters, Stephen Charlton, and Edmund Scarburgh. But whatever the reason behind the travels, they expanded a potentially limited knowledge of the world off the Eastern Shore.

The reverse also held true; by means of their travels, residents brought a knowledge of their new home to people who knew little or nothing about it. They also expanded the network of personal contacts that could be tapped for individual purposes. The same ends were accomplished by those landholding residents who moved off the Eastern Shore. Like those immigrants who brought with them knowledge of and personal contacts with the areas they had left, emigrants from the Eastern Shore departed with the same sort of knowledge and contacts. Of the 315 adult resident landholders, slightly more than 7 percent disappeared abruptly from the official record. Whether they died or moved cannot be determined with certainty, but probably the majority of them moved. Except for the

45. For other references to men serving in a military capacity on the Western Shore, see CCR-1, p. 109, CCR-3, p. 14, fols. 14, 15, pp. 22, 100. See also CCR-2, p. 383; and H. R. McIlwaine, ed., "Acts, Orders, and Resolutions of the General Assembly of Virginia: At Session of March 1643–1646," *VMHB*, XXII (1915), 231–232.

46. CCR-1, pp. 69–70, 85, 86, 99, CCR-2, p. 222, CCR-3, fol. 3, p. 25, CCR-4, p. 102, fol. 154, CCR-5, fols. 5, 131.

twenty-three individuals in this group, it is always possible to identify the death of a landholder. References to widows, orphans, creditors, estate settlement, or some other indicator of mortality provide irrefutable evidence. The complete absence of such references for the twenty-three individuals who disappeared from the court record suggests that all or at least a large proportion of them moved.

Twenty other adult landholders, slightly more than 6 percent of the total number, unquestionably moved off the Eastern Shore. Eight of the twenty moved to the Western Shore of Virginia, eight went to Maryland, and one left for the West Indies; three more emigrated without leaving a trace of where they settled subsequently. These twenty individuals left behind them networks of personal contacts formed over a period of many years: they had lived on the peninsula a median of thirteen years before they moved.[47] After such a long period of residence, it is not surprising that, almost without exception, those residents who moved maintained some subsequent contact with people on the Eastern Shore. Thus, more than seven years after William Epes emigrated, he still owned land on King's Creek. William Stone handled his business affairs for at least ten years after Epes's departure. Stone, in turn, maintained contacts with individuals on the Eastern Shore after he moved to Maryland and became governor there. Several matters continued to draw his attention to his former residence: transactions involving his large acreage, the collection of debts due to him, former official responsibilities, and ties of friendship.[48]

Although the extralocal contacts of any one individual might not have been numerous or frequent, the sum total of these links served to integrate the Eastern Shore into the larger Atlantic world. For avenues of communication, the colonists relied on available shipping. Individuals maintained contact by personal travel, correspondence, and word of mouth. Ties included those between business associates, friends, and

47. This figure contrasts rather sharply with the 6-year median residence for the 23 landholders who disappeared from the official record without any reference to death or mobility. A briefer period of residence may help to explain their unrecorded disappearance. Living on the Eastern Shore for 6 rather than 13 years meant that they had a shorter time to form contacts and become enmeshed in local networks. With fewer ties to the peninsula's population, this group of emigrants probably had less reason to maintain contacts there. This pattern would have reduced the chance that they would be mentioned subsequently in the county court books.

48. Epes: CCR-2, p. 141; Nugent, ed., *Cavaliers and Pioneers*, I, 163. Stone: CCR-3, pp. 199, 212, fol. 225, CCR-4, p. 7, p. 31–fol. 31, fol. 80, p. 121, fol. 139, p. 145–fol. 145, fol. 194–p. 195, CCR-5, fol. 4–p. 5, fols. 69, 131.

relatives. The importance of these networks is reflected in the notable hospitality extended to visitors on the Eastern Shore and elsewhere in the Chesapeake.[49] Institutional ties also bound the peninsula's inhabitants to the outside world. Residents served as councillors and burgesses in James City, brought cases before the colony's quarter court, and fought side by side with other Virginians against the Indians.[50]

49. Hammond, *Leah and Rachel*, 19, in Force, ed., *Tracts and Other Papers*, III; Colonel Norwood, *A Voyage to Virginia*, 48–49, *ibid.*, III.

50. McIlwaine, ed., *Minutes of the Council and General Court*, 24–25; William Waller Hening, ed., *The Statutes at Large: Being a Collection of All the Laws of Virginia*, I (New York, 1823), 141.

7 Institutions and the Societal Network

DESPITE THE peninsula's integration into the network linking the Atlantic world, the everyday experience of an ordinary landholder took place within a very few miles of his residence. With the exception of merchants and commissioners, most individuals were not drawn more than a few miles from their homes by ties of kinship, friendship, and economic necessity. Did any other purposes serve to expand these constricted personal networks? What role did the institutions of government, religion, and militia play in bringing together inhabitants from different parts of the country?

Through midcentury, arrangements for government were adapted to both the total number of inhabitants to be governed and their settlement pattern. In early 1625 approximately fifty people lived on the Eastern Shore.[1] They were concentrated on and around two tracts that the Virginia Company had assigned for its own financial support and for support of the secretary of the colony. The dissolution of the Virginia Company left these inhabitants without any officially recognized local authority. As a temporary measure, "u[n]till there be some order taken for a Comyssione for determininge of pettie differences at *Accomack*," the governor and Council in March 1625 authorized Captain William Epes, who had acted as commander of the Eastern Shore at least since 1623, "in the meane tyme" to exercise "full power and Authority to Administer an oath to any persone or persones there inhabitinge for the better decidinge of any smale cause (that may there arise) by way of Compremise, and for savinge the Charge and trouble of Sendinge up of witnesses" to James City.[2] Significantly, this passage from the minutes of the Council and General Court of Virginia came directly after a reference to the immigration of planters into Accomack. Apparently the colony's officials were interested in the good governance not only of the earlier resi-

---

1. Fifty-one people were listed in the Muster of early 1625. Annie Lash Jester and Martha Woodruff Hiden, comps., *Adventurers of Purse and Person: Virginia, 1607–1625* ([Richmond, Va.], 1964), 66–69.

2. H. R. McIlwaine, ed., *Minutes of the Council and General Court of Colonial Virginia, 1622–1632, 1670–1676* (Richmond, Va., 1924), 50. For Epes's earlier service, see "Wyatt Manuscripts," *WMQ*, 2d Ser., VIII (1928), 56.

dents, many of whom had been Company tenants, but also of these more recent immigrants.

As we have seen, the number of people on the Eastern Shore continued to grow, as did the area of settlement. From 1625 to 1627 new landholders took up acreage near the original settlement on Cherrystone and King's creeks. In late 1627, however, reports reached the governor and Council that "divers planters at *Accawmacke* doe intend at the *old plantation* Creeke and at *Magety*-Bay on that shoare to erect some new plantations and to seat themselves in such sort as may be both inconvenient and dangerous." The General Court refused to permit this expansion of settlement and tried to keep the planters "as much as may be, seated closely together." During the next five years, despite this initial prohibition, officials at James City approved several claims for land on the peninsula formed by Old Plantation Creek and the Chesapeake Bay. This land was easily accessible to the original settlement, and population remained concentrated enough to allow local administration of justice to remain in the hands of a single individual.[3]

As population increased on the Eastern Shore and in the rest of Virginia, there developed a need for a more elaborate local administration of justice. In February 1632 the Virginia Assembly passed an act to provide for monthly courts in "remote parts" of the colony including the Eastern Shore.

> Whereas for the greater ease of the inhabitants in divers parts of this colony, and for the better conservation of the peace, and due execution of such lawes and orders, as are or shall be established for the government of the people, and the inhabitants of the same.... Theire shall be mounthlie corts, and oftener uppon extraordinarie causes requiring and agreed uppon by the major part of the comissioners, held and kept in some of the remote plantations.

After specifying the jurisdiction, duties, and oath of the commissioners of the monthly courts, the act listed the names of those appointed for each of the five "remote parts."[4]

By 1634 local administration of justice was established throughout

3. McIlwaine, ed., *Minutes of the Council and General Court*, 156. After Epes left the Eastern Shore, Thomas Graves was appointed commander (*ibid.*, 165).

4. Although the act establishing monthly courts in 1632 cites a similar order of Mar. 5, 1623, there is no evidence that this earlier order was implemented. William Waller Hening, ed., *The Statutes at Large: Being a Collection of All the Laws of Virginia*, I (New York, 1823), 168–169.

Virginia. The colony leadership had divided Virginia into eight "shires" (including one for "Accawmacke"), designated local officials, and defined the jurisdiction of the local courts. Although the Virginia Assembly tinkered with the details of jurisdiction over the next twenty years, the basic structure of local judicial administration remained intact.[5] It did so not only because of its similarity to the English local system and consequent familiarity to the colonists but also because it could readily be adapted to a growing population and expanding area of settlement. The history of changes in court personnel and local subdivisions on the Eastern Shore evidences the flexibility of the system. These changes also reveal something about the role of the county court in fostering the development of the societal network.

The steadily increasing population on the Eastern Shore flowed initially south and then north of the original area of settlement, with people preferring to live on the bayside.[6] As people moved to new areas, colony officials tried to adapt local government to the enlarging settlement. One way was to delegate limited authority to individual commissioners and to promote convenient access to them. Examining where the members of the county bench lived at five-year intervals reveals that the colony officials succeeded in dispersing representatives of local authority through-

5. *Ibid.*, 168–169, 224, 273, 345–346; CCR-2, pp. 177–179; Warren M. Billings, ed., "Some Acts Not in Hening's *Statutes*: The Acts of Assembly, April 1652, November 1652, and July 1653," *VMHB*, LXXXIII (1975), 70.

6. Maps 4–7 suggest the rapidity and extent of this expansion, but it must be emphasized that these maps depict the progress of land acquisition and not the distribution of population. It is impossible to identify accurately where all people lived. Yet, with two reservations, the land acquisition maps can be used as a rough guide to the spread of population. First, people generally seated themselves on the peninsula's bayside, where sheltered creeks allowed more convenient contact with the rest of Virginia. The innumerable references to people walking, boating, and meeting up and down the western side of the peninsula reflect the preference for bayside residence. This contrasts sharply with the very few references to such occurrences on the seaside. In addition, contemporary accounts testify to the planters' preference for locating near navigable waterways such as those on the bayside; see *A Perfect Description of Virginia* . . . , 6, in Peter Force, ed., *Tracts and Other Papers, Relating Principally to the Origin, Settlement, and Progress of the Colonies in North America, from the Discovery of the Country to the Year 1776*, 4 vols. (Washington, D.C., 1836–1847), II; and John Hammond, *Leah and Rachel; or, The Two Fruitfull Sisters Virginia, and Maryland* . . . , 18, *ibid.*, III. Thus, while people acquired land on the seaside, they very rarely seated there. A second reservation about the use of the land acquisition maps to suggest the spread of population is that they exaggerate the rapidity of that movement. For example, in 1635 four landholders were responsible for expansion on the southern tip of the peninsula, along the seaside, and at Hungars Creek. Meanwhile, more than 400 people were concentrated in the older area of settlement on King's, Cherrystone, and Old Plantation creeks.

Map 8. Residential Locations of Commissioners, 1635

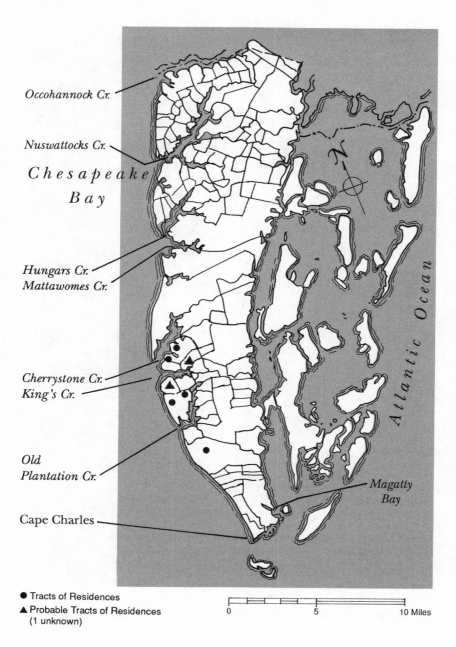

Occohannock Cr.

Nuswattocks Cr.

C h e s a p e a k e
B a y

Hungars Cr.
Mattawomes Cr.

Cherrystone Cr.
King's Cr.

Old
Plantation Cr.

Cape Charles

Atlantic Ocean

Magatty
Bay

● Tracts of Residences
▲ Probable Tracts of Residences
   (1 unknown)

0   5   10 Miles

Map 9. Residential Locations of Commissioners, 1640

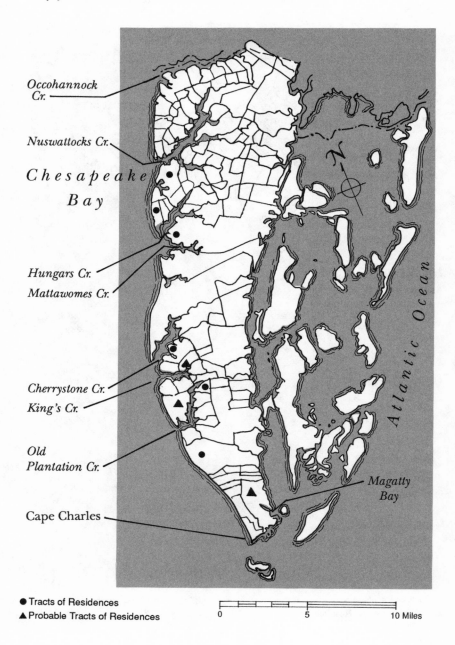

Occohannock Cr.

Nuswattocks Cr.

Chesapeake Bay

Hungars Cr.

Mattawomes Cr.

Cherrystone Cr.

King's Cr.

Old Plantation Cr.

Cape Charles

Atlantic Ocean

Magatty Bay

N

● Tracts of Residences
▲ Probable Tracts of Residences

0   5   10 Miles

Map 10. Residential Locations of Commissioners, 1645

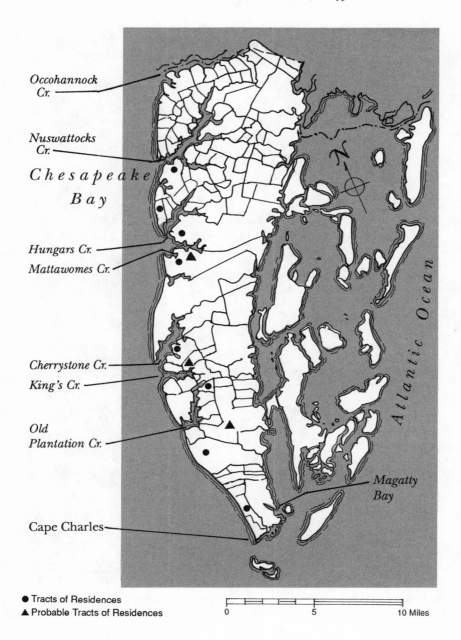

Occohannock Cr.

Nuswattocks Cr.

C h e s a p e a k e   B a y

Hungars Cr.

Mattawomes Cr.

Cherrystone Cr.

King's Cr.

Old Plantation Cr.

Magatty Bay

Cape Charles

Atlantic Ocean

● Tracts of Residences

▲ Probable Tracts of Residences

0   5   10 Miles

Map 11. Residential Locations of Commissioners, 1650

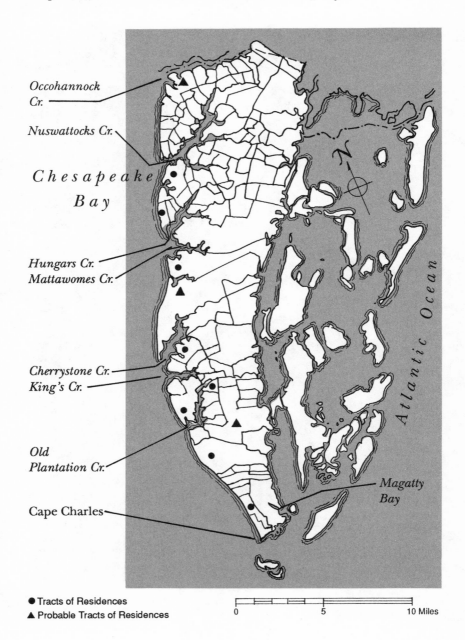

Occohannock
Cr.

Nuswattocks Cr.

C h e s a p e a k e
B a y

Hungars Cr.
Mattawomes Cr.

Atlantic Ocean

Cherrystone Cr.
King's Cr.

Old
Plantation Cr.

Magatty
Bay

Cape Charles

● Tracts of Residences
▲ Probable Tracts of Residences

0   5   10 Miles

Map 12. Residential Locations of Commissioners, 1655

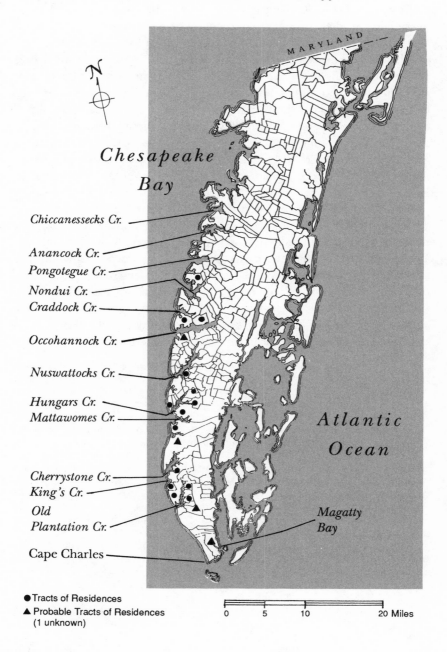

Chesapeake Bay

MARYLAND

Chiccanessecks Cr.

Anancock Cr.
Pongotegue Cr.
Nondui Cr.
Craddock Cr.

Occohannock Cr.

Nuswattocks Cr.

Hungars Cr.
Mattawomes Cr.

Atlantic Ocean

Cherrystone Cr.
King's Cr.
Old Plantation Cr.

Magatty Bay

Cape Charles

● Tracts of Residences
▲ Probable Tracts of Residences
   (1 unknown)

0   5   10   20 Miles

out the area of settlement. As people moved away from previously settled areas, individuals living in their midst were appointed to be commissioners. Studies of county courts elsewhere in the Chesapeake have
also discovered a similar geographic dispersion of local officials.[7]

When a commissioner died, he was replaced with someone living
nearby. For example, William Roper sat as a commissioner of the county
court from 1637 until his death in late 1650. During this entire period,
he lived at the head of Old Plantation Creek. Less than a year after Roper
died, the governor and Council of Virginia appointed Thomas Hunt to
the commission. Hunt lived less than a mile south of Roper's plantation
on Old Plantation Creek. He had lived on the Eastern Shore at least as
long as Roper but was appointed to serve as a commissioner only after
Roper's death left a vacancy in the area of his residence. Another example of the same phenomenon occurred in 1655 after the death of Stephen
Charlton, who had been on the county commission since 1640. His
home was on the southern tip of land at the mouth of Nuswattocks
Creek. Less than six months after Charlton's death, Levin Denwood was
appointed to take a seat on the commission. Denwood lived on the
opposite side of a small creek bordering Charlton's tract but also on the
south shore of Nuswattocks Creek.[8] He had been in the county at least
as long as Charlton but, like Thomas Hunt, was asked to serve as a
commissioner only after a local vacancy had occurred.[9]

7. Tracts of residence were located where possible for members of the county bench
holding commissions as of May in each fifth year. Although other variables—wealth,
family, political connections—may have influenced the appointment of commissioners, the location of residence emerges as a significant determinant. If the pattern
observed on the Eastern Shore was representative of the experience in the rest of
Virginia, the distribution of commissioners' residences can be used to gauge the progress of land acquisition and the distribution of population.

For courts elsewhere, see Wesley Frank Craven, *The Southern Colonies in the Seventeenth Century, 1607–1689* (1949; reprint ed., Baton Rouge, La., 1970), 168, 204;
Lois Green Carr, "The Foundations of Social Order: Local Government in Colonial
Maryland," in Bruce C. Daniels, ed., *Town and County: Essays on the Structure of
Local Government in the American Colonies* (Middletown, Conn., 1978), 79–81;
and Robert Wheeler, "The County Court in Colonial Virginia," in Daniels, ed., *Town
and County*, 116.

8. Roper: CCR-1, p. 71, CCR-3, pp. 223, 236; Nell Marion Nugent, ed., *Cavaliers
and Pioneers: Abstracts of Virginia Land Patents and Grants*, I, *1623–1666*, II,
1666–1695 (Richmond, Va., 1934, 1977), I, 46, 482. Hunt: CCR-2, pp. 306–307,
CCR-4, p. 49–fol. 49; Nugent, ed., *Cavaliers and Pioneers*, I, 46. Charlton: CCR-1,
p. 159, CCR-4, fol. 91, CCR-5, fol. 61, p. 76; Nugent, ed., *Cavaliers and Pioneers*, I,
82, 129. Denwood: CCR-5, fol. 133; Ralph T. Whitelaw, *Virginia's Eastern Shore: A
History of Northampton and Accomack Counties*, 2 vols. (Richmond, Va., 1951), I,
440.

9. For a similar observation for Maryland, see Carr, "The Foundations of Social

A passage from John Hammond's *Leah and Rachel*, printed in London in 1656, suggests the function of a geographic dispersion of commissioners. In Virginia, "Justice is . . . duly and daily administred; hardly can any travaile two miles together, but they will finde a Justice, which hath power of himself to hear and determine mean differences, to secure and bind over notorious offenders." Hammond's statement summarizes the benefits of having commissioners scattered throughout the area of settlement. Individual commissioners had the power to take depositions outside a court setting.[10] This was a great convenience for deponents who were ill, who planned to travel off the Eastern Shore before the next court day, or who for whatever reason could not attend the court where their depositions would be needed. Further extending the power of individual commissioners, the Assembly of March 1643 passed an act giving exclusive jurisdiction over cases involving debts under the value of twenty shillings to whichever commissioner lived nearest the creditor.[11] This measure allowed a quick and convenient resolution of minor financial disputes. In settling such cases out of court, the procedure reduced the necessity for the people involved to attend the meetings of the full commission. Similarly, servants with complaints about their treatment at the hands of their masters had quick and convenient recourse to the commissioner living nearest them. Debtors not contesting the claims of their creditors could verify the debt with one of the commissioners of the quorum. These and other powers allowed individual commissioners on the Eastern Shore and elsewhere throughout the Chesapeake to handle certain issues out of court and thereby reduce the work load at official meetings of the county commission.[12]

The scattering of commissioners throughout the area of settlement

---

Order," in Daniels, ed., *Town and County*, 80–81. In identifying reasons for the appointment of justices in Virginia, Philip Alexander Bruce ignores this geographic factor, in *Institutional History of Virginia in the Seventeenth Century*, 2 vols. (New York, 1910), I, 488–489.

10. Hammond, *Leah and Rachel*, 15, in Force, ed., *Tracts and Other Papers*, III; CCR-1, pp. 6, 48, 119, CCR-2, pp. 95–96, 177–179, 186–187, 213–214, 242–243, 358–359. In 1645 the Assembly passed an act requiring two commissioners to be present when depositions were taken, but the commissioners did not always obey this law. In 1652 the commissions issued by Governor Richard Bennett suggest that individual commissioners were empowered to take depositions (Hening, ed., *Statutes at Large*, I, 304; CCR-3, fol. 57–p. 58, CCR-4, p. 117–p. 118).

11. Hening, ed., *Statutes at Large*, I, 273.

12. Billings, ed., "Some Acts Not in Hening's *Statutes*," *VMHB*, LXXXIII (1975), 33, 39, 53; Craven, *Southern Colonies*, 169–170, 285–286; Carr, "The Foundations of Social Order," in Daniels, ed., *Town and County*, 79; Wheeler, "The County Court in Colonial Virginia," in Daniels, ed., *Town and County*, 116.

served other purposes as well as those related to the administration of justice. In 1640 Governor Francis Wyatt issued a proclamation concerning the regulation of tobacco production. To enforce these provisions, Wyatt ordered the commissioners of each county to subdivide their jurisdictions so that each commissioner would be responsible for viewing the tobacco crop from house to house in his own area.[13] In 1644, following the Indian uprising on the Western Shore, the governor and Council ordered the counties to prepare for their own defense. In accordance with this order, the commander and commissioners on the Eastern Shore divided the county into designated areas, in each of which there resided one or two commissioners responsible for overseeing the preparation.[14] In addition (although discussed more fully below), it is worth mentioning here that individual commissioners were included in the organization of the militia near where they lived. The commissioners performed other local duties as well. In 1646 the county was divided into four precincts for the purpose of compiling exact tithable lists, and one or two commissioners resident within each precinct were responsible for making the lists. Finally, when Virginia succumbed in 1652 to the force of an ascendant Parliament and recognized the English Commonwealth, inhabitants who had not signed the engagement, which signified their support of the new order, were commanded to report to the nearest commissioner to do so.[15]

The commissioners, by performing many official tasks in the vicinity of their residences, helped to make government services available more quickly and conveniently. Residents were spared the time and expense of attending a court meeting that might take place at a not inconsiderable distance and have a full calendar extending over several days. Furthermore, inhabitants seeking redress in minor affairs or needing the attention of local officials in a variety of matters did not have to wait until the next meeting of the county commission. For example, when John Nuthall's servant was found dead in 1647, Nuthall's neighbors insisted that before burying the body he summon William Stone or William Andrews, both commissioners who were his neighbors. At a meeting of the county court on December 28, 1655, the commissioners ordered that Stephen Horsey and John Ellis, appraisers of the estate of William Moulte, take

13. CCR-2, pp. 106–108.
14. CCR-2, pp. 359–360.
15. Militia: CCR-2, pp. 359–360, CCR-4, p. 47, p. 117–p. 118. Precincts: CCR-3, p. 45. Commonwealth: CCR-4, fol. 66.

Table 19. Growth of the County Court

	Frequency of Court Meetings			
Period	No. of Months per Year: Mean (Median)	Months per Year with More than One Meeting: Mean (Median)	Days per Year: Mean (Median)	Maximum No. of Commissioners: Mean (Median)
1636–1640	8.2 (8)	.4 (0)	8.6 (8)	7.4 (7)
1641–1645	8.8 (10)	2.6 (2)	11.6 (12)	10.8 (11)
1646–1650	8.6 (9)	4.0 (4)	13.4 (14)	11.8 (11)
1651–1655	10.2 (10)	8.0 (7)	23.0 (20)	16.8 (18)

their oaths before the magistrates living near them. At the same court, Olive Poulton was given custody of her children and possession of cattle belonging to them; she was instructed to contact the nearest magistrate should her ex-husband attempt to harass her or her children.[16]

Moreover, the saving of time and expense accrued not only to the inhabitants but also to the court itself, whose work load grew steadily. The number of people to be governed increased more than 250 percent from 1632, when a commission first sat, to 1655. In addition, the area seated by these people expanded dramatically. The court's work load included a multitude of actions involving land disputes, servant problems, debtor-creditor relations (by far the largest category), and many other issues.[17] The growth in the court's work load is reflected in an increase in the number not only of months and days per year when the court sat but also of commissioners sitting. In 1636 the six commissioners of the court sat for one day in each of six months. In 1642 there were eleven commissioners, who met in ten of the twelve months of the year. Multiple sittings in four months that year meant that the court sat for a total of fifteen days. It must have been a realization of this increasing

16. CCR-3, p. 116–fol. 118, CCR-6, fol. 21, p. 22.

17. For an overview of the work load of the Eastern Shore county court during the 1630s, see George B. Curtis, "The Colonial County Court, Social Forum and Legislative Precedent: Accomack, Virginia, 1633–1639," *VMHB*, LXXXV (1977), 274–288.

burden that prompted the Assembly to enact legislation transferring limited authority to individual commissioners in March 1643. Significantly,
and surely not coincidentally, this same act ordered that the court meet
only six times each year.[18] Presumably, individual commissioners would
now handle some of the cases slowing the court's completion of its work.
This attempt succeeded temporarily. For a number of years, the court's
calendar stabilized. In 1644, the year after the Assembly acted, there
were still eleven commissioners, but they only gathered for a court in six
months of the year and for a total of nine days.

The relief was temporary, however. During the next six years, while
the number of commissioners stayed about the same, the number of
months and days for sitting increased gradually until by 1650 the court
sat in eight months for a total of thirteen days. From 1651 through 1655,
there was a dramatic increase in all indicators. In 1655, nineteen commissioners held courts each month with multiple sittings in eleven months,
resulting in a total of thirty-four court days. These developments were
not unique; elsewhere in the Chesapeake, county courts also were expanding and becoming busier.[19]

At the same time that this marked increase in the number of commissioners and court sittings occurred, the numerically and geographically
expanding population prompted the commissioners to convene courts in
different locations in order to save people long trips to a stationary place
of meeting. This phenomenon also characterized other counties in the
Chesapeake region.[20] On the Eastern Shore, originally the court had met
at the secretary's land, called "the Towne," between Cherrystone and
King's creeks. When the center of population shifted to Old Plantation
Creek, the court held its sittings there. But as more people settled to the
north on Hungars and Nuswattocks creeks, court occasionally met at a
commissioner's house in that area. By 1649 the shift of population to the

18. Hening, ed., *Statutes at Large*, I, 272–273. The Assembly also sought to regu-
larize the days on which individual county courts would meet. Northampton County
was assigned the 28th of the month. The local commissioners, however, met when it
was convenient for them. From April 1643 to the end of 1644, they met on or within
three days of the designated day (that is, the 28th) only one-third of the times they sat.

19. These figures for the size of the county commission refute contentions that the
number of commissioners hovered around eight (Bruce, *Institutional History of Virginia*, I, 492; John Fiske, *Old Virginia and Her Neighbors*, 2 vols. [Boston, 1902], II,
38–39). Wesley Frank Craven, in a brief analysis of the York County commission,
noted the increase in number of commissioners from the 1630s through 1660. He
surmised that "the convenience of local communities in having a resident magistrate
was a chief, if not the chief, factor operating to increase the number of commissioners" (*Southern Colonies*, 267–268n).

20. Craven, *Southern Colonies*, 168, 204.

north made this ad hoc arrangement no longer appropriate. The commissioners issued an order that in the future the court would meet alternately in one of two places: the "poynt house" ordinary on Old Plantation Creek or Walter Williams's house at Nuswattocks Creek. In practice, there were exceptions to this pattern, but the substitute locations were generally on one of the designated creeks.[21]

In March 1652 the commissioners ordered "for the conveniency of the people of the county" that the court would meet at the house of Walter Williams. The latter received a license to keep an ordinary provided that the accommodations were adequate for the court and that he "not . . . suffer any persons to committ or Act any misdemenors or (contrarye to sobrietye) to abuse themselves by inordinate drinkeinge either upon Sabboth dayes, Court dayes (or att other tymes)."[22] It is unclear whether this order was meant to establish a single court seat for the entire county at Williams's ordinary or merely a court seat for the northern part of the county. Certain evidence suggests that it was to serve as the court seat for the whole county. First, until another change was ordered in the location of the county court, there is no reference to the court's convening anywhere else. Before the decision about meeting at Williams's ordinary and after the reversal of that decision, there are frequent references to other locations where the court sat. Second, the court seems to have lost a place to sit on Old Plantation Creek when John Dixon closed the Point House ordinary around 1650. The third bit of evidence suggesting that the court was stationary for this period is a 1654 petition of Walter Williams in response to the prospect of the court's meeting elsewhere than at his ordinary. In July 1653 it was ordered that the court rotate among locations on Cherrystone, Hungars, and Occohannock creeks. Nine months later Williams petitioned the court to complain of his reduced profits resulting from this change. Aware that few places could accommodate numerous people on a court day and "noteinge the conveniency of the place for all the Inhabitants of this County (as bussines maye require att Court tymes) To Congregate themselves and attend the Courts," the commissioners ordered that for the rest of the year the court would convene at Williams's house "except any matters of consequence or concernment shall interveene for a particular Court to bee called att some other place."[23]

21. Whitelaw, *Virginia's Eastern Shore*, I, 246–247; CCR-3, p. 174.

22. CCR-4, fol. 66–p. 67.

23. CCR-5, p. 4. For the July 1653 order, see CCR-4, p. 180. For the political context of these orders, see Chapter 8.

Table 20. Attendance at Court

Status of Attendance	1636–1640	1641–1645	1646–1650	1651–1655
Adjusted for Travel, Unadjusted for Multiple Sittings				
Possible attendance, in commissioner-months	203	248	256	433
Actual attendance, in commissioner-months	163	177	159	277
Commissioners attending in given month	80.3%	71.4%	62.1%	64.0%
Unadjusted for Travel, Unadjusted for Multiple Sittings				
Possible attendance, in commissioner-months	296	472	486	808
Actual attendance, in commissioner-months	215	275	259	425
Commissioners attending in given month	72.6%	58.3%	53.3%	52.6%
Adjusted for Travel, Adjusted for Multiple Sittings				
Possible attendance, in commissioner-meetings	208	276	304	564
Actual attendance, in commissioner-meetings	168	187	176	300
Commissioners attending a given meeting	80.8%	67.8%	57.9%	53.2%
Unadjusted for Travel, Adjusted for Multiple Sittings				
Possible attendance, in commissioner-meetings	303	526	575	1060

Table 20. *Continued*

Status of Attendance	1636–1640	1641–1645	1646–1650	1651–1655
Actual attendance, in commissioner-meetings	222	294	286	464
Commissioners attending a given meeting	73.3%	55.9%	49.7%	44.2%

Notes: *Commissioner-months* is the product of number of months that court met times the number of commissioners. *Commissioner-meetings* is the product of number of meetings of court times the number of commissioners. *Travel adjustment* deducts possible and actual attendance for the whole year for commissioners known to be traveling off the Eastern Shore or serving as sheriff part of that year, as such absences would be indistinguishable from absences for other reasons. *Multiple-sittings adjustment* attempts, when the court met several days in one month, to differentiate which were in fact one sitting and which were multiple sittings in different locations.

An act of the Virginia Assembly altered this arrangement in March 1655. The statute called for a jurisdictional division of the county, with the line drawn along Hungars Creek. The county commissioners were to alternate their meetings, one meeting in the southern part of the county to be followed by one in the northern part.[24]

As the area of settlement expanded and the county court met more frequently, the share of commissioners present in any given month dropped steadily. Between 1636 and 1640, 72.6 percent of the total commission sat in any given month when a session gathered. Trying to adjust this figure for the fact that the court sometimes met more than once each month results in a slightly higher figure of 73.3 percent of the total commission at any given meeting of the court. By the period between 1651 and 1655, these figures had fallen to 52.6 percent per month, or 44.2 percent per meeting.

This drop in attendance is independent of any bias because of the travels of commissioners off the Eastern Shore. It also is unaltered even when absences are due to a commissioner's not sitting because he was serving as sheriff.[25] Thus, eliminating for each commissioner any year in

24. Hening, ed., *Statutes at Large*, I, 409.
25. A sheriff could not sit as a justice until his term as sheriff was finished. Cyrus

which travel or appointment as sheriff could account for his absences does not change the trend. Between 1636 and 1640, 80.3 percent of the commissioners could be expected to appear at court in any given month (80.8 percent at any given meeting). By the period 1651–1655, attendance had dropped to 64 percent per month (53.2 percent per meeting).

It may have been this drop in attendance as much as the growing burden of litigation that prompted the appointment of an increasing number of commissioners in order to ensure an adequate number at each court sitting. Apparently the high rate of absenteeism on the Eastern Shore was not unique. The Virginia Assembly of 1647 passed an act providing for fines payable by commissioners failing to appear at court. In 1649 the commissioners of Northampton County took cognizance of this act and ordered its enforcement. Yet the effort to compel more frequent attendance failed.[26]

Why did increasingly more commissioners absent themselves from meetings of the court? The major factor was the distances to be traversed. Given the state of land and water transportation, members of the commission were averse to traveling great distances to join their brethren on the bench. For example, when the court met at Stephen Charlton's house on Nuswattocks Creek in March 1647, all commissioners living south of Hungars Creek were absent. A meeting in February 1651 at Nathaniel Littleton's house south of Old Plantation Creek failed to attract any commissioner living north of King's Creek. This pattern was broken on occasion by the presence of one commissioner who lived at a greater distance from the court. Thus, when Nathaniel Littleton convened a meeting of the court at his house in August 1649, the only commissioner to attend from north of Cherrystone Creek was Stephen Charlton. When the court met at Cherrystone Creek in November 1655, all except one of the commissioners who attended lived between Hungars and Old Plantation creeks.[27] The exception was Samuel Goldsmith, who lived on Nondui Creek, more than twenty miles distant.

A commute of this distance was quite unusual, as is reflected in Gold-

Harreld Karraker, *The Seventeenth-Century Sheriff: A Comparative Study of the Sheriff in England and the Chesapeake Colonies, 1607–1689* (Chapel Hill, N.C., 1930), 70, 109.

26. CCR-3, p. 174; Hening, ed., *Statutes at Large*, I, 350. This act was renewed in 1652 (Billings, ed., "Some Acts Not in Hening's *Statutes*," *VMHB*, LXXXIII [1975], 61–62). For a similar increase in absenteeism on the York County commission, see Craven, *Southern Colonies*, 267–268n.

27. CCR-3, fol. 78a, pp. 179, 216, CCR-6, p. 13–p. 14.

smith's attendance record. When he first took his seat as a commissioner in July 1653, Goldsmith lived farther north than any other commissioner.[28] His residence was in a newly settled area that needed a conveniently situated representative of authority. Unfortunately for Goldsmith, his location made it very difficult for him to be present at sessions of the county court. Excluding the period from March 1654 to February 1655 when he may have been traveling off the Eastern Shore, Goldsmith attended eight of the fourteen court meetings whose locations can be identified. Seven of the fourteen meetings were held at Occohannock Creek and an equal number elsewhere. Goldsmith was at six of the seven at Occohannock Creek, not far from his residence, but he attended only two of the seven held south of that waterway.

In many ways, the administration of justice on the Eastern Shore was sensitive to the needs of an increasing population dispersing itself over an ever-widening area. Commissioners were given individual powers and appointed with an eye to their being scattered throughout the settled part of the peninsula. Thus it was unnecessary for those individuals requiring the services of the commission for relatively minor matters to travel to the court when it met. The arrangement also helped to lighten somewhat the increasingly heavy work load that forced the commission to sit for longer and longer periods each year. In order to reduce the settlers' inconvenience and loss of time arising from attendance at court, the commissioners met in different parts of the county. This rotation also served the interests of the commissioners themselves, who were inconvenienced by their attendance at distant courts. As time passed, these judicial officers began to attend, virtually exclusively, only those courts that met in their part of the county. This habit led to a steady increase in absenteeism.

Shaping the administration of justice to the needs of a changing population had a profound impact on the societal network of the Eastern Shore by reducing the importance of networks centered on a countywide institution. In view of the decreasing attendance of commissioners at distant courts, it should not be a great surprise that people were loath to travel any farther than absolutely necessary in order to avail themselves of the power of the local court. This conclusion is substantiated by an analysis of the identifiable residential locations of all landholders appearing before courts whose places of meeting are known definitely. Almost without exception, people brought their cases to the nearest possible court. This practice was convenient not only for the principals in-

28. CCR-4, p. 180.

volved in a suit but also for those who had to appear as witnesses.[29] Besides the difficulty of travel, individuals had to consider the problem of accommodations during court sittings that could last two and sometimes three days.

Although not major occasions for countywide gatherings, sessions of the county court did provide an opportunity for those who did attend to meet people living beyond the familiar world of friends, neighbors, and kin. Occasionally litigants had to travel quite a distance to reach a stationary court. In addition, evidence on the locations of residences of jurors suggests that until 1650 the members of any given jury frequently came from widely scattered parts of the county. By the early 1650s, however, a division between northern and southern court sittings was evident as well in juries drawn from approximately the same areas. The exercise of the right to vote also may have attracted people to attend the court from distances greater than those for ordinary court meetings. During this period the "inhabitants and freemen" of the whole county gathered to vote for burgesses to represent the Eastern Shore in the Virginia Assembly.[30] By act of the Assembly in 1646, voting was to be by voice rather than by writing (which encouraged absentee ballots). This change, in conjunction with a fine for not attending elections, may have spurred more people to appear in person. Court day on the Eastern Shore and elsewhere in the Chesapeake region could be important in introducing people, albeit infrequently, to residents living outside the more restricted world of everyday acquaintances and family.[31] The coun-

29. When combined with the evidence of increasing absenteeism on the part of commissioners, this reluctance on the part of those seeking justice to travel any farther than necessary undermines the belief that meetings of the county court provided important opportunities for countywide contact during this period. Fiske, *Old Virginia and Her Neighbors*, II, 42–43; Oliver Perry Chitwood, *Justice in Colonial Virginia* (Baltimore, 1905), 94–95; Jennings Cropper Wise, *Ye Kingdome of Accawmacke; or, The Eastern Shore of Virginia in the Seventeenth Century* (Richmond, Va., 1911), 327–329; "History of York County in the Seventeenth Century," *Tyler's Quarterly*, I (1919), 265; Albert Ogden Porter, *County Government in Virginia: A Legislative History, 1607–1904* (New York, 1947), 16.

30. CCR-1, pp. 63–64, 153, CCR-2, pp. 255, 407, CCR-4, fol. 63. In 1653, "upon the desire of this County of Northampton," the commissioners ordered that the court meet at Cherrystone, Hungars, and Occohannock creeks in succession and that "these places of the Courts to bee the places for the chooseinge of Burgesses for those several parts." Existing evidence suggests, however, that this plan was not put into effect. There was no meeting of the Assembly between this order and November 1654, for which burgesses were selected by the usual method. CCR-4, p. 180, CCR-5, p. 60.

31. Hening, ed., *Statutes at Large*, I, 333–334; Darrett B. Rutman and Anita H. Rutman, *A Place in Time: Middlesex County, Virginia, 1650–1750* (New York, 1984), 125–126.

ty court, although not a potent force as a single center for countywide contacts, nevertheless shaped the societal network by occasionally drawing settlers out of their more narrow individual networks.

The religious establishment on the Eastern Shore played a similar role. As with the institution of civil authority, the religious establishment shaped itself to the growth and spread of population.[32] Richard Bolton, the first minister on the peninsula, arrived around 1623 and served a population concentrated around King's and Cherrystone creeks. By 1632 William Cotton was minister, and the county court record mentions churchwardens in 1633. In 1635 a "formal" vestry was appointed. As a result of population growth, the inhabitants decided in the late 1630s to build a new church, probably a larger and more substantial structure in the same location as the first church on King's Creek.[33] Meanwhile, more and more people settled to the north on Hungars Creek. In an effort to accommodate residents there, Cotton in 1639 agreed to preach to them once a month. This agreement was legitimized by an act of the Assembly seven years earlier: "Because in this colony the places of their cure are in many places ffar distant, *It is thought fitt* that the mynisters doe soe divide theire turnes as by joynt agreement of the parishioners they should be desired."[34] Although convenient for all concerned, the agreement meant that the people of the county did not worship together.

The year after agreeing to preach at Hungars Creek, William Cotton died, but his office did not remain vacant for long.[35] The following spring, John Rosier's name first appeared in the court record. He had

32. The most informative discussion of the religious establishment on the Eastern Shore is in Whitelaw, *Virginia's Eastern Shore*, I, under N20, N30, N72, and N75, and II, 1391–1397. Two articles by George Carrington Mason—"The Colonial Churches of the Eastern Shore of Virginia," *WMQ*, 2d Ser., XX (1940), 449–474, and "The Six Earliest Churches on the Eastern Shore of Virginia," *WMQ*, 2d Ser., XXI (1941), 200–207—are both flawed, although in the latter, Mason attempted to correct errors in his earlier piece.

33. "Wyatt Manuscripts," *WMQ*, 2d Ser., VIII (1928), 56; Whitelaw, *Virginia's Eastern Shore*, I, 140; CCR-1, pp. 1, 39–40, 117. The interpretation that follows in the text contradicts the arguments of several other historians, but it is the only internally consistent one and fits all available evidence. References to a church as early as 1634 could only be to a structure on King's Creek, the point where the population was centered at the time. A contemporary reference to the palisades around the church is further proof that the church was built on King's Creek, because it indicates a concern for security dating from a period prior to settlement elsewhere on the Eastern Shore. CCR-1, pp. 15, 22, 28.

34. CCR-1, pp. 156, 159; Hening, ed., *Statutes at Large*, I, 157, 181.

35. He made his will Aug. 20, 1640. At the time, he was "weake in body." Apparently he died shortly thereafter, because he never appeared again in the court record, which had witnessed his active presence before that date. CCR-3, p. 55.

been identified two years before as a "clerk," or cleric, living at Warros-quyoake, on the south side of the James River. Although not identified as a cleric on the Eastern Shore until March 1642, Rosier may have served in a religious capacity from his first arrival. Indicative of this is a court order made less than three months after his appearance in the record, following almost a year during which there had been complete silence about anybody or anything relating to the religious establishment. Very simply, the commissioners, in an effort to punish several offenders, or-dered them to "meete at the parish Church of Ackowmack . . . and there Cutt up all the weedes as well about the Church as allso the Church paths neare adjacent thereto." Could it be that the church grounds had been neglected in the absence of services there and, with a new cleric, the area needed sprucing up? It is quite possible and becomes more likely when it is noted that Rosier purchased land on King's Creek near the church just before the court's order.[36]

In the meantime, a second cleric appeared in the official record. Na-thaniel Eaton, fleeing debt and an unsavory reputation in New England, was first mentioned in late 1640. He may have known William Cotton already, because Eaton's father and Cotton's mother both were from Cheshire, England. After Cotton died, Eaton married his widow, Ann. Surviving evidence indicates that Nathaniel Eaton and John Rosier both may have served as clerics.[37] But Eaton did not remain on the Eastern

36. CCR-2, pp. 105, 109–114, 144; Dorothy O. Shilton and Richard Holworthy, eds., *High Court of Admiralty Examinations, 1637–1638* (London, 1932), 106–107; Nugent, ed., *Cavaliers and Pioneers*, I, 163. It seems obvious that attention to weeds around the church would be a continuing activity and one of special importance after a period of neglect. But Whitelaw and Mason both use this evidence to support an argument that the weeds were being removed from the area around a new church on Old Plantation Creek. This would mean that it had taken three years—an unusually long time—between the first references to fund raising and construction in order to complete a new church. Most important, they ignore the evidence of Rosier's buying land on King's Creek, where the church was in fact located. Finally, there are no references to a church on Old Plantation Creek, but there are such references for one on King's Creek. Whitelaw and Mason (who follows Whitelaw's lead) assume the move to Old Plantation Creek happened because of the normal proximity of church and court. Such proximity might occur, as it did when the church and court were located at Hungars Creek; but proximity was not always the case. The court was fairly mobile, because it could house itself virtually anywhere, but the church was not so fortunate. Although the commissioners decided to meet on Old Plantation Creek, there is no evidence that the parishioners decided to undertake a new building pro-gram to do the same. Whitelaw, *Virginia's Eastern Shore*, I, 122, 247; Mason, "The Colonial Churches of the Eastern Shore of Virginia," *WMQ*, 2d Ser., XX (1940), 455; Mason, "The Six Earliest Churches on the Eastern Shore of Virginia," *WMQ*, 2d Ser., XXI (1941), 200–203.

37. P. W. Hiden, "Three Rectors of Hungar's Parish and Their Wife," *WMQ*, 2d

Shore for long. It is possible that his reputation finally caught up with him. Or residents on the peninsula may have been shocked at Eaton's usurping his infant stepdaughter's landed inheritance and selling it. Although she eventually recovered her claim, Eaton's act probably alienated some of the most important people on the Eastern Shore. William Stone and William Roper, both commissioners on the court, were William Cotton's brothers-in-law and overseers of his will.[38] Evidence of conflict between John Rosier and Nathaniel Eaton appears late in 1642, when Rosier was identified as "Minister of God's Word," a title more elaborate than any formerly used and suggestive of a pugnacious assertion in defiance of all contenders. A January 1643 court order involving "the minister of this County of Northampton" also reflects an exclusive claim by a single person. This must refer to Rosier, because, although he and Eaton both were clerics by profession, only Rosier had been referred to as minister on the Eastern Shore. Two months later arbitrators were chosen to settle a dispute between Rosier and Eaton about the county tithes for 1642 and 1643. This was the last reference to Eaton's being on the Eastern Shore. He next tried his luck over the bay.[39]

The arbitrators' division of tithes between Rosier and Eaton in late March 1643 may have reflected action that same month by the Virginia Assembly, which divided the Eastern Shore into two parishes with the border at King's Creek. The Assembly gave as its reason the extent of the county as people moved north on the peninsula. Nevertheless, despite this administrative division, only one minister officiated on the Eastern Shore until 1652. Following Nathaniel Eaton's departure, John Rosier served alone until early 1647, after which he moved across the bay.[40]

Ser., XIX (1939), 35–36; CCR-2, p. 34, CCR-3, p. 55; Nugent, ed., *Cavaliers and Pioneers*, I, 135. In early 1642 the court ordered Eaton be paid tithes from the estate of John Angood. Presumably these tithes were owed to him rather than to the estate of William Cotton, whose name is not mentioned (CCR-2, p. 143). Arbitrators chosen by Eaton and Rosier divided the tithes for 1642 and 1643 between them (CCR-2, pp. 331–332).

38. Nugent, ed., *Cavaliers and Pioneers*, I, 135; CCR-1, pp. 7–8, 71, CCR-3, p. 55; Whitelaw, *Virginia's Eastern Shore*, I, 356.

39. CCR-2, pp. 220–221, 235–236, 331–332; Whitelaw, *Virginia's Eastern Shore*, I, 154–155; Nugent, ed., *Cavaliers and Pioneers*, I, 174. Ann (Graves) Cotton-Eaton either did not move to the Western Shore with her husband or she returned by herself very quickly. She subsequently married Francis Doughty, another Eastern Shore minister. Significantly, before entering into marriage with Ann, Francis had to sign a statement disavowing any claims either to her estate or to the estate of her children. CCR-3, p. 70, fol. 169, p. 170, fol. 201, p. 227, CCR-4, fol. 23, p. 84, CCR-7, fol. 20, p. 48.

40. Hening, ed., *Statutes at Large*, I, 249. In February 1647 Rosier sold his land to

Toward the end of Rosier's service, there appeared the first definite reference to a church building for the Upper Parish on the neck of land between Hungars and Nuswattocks creeks. Within a few months of Rosier's departure, Thomas Palmer, who had arrived on the peninsula in late 1646, was referred to as minister.[41] In late 1647 the Virginia Assembly, possibly in response to the continually increasing number of people in the northern part of the county, moved the dividing line between the two parishes six miles to the north to an inlet between the tracts originally claimed by Thomas Savage and George Yeardley. Yet Palmer continued to be the only minister. He served in that office until 1650 and then left the Eastern Shore. His successor, John Armourer, first appeared in the county record in early 1651 but was gone by the beginning of the next year.[42]

Part of the reason for the rapid turnover of ministers may have been the arduous duty imposed on them by having to serve two parishes requiring extensive travel.[43] This strain would help to explain the developments of early 1652, immediately after Armourer's departure. In the first few months of that year, there are references to two separate and geographically distinct vestries, one for the Lower and one for the Upper Parish. The membership of these two vestries was drawn from within the

Randall Revell (CCR-3, fol. 61–p. 61 [sic]). Rosier appointed Revell to act as his attorney, which Revell did in June of that same year (CCR-3, fols. 69, 87, p. 100, fol. 139). Rosier lived on the Northern Neck as early as February 1648 and patented land there in 1650 and 1654. William Hand Browne, ed., *Archives of Maryland*, IV, *Judicial and Testamentary Business of the Provincial Court, 1637–1650* (Baltimore, 1887), 378, which records a letter of attorney (witnessed by Randall Revell) from William Stone to his "loving ffreind" Rosier; Nugent, ed., *Cavaliers and Pioneers*, I, 205, 304.

41. CCR-3, fol. 62–p. 63, pp. 105, 115.

42. H. R. McIlwaine, ed., "Acts, Orders, and Resolutions of the General Assembly of Virginia: At Sessions of March 1643–1646," *VMHB*, XXIII (1915), 249. Palmer: CCR-3, p. 199, fol. 208, p. 210. Armourer: CCR-4, p. 81, p. 172–p. 173, CCR-5, fol. 69.

43. Whitelaw identifies John Rosier and John Armourer as ministers of the Lower Parish and Thomas Palmer as minister of the Upper Parish (*Virginia's Eastern Shore*, II, 1397). Given that their tenures were sequential rather than overlapping, it seems likely that these three served both parishes. Although each might have lived within one of the two parishes, he probably performed some religious services for the other as well. One bit of evidence suggests that this was the case. In relation to a case of adultery in 1648, Palmer is identified simply as "Minister" while Richard Smith and Stephen Horsey are called "Churchwardens of the Upper parish." Apparently Palmer was minister for both parishes, although he did live on Hungars Creek in the Upper Parish. CCR-3, p. 148–fol. 149.

respective parishes. At the same time, Thomas Higby is mentioned as minister for the Lower Parish and Thomas Teackle for the Upper. This separation was of great importance. Previously there had been one vestry and one minister for two parishes.[44] Now a division of church officials corresponded to the parish division. After 1652 each parish functioned autonomously. For example, within two months of Thomas Higby's death, "it was agreed by the Commissioners and howsekeepers of the lower parish of Northampton County. To accept of Mr. Francis Dowty for their Minister." When Thomas Teackle and Edmund Scarburgh were in conflict, "the Inhabitants of Nuswattocks parish" petitioned in behalf of their minister.[45]

By the mid-1650s, as people moved north of Occohannock Creek, actions were taken toward the formation of another parish in that area; but this movement toward further fragmentation seems to have lost momentum. Yet it is unlikely that people too far north of that creek traveled to the Upper Parish church. Perhaps they did what Colonel Norwood had done when he stayed at the house of Jenkin Price on Nondui Creek several years earlier; as reported by Norwood, "We were not yet arrived to the heart of the country where there were churches, and ministry perform'd as our laws direct, but were glad to continue our own chaplains, as formerly."[46]

44. Lower and Upper Parish Vestries: CCR-4, p. 73, fol. 86. Higby: CCR-4, p. 73. The first reference to Higby as being on the Eastern Shore was in 1649. In the fall of 1650, he sued Susanna Brothers for allegedly breaking a contract to marry him. He lost his suit but gained an alternate bride by early the next year, when he married Ann, the widow of John Wilkins (CCR-3, pp. 141, 232, CCR-4, p. 8). Higby appeared frequently before the court. His litigious record included, among other conflicts, a battle with his stepson-in-law. In addition, Higby and his wife were in court several times for slandering Grace and Obedience Robins, two of the oldest and most respected residents of the county (CCR-4, pp. 8, 10, 11, 141).

Teackle: CCR-4, fol. 86. The first reference to Thomas Teackle's being on the Eastern Shore was only 10 days before his mention as minister. He was a cousin of Obedience Robins and a royalist refugee from England. CCR-4, p. 18–fol. 18; Whitelaw, *Virginia's Eastern Shore*, I, 639; VMHB, XXII (1914), 84–85.

All references before 1652 are to "the" vestry, indicating a single body. CCR-3, pp. 2, 18, fol. 54–p. 55, pp. 100, 170, fol. 186.

45. CCR-5, p. 94–fol. 94, p. 105–fol. 105, p. 117. For Higby's death, see CCR-5, p. 56, fol. 116. On June 8, 1657, Doughty signed a contract relating to his upcoming marriage to Ann (Graves) Cotton-Eaton, widow of two former Eastern Shore ministers (CCR-7, p. 48). For Doughty's earlier career, see Jessica Kross, *The Evolution of an American Town: Newtown, New York, 1642–1775* (Philadelphia, 1983), 3, 44.

46. Colonel Norwood, *A Voyage to Virginia*, 48, in Force, ed., *Tracts and Other Papers*, III. On formation of another parish, see Hening, ed., *Statutes at Large*, I, 374.

All of these developments were detrimental to the fostering of a countywide societal network. After 1639, people worshiped in two, and eventually three, separate places. As of 1652 each parish had its own minister and vestry. Yet, although the peninsula's religious life fragmented in this way, the church was an integrative social force within its divisions. Each parish was larger than the interactional networks of most individuals, and therefore attendance at church served to broaden an individual's range of contacts. Churches elsewhere in the Chesapeake performed the same function. Although it is difficult to determine how many people went to church how often, it is suggestive that the commissioners, in order to disseminate certain orders, directed that they be published in the churches of the county.[47]

Compared to the role of court and church in broadening the range of

---

At a county court of May 7, 1655, the commissioners ordered construction of a church at Occohannock Creek. This was in response to an act concerning the location of public facilities passed by the Virginia Assembly in March 1655. (The date of this act was incorrectly reported by the Northampton County clerk as March 20, 1655/6.) CCR-5, fol. 133; Hening, ed., *Statutes at Large*, I, 413–414.

Richard Vaughan, in his will of Nov. 23, 1655, bequeathed 1,000 pounds of tobacco to the building of a church. This was probably to be at Occohannock Creek, where he lived, a contention supported by the fact that he had been one of the commissioners present at the May meeting ordering its construction (CCR-5, fol. 101–fol. 102, fol. 133). It is important at this point to clarify a clerical error in this will that has led to some confusion. The date when it was written was entered by the clerk as being Nov. 23, 1645. Internal evidence, however, refutes this date. In mentioning "Alice Major (daughter in Lawe [that is, stepdaughter] to Major Thomas Johnson)," the will automatically must be dated at least after 1648, in which year John Major died and his widow married Thomas Johnson (CCR-3, fol. 133–p. 134, fol. 152, CCR-4, fol. 132). Richard Vaughan's presence at the court meeting of May 7, 1655 establishes the date of his will as Nov. 23, 1655. It was probated five months later (CCR-5, fol. 101–fol. 102). The importance of this point arises from the fact that G. C. Mason cites the earlier date of 1645 as evidence of an intention to build a church at Occohannock Creek in the mid-1640s. This was hardly likely, as settlement was virtually nonexistent there at the time. On the other hand, Ralph T. Whitelaw, by accepting the date of 1645, interprets Vaughan's bequest to mean that there was no church at Nuswattocks Creek as of that date and that the tobacco was to fund the building of one there. G. C. Mason, in an effort to correct certain errors in his first article, wrote a supplementary one in which he accepted Whitelaw's explanation. (Mason, "The Colonial Churches of the Eastern Shore of Virginia," *WMQ*, 2d Ser., XX [1940], 467; Whitelaw, *Virginia's Eastern Shore*, I, 408; Mason, "The Six Earliest Churches on the Eastern Shore of Virginia," *WMQ*, 2d Ser., XXI [1941], 206). It should be noted that Whitelaw doubts that the area around Occohannock Creek was a separate, functioning parish until the division of the Eastern Shore into two counties (*Virginia's Eastern Shore*, II, 1395).

47. Rutman and Rutman, *A Place in Time: Middlesex County*, 120–125; CCR-4, fol. 66, CCR-5, p. 22.

contacts of Eastern Shore residents, the militia was the weakest integrative force. In fact, the militia seems to have been virtually moribund through midcentury. The Virginia Assembly in 1632 enacted legislation requiring that "the comanders of all the severall plantations, doe upon holy days exercise the men under his comand." In 1634, when the Eastern Shore became one of the first eight shires, William Claiborne received the appointment as lieutenant there. A member of the Virginia Council, Claiborne had extensive mercantile interests, including an important trading post and settlement on Kent Island in the upper Chesapeake Bay. As his deputy he appointed Obedience Robins "to perform all such services . . . to be done in that office."[48] Despite this initial legislation and organization, no evidence exists suggesting that the militia ever met to drill: no deposition mentioning travel to or from training, no fine for absenteeism, no drunken incident, no reference to a gathering. In the absence of a threatening impetus—that is, Indians or foreigners—there was no incentive to gather.[49]

In 1642, just after he arrived in Virginia, the new governor, Sir William Berkeley, attempted to resuscitate and reform the system of militia training. In an order signed July 2, 1642, Berkeley stated that "for the directing and teaching of the people in the use and exercise of their Armes and the disipline thereunto belonging The Governor and Counsell . . . have thought Fitt to reduce the people into Companyes under the Commaund and leading of Severall Companyes." To take charge of the inhabitants between King's Creek and Hungars Creek, Berkeley appointed Francis Yardley, the brother of Councillor Argoll Yardley, who lived in that precinct. Francis Yardley received authority to appoint subordinate officers, exercise his company once a month, and levy a special tax to raise funds for the purchase of a drum, colors, and tent.[50] Again, no evidence of compliance exists.

The next effort to give life to a militia establishment arose in response to an Indian attack against the Western Shore settlers in April 1644. Less

48. Hening, ed., *Statutes at Large*, I, 174–175, 200; CCR-1, p. 17. See John Herbert Claiborne, *William Claiborne of Virginia, with Some Account of His Pedigree* (New York, 1917), for Claiborne's Kent Island involvement.

49. The two most detailed studies of the Virginia militia in this period both emphasize the formal militia organization and assume that practice followed prescription: Frederick Stokes Aldridge, "Organization and Administration of the Militia System of Colonial Virginia" (Ph.D. diss., American University, 1964), 48–53; William L. Shea, *The Virginia Militia in the Seventeenth Century* (Baton Rouge, La., 1983), 57, 138.

50. CCR-2, pp. 176–177.

than two weeks later and by an "expresse order from the Governor and the Counsell for Reduceing the stragling and Remote Plantations into Convenient and defensive bodyes," the county court issued instructions for militia organization. According to this plan, the commissioners divided the Eastern Shore into six jurisdictions: (1) from Cape Charles to the mouth of Old Plantation Creek, (2) from there to the south side of King's Creek, (3) next the area on both sides of Cherrystone Creek, (4) then from the head of Cherrystone Creek to the south side of Mattawomes Creek, (5) from the north side of the same creek to the south side of Hungars Creek, (6) and finally from the north side of Hungars Creek to Nuswattocks Creek. One or two commissioners lived within each of these areas; and, for their respective jurisdictions, they were put in charge of directing the residents "how and in what convenient manner [they] shall joyne themselves togeather." Punishments were stipulated for uncooperative individuals.[51]

This plan reflects the knowledge and experience of the local officials who designed it. The areas defined were small and did not require travel more arduous than that involved in an individual's personal network. In order to avoid forcing residents to travel by water, the commissioners used waterways to define rather than to divide each militia jurisdiction. The instructions did not provide for frequent meetings or, for that matter, any at all. And inasmuch as the Indians on the Eastern Shore did not participate in the attack on the colonists and showed no inclination to join in after the fact, no urgent reason prompted implementation of the commissioners' system. An ad hoc response to events on the Western Shore and the order of the governor and Council, the plan languished.

It is interesting to contrast these abortive organizational attempts either dictated or initiated by officials at James City with the response of the Eastern Shore settlers to a military threat on the peninsula. In May 1649 the commissioners perceived that the county was in a "dangerous condition" for reasons that were not stated but that may have involved the execution of Charles I four months earlier. But they did not issue a call for the militia to gather. Instead, they ordered the populace to be

51. CCR-2, pp. 359–360. See also Alf J. Mapp, Jr., *The Virginia Experiment: The Old Dominion's Role in the Making of America (1607–1781)* (La Salle, Ill., 1974), 125. This Eastern Shore militia organization refutes Frederick Stokes Aldridge's claim that commissioners were not appointed as militia administrators until the Commonwealth period ("Organization and Administration of the Militia System of Colonial Virginia," 61–62).

properly armed and watchful, and they authorized William Roper to take a muster of the number of men fit to bear arms and to check that all weapons were in good repair.[52]

Two years later Governor Berkeley again issued instructions for the organization of the militia on the Eastern Shore. He may have renewed his efforts either in anticipation of a conflict with the parliamentary forces then on their way to Virginia or in response to increased friction between the settlers and Indians in Northampton County. The plan of organization was virtually the same as that designed by the commissioners in 1644. Now there were seven (instead of six) jurisdictions, or "precincts." Boundaries were shifted slightly in order to accommodate the new settlement north of Nuswattocks Creek. With a single exception, one commissioner was appointed to be captain of militia for each precinct. The exception was Samuel Goldsmith, the most eminent individual living in the precinct farthest north; he would become a commissioner within two years. Berkeley's efforts seem to have generated some activity; but less than two months later, some militia captains were complaining that "many of the Inhabitants . . . which are listed both for horse and foote have neglected to attend their Captain (upon the dayes appointed to exercise)."[53]

In October 1652 Richard Bennett, the new governor of Virginia under the authority of Parliament, sent to Northampton County the list of newly appointed officials, both civil and military. All of the commissioners were reappointed except for Thomas Hunt, who was renamed the following July. Five commissioners were added. The new militia organization involved a division of the county at Hungars Creek, with four senior commissioners appointed to military office in each of the two parts of the county. But as in the past, there was little effort at active training. Three years after Bennett's naming of militia officers for the two divisions, a threat of Indian attack prompted a flurry of activity in an attempt to begin training the troops.[54]

In the formative years of societal development on the Eastern Shore, the institutions of militia, church, and court were not of great impor-

52. CCR-3, p. 171, p. 174–fol. 174, fol. 175.

53. CCR-4, p. 22, p. 36–fol. 36, p. 37, p. 40–fol. 40, p. 47, fol. 80 (for quotation), p. 180.

54. CCR-4, p. 117–p. 118, p. 180, CCR-6, fol. 27. It is worth noting that the general militia in England seems to have been equally moribund. See Esther A. L. Moir, *The Justice of the Peace* (London, 1969), 68; Shea, *Virginia Militia*, 2–3.

tance as nodes for the formation of countywide networks of interaction. The history of the development of a militia system on the peninsula reveals an institution lacking any unifying importance. If people served at all, they did so sporadically and locally in response to perceived crises. Compared to the militia, the structure of religious observance provided an enduring framework for contact. But as a consequence of parish divisions made in response to the increase and shifting geographic concentration of population, not all of the residents worshiped together. Within each parish, however, the church did provide to those who attended a focal point for meeting people outside the daily range of contact. The local court structure also accommodated itself to the movements of population. The commissioners, by exercising certain powers individually and moving the location of sittings, provided a convenient, flexible system of justice. Yet, by bringing justice to their constituents instead of forcing people to attend one central court, the commissioners significantly restricted the geographic area for which court day could serve as a unifying occasion. Nevertheless, as with the religious establishment, attendance at court occasionally served to bring together people who might not have had contact within their individual interactional networks.

8 The Societal Network and the Role of Authority

GRADUALLY, A CLEARER VIEW of Eastern Shore society from 1625 to 1655 begins to emerge. Most important, the kinship, affectional, and economic networks of a vast majority of landholders extended no further than a few miles from their residences. For the most part, relatives lived nearby. Neighbors, whether or not they were relatives, were the main source of companionship, support, and services. The interactional network of the peninsula's landholders can be visualized as a series of overlapping circles, each centered on an individual landholder. Of course, the shape of each person's web of contacts varied in response to a number of factors, including occupation, personal initiative, official position, and ease of travel. But the schematic visualization approximates the overall pattern. Understanding it is essential before probing the changes wrought as more people settled on the Eastern Shore and spread over a wider area.

One precondition for this localized pattern of contact was an even development of land resources. The colonists generally patented acreage adjacent to land previously claimed and thus concentrated themselves more than if they had established themselves on tracts beyond the settled boundary. In addition, the settlers' preference for waterside locations maximized the integrative potential of the numerous creeks, branches, inlets, and bays. Whether landholders claimed contiguous acreage and settled adjacent to one another for purposes of protection, companionship, or the need for services, the orderly, contiguous spread of settlement along waterways did promote contacts among them.

Such contacts aided socialization by promoting the definition of acceptable as well as unacceptable behavior in the nascent society. Although lacking the strong sense of communal purpose generally associated with New England town societies and although too new to have established commonly recognized and authoritative local traditions, Eastern Shore society was not a chaotic assemblage of individuals, each living an isolated existence, seeking his own ends, oblivious to the restrictions imposed by the presence and opinions of others. Neighbors married, exchanged visits and favors, traded goods, and performed services for one another. On the other hand, they occasionally appeared as adversaries in court proceedings for assault, slander, theft, and breach of contract. But it is possible to overemphasize these divisive actions simply because they were amply recorded in the county court record, whereas actions promoting a sense of responsibility and obligation to others are too easily neglected because they were not.

The Eastern Shore court record reveals the local give-and-take and the networks of contact of the landholders who settled there. The organic development of these networks was based on proximity and need and shaped by geography. It was a natural, unarticulated process but nevertheless of crucial significance for understanding the centripetal force holding together Virginia's nascent society. Contact with landholders living nearby allowed for the definition of behavioral norms and the maintenance of those norms through neighborly oversight. In the face of a high mortality rate and an unending influx of immigrants, the development of a local culture was indispensable for countering a potentially destructive individualism.

This visualization of grassroots networks and how they functioned to promote stability is the first step toward understanding the growth and development of Eastern Shore society. The next step is to consider what impact the spread of settlement had on that society. In 1635 about four hundred people lived around Cherrystone, King's, and Old Plantation creeks. In such a small area, personal networks overlapped and created a densely interconnected societal web embracing the entire settled area. This situation changed after 1635, when land policy was clarified. During the next twenty years people occupied land extending from the southern tip of the peninsula to far north of Occohannock Creek. Although each person maintained a network of contacts extending several miles from his residence and although these networks still overlapped one another, no longer was there a dense interconnection of contacts linking together landholders at the extremities of settlement.

During this period, institutional development, which had previously been tentative and slow, proceeded rapidly. In the period 1635–1655, the Virginia Assembly, composed of county dignitaries well aware of local needs, shaped the governmental and religious structures to the reality of life in a dispersed rural society. On the Eastern Shore, county officials coped in several ways with the increase in both population and area of settlement. In order to reduce the load of business at meetings of the county court, the Assembly had granted special judicial, administrative, and oversight powers to individual commissioners acting out of court. The effectiveness of this maneuver was magnified on the Eastern Shore, because the commissioners who were appointed lived in homes scattered the length of the county, thus maximizing their accessibility to the governed. Although minor matters were thereby removed from the court docket, there remained the problem of how the county court could best serve the needs of a dispersed population when the issue was not within the purview of an individual commissioner. The Eastern Shore answer was a county court that rode circuit. Meeting in two or three fixed locations or at some special place for a "particular court," the commissioners brought government to the governed and so reduced the travel required for people to avail themselves of the power of the court. But these particular courts, along with the fact that people did not have to bring minor matters to the court at all, reduced the integrative potential of the county court as a single focus for the interactional networks of the county's residents. The same result attended the decisions by local religious officials, first, to hold services in more than one location and, then, to divide the county into more than one parish. Both governmental and religious institutions were shaped to the needs of an ever larger, more dispersed population, but they were not designed to promote the social integration of the entire county. Given the size of the settled area and the limitations of transportation, such integration was not possible.

The view of society from the grassroots level emphasizes restricted individual networks and a potential for the fragmentation of county society, but other factors promoted long-range contacts and societal integration. Some individuals, especially merchants and commissioners, had personal networks extending distances greater than those for other landholders. These ties served to link parts of the county that otherwise would have remained isolated from one another. In addition, attendance at church and court, although not bringing together the whole county, broadened the web of contacts for an individual.

Moreover, the institutional structures, in spite of their failure to bind together inhabitants from all parts of the peninsula, had a profound impact on the development of the county's society. Those appointed to serve as vestrymen or commissioners were generally individuals with the broadest interactional webs and represented an integrative force in their own right. But as institutional officials, they magnified their influence.

Their authority to wield power and their effective exercise of that power were preconditions for social stability.

The members of the county commission were distinguished from their fellow residents on the Eastern Shore in a number of ways that enhanced their authority as county officials. In any given year from 1635 through 1650, the average landholding of a commissioner was 224–290 percent greater than for all landholders (median 272–514 percent greater). In 1655 the average fell to 221 percent (median 263 percent) because of the expansion of the court and the appointment of additional commissioners to fill not only these positions but also those left vacant by older commissioners who had died.[1] In addition to greater landed wealth, commissioners also had economic networks far more extensive than those of the average Eastern Shore resident. Not surprisingly, as the average and median ages of the commissioners increased, so too did the frequency of their having a nuclear family (eventually reaching 100 percent) as well as other relatives on the Eastern Shore.[2] Clearly, the commissioners were successful economically and demographically. Compared to their fellow Eastern Shore residents, they were wealthier, survived to a greater age, enjoyed the presence of more family and kin, and stood at the center of broader economic networks. Furthermore, not only did the economic networks of the commissioners interlock with one another, but so too, increasingly, did their kin networks. These ties consisted of blood relationships as well as quasi-relationships, such as godparentage.[3]

To be effective, a commissioner or justice needed respect; and experi-

1. For landholdings 1635–1655, cf. table 8. Elsewhere in the Chesapeake, wealth characterized those who held commissions of the peace, and it helped generate respect for the bench. Lorena Seebach Walsh, "Charles County, Maryland, 1658–1705: A Study of Chesapeake Social and Political Structure" (Ph.D. diss., Michigan State University, 1977), 383–384; Lois Green Carr, "The Foundations of Social Order: Local Government in Colonial Maryland," in Bruce C. Daniels, ed., *Town and County: Essays on the Structure of Local Government in the American Colonies* (Middletown, Conn., 1978), 80–81.

For 1655: Wesley Frank Craven noted a similar turnover in personnel on the York County commission in the mid-1650s, in *The Southern Colonies in the Seventeenth Century, 1607–1689* (1949; reprint ed., Baton Rouge, La., 1970), 368n.

2. On economic networks, see Chapter 5. Actually, the average and median ages in 1655 probably would drop slightly if the ages of more of the new commissioners were known. Table 21 shows the average and median ages for only 7 of a possible 18 commissioners.

3. For a comparable review of the commissions of four other Virginia counties, see Warren M. Billings, "The Growth of Political Institutions in Virginia, 1634 to 1676," *WMQ*, 3d Ser., XXXI (1974), 236–237.

Table 21. Members of the Commission

Measure	Year (No. of Commissioners)				
	1635 (7)	1640 (10)	1645 (12)	1650 (11)	1655 (18)
Acres held					
Average					
Minimum	583	1,222	1,650	1,810	1,528
Maximum	583	1,256	1,709	1,905	1,568
Median					
Minimum	250	1,200	1,500	1,450	1,050
Maximum	250	1,200	1,500	1,775	1,100
(No. calculated)	(4)	(9)	(11)	(10)	(14)
Years as commissioner					
Average	2.3	4.9	7.8	9.6	6.7
Median	2.0	7.0	8.0	9.0	4.0
(No. calculated)	(7)	(10)	(12)	(11)	(18)
Years as landholder					
Average	5.2	6.1	11.3	13.7	13.2
Median	6.0	4.0	10.0	13.5	11.5
(No. calculated)	(5)	(9)	(11)	(10)	(18)
Years on Eastern Shore					
Average	9.0	10.3	13.9	14.6	16.7
Median	10.0	11.0	12.0	13.5	15.5
(No. calculated)	(6)	(9)	(9)	(8)	(16)
Age in years					
Average	36.7	41.1	41.1	44.3	47.4
Median	35.0	40.0	45.0	50.0	52.0
(No. calculated)	(6)	(7)	(9)	(8)	(7)
Nuclear family	43%	80%	92%	91%	100%
Relatives on Eastern Shore	0%	50%	58%	64%	61%
Relationship to other commissioners					
Real and fictive[a]	0%	30%	58%	64%	50%
Fictive only	0%	10%	42%	45%	22%

Note: Statistics are for commissioners as of December 31 in any given year. Minima and maxima are calculated as in Table 8.

[a]Godparentage.

Table 22. Residence on Eastern Shore before First Holding Office

Attainment of Office	Years before Attaining Office (No. of Individuals)		
	Commissioner (N = 29)	First Major Office (N = 48)	First Office (N = 155)
1626–1630			
Average	4	2	2
Median	4	2	2
(No. calculated)	(1)	(3)	(3)
1631–1635			
Average	7	5.6	4.6
Median	7.5	7	4
(No. calculated)	(8)	(12)	(15)
1636–1640			
Average	3.8	2.7	3.8
Median	4	3	3
(No. calculated)	(4)	(3)	(15)
1641–1645			
Average	6.5	4	6.2
Median	6.5	4	6
(No. calculated)	(2)	(3)	(49)
1646–1650			
Average	7.3	10.4	8.4
Median	6.5	11	7
(No. calculated)	(4)	(11)	(33)
1651–1655			
Average	12.1	10.6	9.1
Median	11.5	11	9
(No. calculated)	(10)	(16)	(40)

Note: Includes resident adult male landholders who lived at least until January 1633 (when the county court record began); excludes those whose names were too common to allow identification with officeholding.

ence (as well as economic position, age, and kin connections) won respect, especially in the new societies of the Chesapeake. On the Eastern Shore, the commission in any given year showed a steady increase in the average and median number of years that its members had lived on the peninsula. This increase occurred even during the early 1650s, when the commission was being expanded and new members added. The commis-

Table 23. Pluralism of Major Officeholding among Landholders, 1630–1655

Service	No.	Proportion of Commissioners	Proportion of Total Major Officeholders
Only as commissioner	6	19%	11%
As commissioner and in another major office	7	22%	13%
As commissioner and in two or more major offices	19	59%	36%
In other major office but not as commissioner	21		40%

Note: Major office includes as councillor, burgess, sheriff, or in vestry.

sioners appointed from 1651 through 1655 had lived on the Eastern Shore for an average of at least 12.1 years (median 11.5 years). Clearly, long-resident landholders were favored for appointment when the commission was undergoing its most important period of expansion and membership turnover.

Economic position, age, kin networks, and experience elevated the commissioners above their fellows on the Eastern Shore and allowed them to assume an elite position similar to that enjoyed by the justices of the peace in England. They could legitimately lay claim to the same deference accorded their brethren on the bench there. Like justices elsewhere, they remained in office, almost without exception, until death.[4] During their careers, they enjoyed the same perquisites of plural office-holding that were enjoyed by justices elsewhere in the Chesapeake. Of those landholders who served as commissioners, 59 percent held two or more other major offices, including councillor, burgess, sheriff, or vestryman. Another 22 percent held only one other major office, and only 19 percent held no other. But the commissioners did not monopolize all major offices. Of landholders who held major office at one time or

4. J. H. Gleason, *The Justices of the Peace in England, 1558–1640* (Oxford, 1969), 57, 96; Billings, "Growth of Political Institutions," *WMQ*, 3d Ser., XXXI (1974), 238.

another, 40 percent were never appointed to the commission.[5] Two-thirds of these twenty-one noncommissioners were major officeholders by virtue of appointment as vestrymen.

In one respect, the situation of the commissioners on the Eastern Shore differed significantly from that in England: Virginia's county elite enjoyed far greater autonomy than was ever available in the mother country. There is little evidence, however, that this relative freedom from oversight led to abuses.[6] In fact, it facilitated the justices' experimentation with local solutions to new problems, a process that characterized other English colonial societies and one that resulted in a more effective dispensation of justice than was currently available in England. These local solutions frequently were enacted into law, a process made easier because the men elected as burgesses were almost invariably the commissioners themselves, the ones most aware of the need for change.[7] The evidence shows that commissioners on the Eastern Shore worked hard, and, if their attendance record is any indication, harder than justices in England. Their position, while prestigious, was also a burden, only slightly compensated for by occasional appointment to the more lucrative office of sheriff. In sum, the prominent local position of the commissioners combined with their effective administration of justice to generate support for and to bolster the authority of the county court.[8]

5. During the period 1658–1680, Lorena Walsh found a far lower concentration of plural officeholding among the justices, but also a far lower participation in major officeholding among nonjustices, with only 20% of those holding major offices being nonjustices ("Charles County, Maryland, 1658–1705," 354). See also Billings, "Growth of Political Institutions," *WMQ*, 3d Ser., XXXI (1974), 237.

6. Cyrus Harreld Karraker, *The Seventeenth-Century Sheriff: A Comparative Study of the Sheriff in England and the Chesapeake Colonies, 1607–1689* (Chapel Hill, N.C., 1930), 156–157. See also Lois Green Carr, "Sources of Political Stability and Upheaval in Seventeenth-Century Maryland," *Maryland Historical Magazine*, LXXIX (1984), 51.

7. Warren M. Billings, "English Legal Literature as a Source of Law and Legal Practice for Seventeenth-Century Virginia," *VMHB*, LXXXVII (1979), 415–416; David Thomas Konig, *Law and Society in Puritan Massachusetts: Essex County, 1629–1692* (Chapel Hill, N.C., 1979), 37; Craven, *Southern Colonies*, 289; George B. Curtis, "The Colonial County Court, Social Forum and Legislative Precedent: Accomack, Virginia, 1633–1639," *VMHB*, LXXXV (1977), 276–277.

8. Curtis, "The Colonial County Court, Social Forum and Legislative Precedent," *VMHB*, LXXXV (1977), 286. Warren Billings argues that the commissioners lacked "a sense of social and political responsibility," in "Growth of Political Institutions," *WMQ*, 3d Ser., XXXI (1974), 237. There is no evidence to support this.

According to J. H. Gleason, "standard attendance" in England was one-quarter of the working commission, which excludes the 16%–39% of the whole commission

But support for local government in the Chesapeake was not simply passive. More than one-half of the landholders on the Eastern Shore shared in the establishment and maintenance of local peace and order by holding some minor or major position of public trust. Twice as many served in minor offices as served in major ones. Some landholders were constables, others churchwardens, but 84 percent of those in minor positions were jurors, sometimes several times over a number of years. In addition, elections for burgesses seem to have drawn together the citizenry. Active participation in public service and in the body politic supported the maintenance of public peace and reflected the recognition of the county court's authority.[9]

The young Virginia gentry recognized the importance of authority in the maintenance of public peace.[10] Such authority was necessary because, although contact promoted social integration, it could lead also to hostility and conflict. In the absence of an effective local police power, the authority of church and county officials stood as a major bulwark against the escalation of hostility to violence and violence to chaos.

For example, both religious and secular authorities acted quickly and conspicuously to investigate accusations of slander and to discipline anyone found guilty. Defamations included a wide variety of topics. Individuals were convicted and punished for falsely accusing their neighbors of sexual improprieties, professional malpractice, abuse of servants, theft, and dishonesty. Those who slandered their neighbors or questioned their background in England quickly found themselves on a ducking stool, in stocks, or wearing a sign that proclaimed their error. As in contemporary

---

who were dignitaries who never attended (*The Justices of the Peace in England, 1558–1640*, 49, 105, 112). Compare table 20, above. Also see Darrett B. Rutman and Anita H. Rutman, *A Place in Time: Middlesex County, Virginia, 1650–1750* (New York, 1984), 161–162. For the burden of being a commissioner and compensation through appointment as sheriff, see Craven, *Southern Colonies*, 281–286; Oliver Perry Chitwood, *Justice in Colonial Virginia* (Baltimore, 1905), 109. On the Eastern Shore, fewer than half of the sheriffs chosen through 1655 were commissioners.

9. See Walsh, "Charles County, Maryland, 1658–1705," 325; Carr, "The Foundations of Social Order," in Daniels, ed., *Town and County*, 89–90; Carr, "Sources of Political Stability and Upheaval," *MHM*, LXXIX (1984), 48–49. See Chapter 7, above, for a discussion of elections. Contests for office seem to have been as rare in the Chesapeake as they were in England in the early 17th century. The franchise, however, was poorly defined and therefore probably exercised by anyone not obviously unqualified. See Derek Hirst, *Representative of the People? Voters and Voting in England under the Early Stuarts* (New York, 1975), 16, 19, 21, 193.

10. John C. Rainbolt, "The Absence of Towns in Seventeenth-Century Virginia," *Journal of Southern History*, XXXV (1969), 346.

ecclesiastical courts in England, there was on the Eastern Shore an emphasis on restoring peace and clearing the reputation of the injured party. To effect the latter, the authorities usually required the slanderer to apologize in a public setting—sometimes at court, sometimes at church, and occasionally at both. These public confessions served not only to defuse potentially explosive situations but also to distinguish acceptable from unacceptable behavior.[11]

Of central and indispensable importance to the effective exercise of authority was the obedience of those governed. Although local officials could rely to some extent on a traditional deference to established authority, they did not lean only on that support. The commissioners of the county court demanded respect. They therefore prosecuted anyone who insulted or obstructed an official of the court in the execution of his office. When Peter Walker insulted the undersheriff Thomas Hatton, the court ordered that Walker pay as a penalty two hundred pounds of tobacco to Hatton and two hundred for the use of the county. But it did not require him to put in security for his good behavior in the future. Shortly thereafter, "by the words and demeanor of the said Peter Walker and manifest assault offered unto the Court . . . whereby [the commis-

---

11. For examples of suits brought against individuals who accused their neighbors of sexual improprieties, see CCR-1, pp. 86–87, 118, CCR-2, pp. 103–104, 189–190, 235–236, 287–288, 292, CCR-3, fol. 62–p. 63, p. 64–fol. 64, p. 65–fol. 65, pp. 157a, 160, fols. 160, 164, pp. 227, 229, CCR-4, p. 42–fol. 45, fol. 87, p. 88–fol. 88. For suits concerning accusations of professional malpractice, see CCR-1, p. 130, CCR-2, pp. 28–29, CCR-4, p. 84, fols. 92, 105. For suits concerning accusations of abuse of servants, see CCR-1, pp. 49, 84. For suits concerning accusations of theft, see CCR-1, pp. 53, 84–85, 92, 115–117, CCR-3, fol. 150, CCR-4, p. 79, fol. 105, p. 107, CCR-5, fol. 146. For suits concerning accusations of lying, see CCR-1, pp. 23, 49, CCR-2, pp. 172–174, 208, 292, 313–314, 315, 384–385, CCR-3, fol. 239, CCR-4, fol. 87, p. 88–fol. 88, fol. 90. For suits involving name calling, see CCR-1, pp. 2, 15, 20, 22–23, 150, CCR-2, pp. 59–60, 201, 396–397, 414. For suits concerning the questioning of background, see CCR-1, pp. 20, 22–23, 115, 118–119, CCR-2, pp. 392–393, 395, CCR-3, p. 135, fol. 135a.

For apologies, see CCR-1, pp. 15, 88, 116–117, CCR-2, pp. 59–60, 104, 235–236, 238, CCR-3, fol. 62–p. 63, p. 229, CCR-4, p. 7–fol. 7, p. 8, p. 42–fol. 45, p. 90, fols. 105, 142, p. 168. See also Clara Ann Bowler, "Carted Whores and White-Shrouded Apologies: Slander in the County Courts of Seventeenth-Century Virginia," *VMHB*, LXXXV (1977), 413–415. Bowler's is the best examination of the way that local officials dealt with the problem of slander. She contrasts ecclesiastical court jurisdiction with manorial court jurisdiction, which emphasized the payment of damages to the injured party. She argues that the latter was not common in Virginia. But, in fact, such monetary penalties were adopted on the Eastern Shore for a short time from mid-1641 to mid-1642 (CCR-2, pp. 104, 172–174). For the role played by the parish in promoting social stability, see Virginia Bernhard, "Poverty and the Social Order in Seventeenth-Century Virginia," *VMHB*, LXXXV (1977), 141–151.

sioners] suspect that the undersheriff may bee further abused and the power of Justice to much undervalued," the court ordered Walker to deposit such security. Nor was the sheriff immune from such abuse. In 1655 Thomas Ball was fined for his contemptuous behavior toward the high sheriff, Francis Pott. After Ball "testifyed his desire to satisfye the Lawe and the person offended," the commissioners reversed the fine, provided that he pay the clerk's charges.[12]

In addition to this concern that the inhabitants treat court officials with due respect, the commissioners also attempted to encourage proper, orderly behavior at court sittings. For example, they punished anyone guilty of swearing or appearing drunk before them. They also frowned on brawling in court. When John Johnson, Sr., struck Richard Hudson during court proceedings, the commissioners ordered him imprisoned until their next sitting. At that time, "takeinge the contempt of the Court into consideration And noteinge the great Indignity thereof reflectinge upon the Authoritye from whome they derive theire power to Negotiate the affayres Committed to their care and trust," they levied against Johnson a heavy fine, which would have been even heavier had he not evinced contrition and submission.[13]

The commissioners reacted with a great deal more severity to court-room actions that posed a direct threat to their authority. People who acted in contempt of court orders received sentences to be whipped or fined. Refusal to obey court orders implied a threat to authority, but some threats were more than implicit. In 1638 "Daniell Cugley did openly taxe this Courte with inj[ustice] and other approbryous speeches." The commissioners ordered the sheriff to take the offender into custody until Cugley confessed his error and paid a fine. Nor did women who challenged the court escape punishment. Alice Robins, who "did in open Court question and disparrage the Commissioners by abusive under-valluing speeches," was towed over Hungars Creek as a punishment.[14] Other individuals who "affronted" the court, "taxed" it with injustice,

12. Walker: CCR-3, pp. 17, 19. Ball: CCR-7, fol. 12. For an attack on the constable, see CCR-1, pp. 71–72.

13. CCR-1, pp. 24, 114, CCR-2, pp. 3, 202, 212, 234–235, 265, 284, 317, CCR-3, fols. 149, 157a, p. 178, fol. 183, p. 232. On Johnson: CCR-5, p. 15, fol. 19. Hudson, who had provoked the attack, also was fined, although less heavily. But the commissioners remitted the fine when Hudson admitted his fault and promised to behave himself with respect to the court. Having done this, the commissioners later removed Johnson's fine and instead ordered him to pay a lesser amount to the sheriff "for publique use of the County." CCR-5, p. 20, fol. 21, p. 58–fol. 58.

14. Contempt: CCR-1, p. 116, CCR-5, fol. 26–p. 27, p. 56. Cugley: CCR-1, p. 114. Robins: CCR-3, p. 148–fol. 149.

or were in "contempt of Authority" received like sentences. But the commissioners tempered their punishments according to the attitude of the culprit. In 1655 the court record notes, "Mr. George Parker hath this day in abusive tearmes affronted the Court and challenged the Authoritye nowe present with doeinge Injustice (which uncivill demenor ought to bee Censured by the Court)." The sheriff arrested Parker, who was ordered to enter into bond ensuring his future good behavior and to pay a fine. At the next court Parker apologized for his offense, and the fine was removed.[15] In the end, whether the court's punishment was meted out or remitted because of a penitent attitude, its authority was affirmed and strengthened.

Moreover, inasmuch as the commissioners punished individuals disrespectful of lower court officials and courtroom protocol, it is not surprising that they did not tolerate personal attacks that touched on their own official position. In court, rude behavior toward a commissioner, an inappropriate comment about his private affairs, or a question concerning his fairness or competence elicited immediate retribution. Whether the offender suffered the penalty or apologized and received a lesser sentence, the commissioners gained by a further definition of the boundary of acceptable courtroom behavior.[16]

There was also concern that the commissioners receive their due respect when outside the courtroom. In 1643 Thomas Parks, in conversation with several other residents, insulted Argoll Yardley's family background, questioned his fairness, and threatened to go to Maryland or to the Indians to receive justice. It was probably the latter statement, involving an appeal to rival regional powers, that prompted the court to order Parks arrested and tried before the governor and Council in the next quarter court at James City. Two months later Parks appeared before the county court for affronting Yardley again as well as the rest of the commissioners. This time he received a whipping.[17]

Ten years later Commissioner John Stringer stopped at the house of

15. CCR-1, p. 137, CCR-4, pp. 226, 227, CCR-5, p. 150, CCR-7, fol. 10, p. 14. Parker: CCR-5, fol. 151, CCR-6, p. 12–fol. 12. See also CCR-7, p. 14.

16. CCR-2, pp. 307–308, CCR-3, fols. 13, 125, CCR-4, fol. 143–p. 144, CCR-5, p. 14.

17. CCR-2, pp. 313–317, 351. A little more than two years later, Parks "abused and defamed" Commissioner Obedience Robins. As a punishment for this and a related offense, the court ordered him whipped. After Parks acknowledged his error, however, the court, with Robins's consent, withdrew his punishment. CCR-3, fol. 2, p. 5.

John Little to request directions to the residence of Francis Stockley. As detailed in Stringer's petition to the court, Little attacked him with

> such abusive languidge and opprobrious speeches from him, tending to your petitioners great disgrace, insomuch That if true, He [Stringer] is altogether incapable of the place of Justice, whereunto hee is Invested to doe equall right to all that shall come unto him for the same.

Although part of Little's fine was remitted after his contrite appearance at court, he still received a severe punishment.[18]

On the same day that this case concluded, another began involving Thomas Higby's questioning of the justice dispensed by Obedience Robins. Preceding its order that depositions be taken in the incident, the court noted "that words and Actions of this consequence Reflect to the dishonor of the Government and undervallueinge and publique scandall of all the Magistrates of the County."[19] It is difficult to imagine a more succinct statement of the commissioners' belief that respect for the officer mirrored respect for the office, for the government in general, and for authority in the abstract.

Occasionally individuals would voice thoughts derogatory, not of any particular officer, but of the office, government, or authority in general. These statements usually coincided with periods of particularly unsettled relations with James City or England. Thus, three such cases occurred in 1637. That year marked the return from England of the hated Governor John Harvey, ousted from office two years before by his own councillors and allowed to leave Virginia and argue his case before the king and Privy Council. Won over less by Harvey's arguments than by the evil consequences that might follow an unpunished overthrow of a royal official, Charles I ordered Harvey back to his post.[20] In a period of less

18. CCR-4, pp. 99, 141, fol. 141–p. 142.
19. CCR-4, p. 141. This incident and the one involving Little and Stringer, as well as others on record, refute Philip Alexander Bruce's assertion that cases concerning insults to commissioners out of court were heard by the General Court rather than the county court (*Institutional History of Virginia in the Seventeenth Century*, 2 vols. [New York, 1910], I, 512).
20. For a brief account, see Alf J. Mapp, Jr., *The Virginia Experiment: The Old Dominion's Role in the Making of America (1607–1781)* (La Salle, Ill., 1974), 103–121. It is worth noting that, according to Harvey's declaration to his English superiors, the colonists on the Eastern Shore had refused to sign the petitions circulated in opposition to him (W. Noel Sainsbury, ed., *Calendar of State Papers*, Colonial Series, 1574–1660 [London, 1860], 212–213).

than a year following Harvey's landing in Virginia, three Eastern Shore residents uttered statements defiant of authority that resulted in court hearings. The most pointed of these was Thomas Powell's blast against Harvey. Powell reportedly said that Harvey "would stint the Country in planting, that it wold undoe a number of poore men, but the great ones wold not care soe much for it, for they wold goe up with a Guard of men." Powell's derogatory reference to stinting, or controlling, tobacco production reflects the general unpopularity of that policy. He based his speculation about the reaction of "the great ones" on experience; in that way they had accomplished their coup of 1635. Damaging as this statement was, Powell did not stop there. He attacked Charles I: "Kinges in former tymes went to the Warres, but this King was fitter for a Ladyes lap." Powell had spoken rashly but does not seem to have suffered any punishment. Maybe the commissioners took into consideration that his comments had been reported by a disgruntled employee. But this fact does not explain the lack of reported punishment in the other two cases.[21] Quite possibly, the commissioners took cognizance of the extraordinary, tense situation in the colony and decided not to press charges against the less than a handful of residents who let off steam in this way. In any event, the circumstances and the response they elicited both were short lived.

This was not true, however, of the crisis of authority engendered by events in England during the 1640s and early 1650s. The prolonged conflict between king and Parliament and the transfer of power to the protectorate threw into question the status of relations between England and Virginia. Following the dissolution of the Virginia Company, the colony had enjoyed a remarkable autonomy and an especial freedom from the sort of interference that had made corporate rule a disaster. Any threat to Virginia's autonomy was viewed as a danger to the colony.[22] It was, by extension, a threat to the political balance of power

21. CCR-1, pp. 72, 78, 84–85, 89. It is possible that these cases all were ordered to be heard before the governor and Council sitting as the General Court, the records of which have survived only in fragments for this period. But the fact that no such order was recorded in any of these cases suggests the explanation that follows in the text.

22. For a discussion of Virginia's autonomy and the impact of events in England, see John Fiske, *Old Virginia and Her Neighbors*, 2 vols. (Boston, 1902), I, 238–239; Percy Scott Flippin, *The Royal Government in Virginia, 1624–1775* (New York, 1919), 31–36; Craven, *Southern Colonies*, 150–172 and chap. 7; Steven Douglas Crow, " 'Left at Libertie': The Effects of the English Civil War and Interregnum on the American Colonies, 1640–1660" (Ph.D. diss., University of Wisconsin–Madison,

within the colony, a balance decidedly in favor of local rather than provincial government. In the course of time, as more people moved further away from James City, the powers of the county magistrates had been increased until they included jurisdiction in civil, criminal, equity, and probate cases. In addition, the commissioners were responsible for maintaining vital records, administering laws requiring oversight (concerning weights and measures, ordinaries, economic regulation, public ways, and so forth), and keeping an official record, especially important in relation to land titles.[23]

The crisis at the summit of governmental authority in England was felt throughout the political structure. An incident that occurred on the Eastern Shore less than a year after the civil war broke out in England illustrates the repercussions of the conflict at the local level. The ship *Reformation* was at anchor with Richard Ingle, a supporter of the parliamentary cause, its master. On board were Argoll Yardley, not only a member of the Virginia Council but also the commander of the Eastern Shore, his brother Francis, and several other people. According to the testimony of several witnesses, Ingle and Francis Yardley argued "concerning the King and Parliament And the said Ingle told the said Yardley saying All those that are of the Kings side are Rattleheads." Argoll Yardley attempted to calm the two men, but they continued to argue. Ingle grabbed a poleax and cutlass and ordered all Virginians off his ship. At this point Argoll Yardley moved toward Ingle, saying, "I arrest you in the King's Name And the said Ingle Answeared saying if you had arrested mee in the King and Parliaments name I would have obeyed it for soe it is now." Having opposed the command of one of Virginia's highest officials and appealed to an authority not recognized in the colony, Ingle was in an untenable position. After threatening Argoll Yardley with his cutlass, he again ordered all Virginians off his ship, weighed anchor, and sailed to Maryland. From there, reports filtered back to the peninsula that Ingle boasted of his opposition to Yardley.[24]

1974), and " 'Your Majesty's Good Subjects': A Reconsideration of Royalism in Virginia, 1642–1652," *VMHB*, LXXXVII (1979), 158–173.

23. See Craven, *Southern Colonies*, 269–280, 289–295; Billings, "Growth of Political Institutions," *WMQ*, 3d Ser., XXXI (1974), 225–242.

24. CCR-2, pp. 301–302, 304–305. A reference to Ingle's encounter on the Eastern Shore appears in William Hand Browne, ed., *Archives of Maryland*, IV, *Judicial and Testamentary Business of the Provincial Court, 1637–1650* (Baltimore, 1887), 233–234, 237–238. Another conflict between Argoll Yardley and Ingle seems to have occurred several months earlier (CCR-2, pp. 269–270). For Ingle's subsequent his-

The breach of authority was serious, but it was of brief duration because Ingle never returned to the Eastern Shore. His ship continued to ply the waters of the peninsula, and he conducted business there for at least another five years, but attorneys handled his affairs.[25]

As the civil war raged in England and rumors of events there reached the Eastern Shore, the commissioners kept a watchful eye on the behavior of the peninsula's inhabitants. In September 1648 they acted promptly to bring to justice John Johnson, who was accused of having "spoken some words tendinge to mutanye."[26] But not until after the execution of Charles I in January 1649 was their authority really questioned. Four months later, citing "the present and dangerous condition wherein this County is nowe stated," the commissioners ordered the residents to arm themselves and appointed William Roper to inspect each individual's supply of weapons and ammunition.[27] While not stated, the danger probably grew out of the events in England.

The precautions of the local magistrates were not unwarranted. Within a period of less than a year, three men challenged the authority of the commissioners. The first incident involved a group of people at Walter Williams's ordinary near the church between Hungars and Nuswattocks creeks, after the Sunday evening religious service. Commissioner Stephen Charlton witnessed a commotion arising from the ordinarykeeper's hesitation to serve any more drinks to the crowd. Despite Charlton's support of this refusal, some of the crowd attacked the ordinarykeeper. Charlton entered the fray and "apprehended one of the actors herein and layd him necke and heeles." But some of the offender's fellow revelers freed him, whereupon Charlton "(in his Majesty's name) required those that were present to ayde him." At that moment, in an attempt to incite the crowd to further opposition, "Olliver Gibbons cryed knock them down, Knocke them downe, Knocke them downe And [Charlton] demandeinge of the said Gibbons howe hee darst saye soe hee answered hee might choose whether hee would obey any of us or not (or words to that effect)." This was a dangerous sentiment. Following Charlton's report of

tory, see Edward Ingle, *Captain Richard Ingle, the Maryland "Pirate and Rebel,"* *1642–1653* (Baltimore, 1884).

25. CCR-2, pp. 330–331, 388–389, 405–406, 437, CCR-3, pp. 13, 46, fol. 56, fol. 84–fol. 87, fol. 130. A year and a half after the incident described here, Argoll Yardley severed all ties with Ingle and had no further contact with him (CCR-2, p. 437).

26. CCR-3, p. 154.

27. CCR-3, p. 171, p. 174–fol. 174, fol. 175.

the incident, Gibbons, "for speeches devuleged by him tendeinge to mutany and resistinge of Authority in contemptious undervallueinge opprobrious termes," was ordered to remain in the custody of the sheriff until the next court and file security for his good behavior.[28]

In October 1649, less than three months after Gibbons's mutinous speech, the Assembly met and passed legislation to deal with the repercussions of events in England. The burgesses began by pointing out that "divers out of ignorance, others out of malice, schisme and faction, in pursuance of some designe of innovation," sought to justify the execution of Charles I and the disinheritance of his son. "And as arguments easily and naturally deduced from the aforesaid cursed and destructive principles, . . . they press and perswade the power of the commission to be void and null, and all magistracy and office thereon depending to have lost their vigor and efficacy." To prevent the consequences of such a line of argument, the Assembly outlawed any effort to justify the late regicide, malign Charles I, or attack the succession of Charles II. Furthermore,

> what person soever, by false reports and malicious rumors shall spread abroad, among the people, any thing tending to change of government, or to the lessening of the power and authority of the Governor or government either in civill or ecclesiasticall causes . . . shall suffer such punishment even to severity as shall be thought fitt, according to the nature and quality of the offence.[29]

Within the next four months, two more breaches of authority occurred on the Eastern Shore. The first involved Peter Walker, now a commis-

28. CCR-3, fol. 177–p. 178, fol. 178. The outcome of this prosecution is unknown. Gibbons, who was a shoemaker, appeared freely before the court the following year (CCR-3, p. 232). It is possible that this affair ended without serious punishment, because it was not until the fall of 1649 that such behavior was outlawed specifically. See the discussion that follows in the text.

29. William Waller Hening, ed., *The Statutes at Large: Being a Collection of All the Laws of Virginia*, I (New York, 1823), 359–361. A much briefer act had been passed 25 years earlier, when the Virginia Company was in serious difficulties. It ordered that "no person within this colony upon the rumur of supposed change and alteration, presume to be disobedient to the present government, nor servants to their private officers, masters or overseers at their uttermost perills." This act was repeated virtually verbatim as part of the codification of laws in 1632. Note that no punishment was prescribed. *Ibid.*, I, 128, 174, 198.

Two months after the Assembly met in 1649, the commissioners of Northampton County proclaimed in a lengthy and elaborately worded statement the accession of Charles II as heir to his father's throne (CCR-3, fol. 192).

sioner, who, "in a disturbinge uncivill manner affronted The Comissioners" in court. Although not exactly a violation of the law passed by the Assembly two months before, Walker's action came at a particularly unsettled period. And unlike Oliver Gibbons, who was a shoemaker, Walker was an official sworn to uphold and administer the laws of the colony. Therefore, his fellow commissioners suspended him from office, committed him to the sheriff's custody until he posted a bond for his good behavior, and sent the record of his action to the governor and Council. The local magistrates also took prompt action to bring to justice Robert Berry, a planter who reportedly "doth demeane himselfe in a contemptious manner And refuseth to submitt to the Kings lawes."[30]

The combination of legislation and local vigilance successfully maintained established authority following the execution of Charles I. For two years after Berry's reprimand, no such incident came before the commission. During that period, Virginia was left in relative peace by the new government in England, which was preoccupied with establishing its authority at home. The next crisis of authority would come in early 1652, when Virginia surrendered to the representatives of Parliament.

But in order to understand the impact of this change on the Eastern Shore, it is necessary to be aware of certain developments on the peninsula from early 1650 to early 1652. Very briefly, the previously stable relationship between the colonists and the Eastern Shore Indians turned increasingly to hostility. As the English claimed more and more acreage, especially in the early 1650s, they encroached further upon the land of the natives, and their claims occasionally rested on fraud and deceit. In a letter to the commissioners in the spring of 1650, Governor Berkeley sent instructions for procedures to follow in order to ensure the fair treatment of the Indians. Local officials complied with his request.[31]

But other areas of conflict between the colonists and natives could not be controlled so easily. Living in greater proximity and already on edge because of the land issue, they interacted with greater friction, especially along the northern edge of settlement. In the summer of 1650, it was rumored that the Indians planned to poison and then attack the English on the peninsula. The commissioners did their best to place the county in a defensive stance. Tensions mounted.[32]

30. CCR-3, fol. 195. Walker sat again as a commissioner two months later (CCR-3, p. 216). Berry: CCR-3, fol. 196, p. 204.

31. CCR-3, fols. 207, 209. See Chapter 2 for a brief synopsis of the Indian-English relationship concerning land.

32. CCR-3, pp. 203, 212, p. 217–fol. 217, fol. 219. In the fall of 1650, an Indian was shot by Elizabeth, wife of Tobias Selby (CCR-3, fol. 226).

On April 28 of the following year commissioners Edmund Scarburgh and Thomas Johnson, with about fifty other men from the area around Occohannock Creek and to the north, attacked the Indians, who in turn marshaled their forces for a concerted assault on the English. What prompted the English attack is not recorded specifically, but there is a reference to Indian "plotts and conspiricyes." Whatever the precise motivation, some of Scarburgh and Johnson's countrymen were not convinced that the breach of the peace was justified. Other Eastern Shore commissioners, including two members of the Council, moved quickly to restore peace. They ordered the sheriff to arrest all Englishmen involved in the assault on the Indians, arranged for their transportation to James City for a trial before the governor and Council, appointed two of their own to prosecute the charges against the culprits, and attempted to appease the Indians.[33] But either they reacted too quickly on insufficient evidence or their opposition presented a better argument in James City, because a council of war with the governor present cleared Scarburgh, Johnson, and the others. According to the judgment of the council, "they did (as Honest and carefull men ought to have done) in such a Case as they did it."[34]

Two months after the proceedings in James City, rumors again circulated on the Eastern Shore "that the Indyans have concluded a confederacie of Acteing a sudaine massacrie." Again the commissioners along the northern edge of settlement, where the threat was most serious, seized the initiative. Scarburgh and Johnson, with the collaboration of two other commissioners, Stephen Charlton and John Stringer, organized a party of armed horsemen "to prevent the Indyans in their intended treacherous plotts and discover those practices (which yet wee are not acquainted with)." A note was appended to the order for mobilization; significantly, in view of the acrimonious outcome of the last such expedition, it recorded that the planned action met with the approval of Nathaniel Littleton and Argoll Yardley, the two Eastern Shore councillors who had raised a question about the propriety of the last such effort.[35] The division among the local officials was healed, and the commission again spoke with a unified authority. It could thereby handle

33. CCR-4, p. 40–fol. 40.
34. CCR-4, p. 22. There is a suggestion that William Andrews, one of the commissioners acting in opposition to Scarburgh, may have been doing so out of economic self-interest. The same council that exonerated Scarburgh forbade Andrews from trading any longer with the Indians (CCR-4, fol. 22).
35. CCR-4, p. 36–p. 37.

more effectively the threatened Indian uprising (which never took place) and the continued friction between the colonists and natives.[36]

But, more important, the resolution of the commissioners' clash over Indian policy prepared them to deal more effectively with a new threat to their exercise of authority. The danger resulted from Virginia's continued refusal to recognize the supremacy of Parliament in England. While affairs in the mother country occupied the full attention of Parliament, Virginia had been allowed to persist in its allegiance to Charles II. Nominally royalist, Virginia's leaders had taken the opportunity of weakened imperial authority to reshape colonial government to their own advantage and to follow their own economic best interest.[37] But in 1651 the imperial legislative body finally turned its attention to Virginia. It sent commissioners to negotiate the surrender of the colony and a transfer of allegiance. Although two members of the commission were lost at sea, the rest arrived in early January 1652 and began their talks with the colony's ruling powers.[38] The issue was of intense concern to all Virginians.

On the Eastern Shore the extraordinary events taking place across the bay prompted the following action on the part of the county court on February 11:

> Upon serious consultation of the importance and consequence of the publique affayres. That there maye bee a fayre correspondencye and right understandinge in such matters as are very necessary to be proposed and withall possible expedition absolute answers returned To those questions much concerne the Peace and saftye of the County . . . ordered That upon monday next (beinge the 16th daye of this month) att the howse of Walter Willyams The mayster of every family in Northampton County and all freemen hereby take notice that they are required to meete the Commander and Commissioners [of the county].[39]

No record exists of what happened at this unprecedented meeting. But the following deposition suggests that those who attended discussed and voted for a surrender to the parliamentary commissioners, and it also

36. CCR-4, pp. 51, 53, fol. 96–p. 98, p. 102.
37. Crow, " 'Your Majesty's Good Subjects,' " *VMHB*, LXXXVII (1979), 159, 173.
38. "Surrender of Virginia to the Parliamentary Commissioners, March, 1651–2," *VMHB*, XI (1903–1904), 33.
39. CCR-4, fol. 79.

reveals the consequent dilemma of local officials who had to exercise power with no explicit authority to do so. The incident took place about three days after the meeting of the inhabitants of the county. Samuel Luddington, acting in his capacity as an officer under the sheriff, was at the house of Commissioner Thomas Johnson, with whom he discussed certain people who were to attend the next court, to be held on February 28, "whereupon Mr. Johnson demanded of this deponent who had Power to Keepe a Court; for (said hee) Wee have given the Power out of our owne hands which is Nullified and abrogated by Declareinge for the Parlament."[40] Johnson's question was both legitimate and pertinent. And his fellow commissioners may have agreed with him, because the court did not meet on the scheduled day.

Fortunately, the colony's situation vis-à-vis Parliament did not remain unsettled much longer. On March 12 the commissioners from England and the governor, Council, and burgesses of Virginia signed articles surrendering Virginia to the control of Parliament. The articles, quite favorable to the colony, made no mention of the continued authority of the local commissioners, but two proclamations issued the next day and recorded in the local county court book reveal at least a de facto recognition of their powers.[41]

Gradually order was restored to governmental processes. The inhabitants of the peninsula signed the "engagement," or statement of loyalty, to the new sovereignty of Parliament. At the next meeting of the county court on March 30, those present elected a new sheriff and burgesses, and the commissioners renewed the appointment of the court clerk and made arrangements for the militia.[42] At the same court, the following was recorded:

> Willinge And Requiringe the Inhabitants to bee obedient to their several Commanders (which have subscribed the Ingagment) As they will answer the contrary att their perill. It is further ordered

40. CCR-4, p. 63. Elizabeth S. Haight argues that Johnson feared that Parliament would nullify the commission's powers; on the contrary, he knew that the act of declaring for Parliament and disavowing the king had already nullified the former authority for the commission. See "The Northampton Protest of 1652: A Petition to the General Assembly from the Inhabitants of the Eastern Shore," *American Journal of Legal History*, XXVIII (1984), 373.

41. CCR-4, p. 66–fol. 66. For the favorable terms of the articles and the subsequent political settlement, see Craven, *Southern Colonies*, 262–263, 265; Crow, " 'Your Majesty's Good Subjects,' " *VMHB*, LXXXVII (1979), 170–171.

42. CCR-4, fol. 63, p. 66, fol. 66, p. 67, fol. 188–p. 189.

that those persons (which have not subscribed the Ingagment) Re-
payre to the next [nearest] comissioner (That hath subscribed) who
is hereby quallifyed to Tender the Ingagment to the Inhabitants.[43]

All but two of the thirteen Eastern Shore commissioners signed the engagement.[44] Their geographic dispersion, and consequent accessibility,
aided in the establishment of the parliamentary government.

It was also at the court meeting of March 30 that steps were taken to
assert local rights. With the question of ultimate authority settled in
England, the inhabitants seem to have felt that it was an opportune time
to readjust the balance of power more in their favor within Virginia.
They proceeded on several fronts. First, they ordered the new sheriff not
to collect the county tax for the time being.[45] They justified this move by
arguing that, with the exception of one Eastern Shore burgess who had
attended the Assembly in 1651, the peninsula had not been represented
since 1647. The taxes that had been authorized and that they viewed as
excessive had been passed without their approval.[46] According to the
complaint, because the Eastern Shore had never received a summons to
send burgesses, "wee did understand and suppose our Countie of Northampton to bee disjoynted and sequestered from the rest of Virginia." In a
bold move toward autonomy, the inhabitants also desired an annual
choice of magistrates within the county, which would have freed these
appointments from the approval of the governor. "And if our Countie
maye not have the priviledge of a peculier Government and propriety (att
present) granted within our precincts," the inhabitants of the county
wanted "all causes, suits or Tryals (of what nature soever) [to] bee Com-
menced and (for future tyme) Determined in our said Countie of Northampton." Finally, those present at the court voiced their support for

43. CCR-4, fol. 66.
44. Commissioner Thomas Hunt did not sign the engagement and did not sit from
February 1652 until his reinstatement in July 1653 (CCR-4, fol. 79, p. 180, fol. 198).
Although Thomas Sprigg was reappointed to the commission in October 1652, he did
not rejoin the commission until after he signed the engagement in July 1653 (CCR-4,
fol. 79, p. 117–p. 118, p. 181, fol. 198).
45. CCR-4, fol. 67–p. 68. A few pages earlier in the court record, the clerk recorded a slightly different version of this decision, that is, that the new sheriff should
collect the tax but not send the tobacco to James City pending further action by the
Assembly on Northampton County's complaints. According to this earlier version,
the question had been debated and decided by the people present and ordered by the
court. CCR-4, p. 66.
46. CCR-4, fol. 67–p. 68. There had been a shortfall in the collection of taxes on
the Eastern Shore the previous year. Questioned about the deficit, the commissioners
had undertaken an audit of the county's public revenues. CCR-4, p. 61, fols. 70, 80.

Richard Bennett to take over as governor.⁴⁷ The degree of fiscal, administrative, and judicial autonomy claimed was truly audacious. The county court record notes that these demands were made by "the Inhabitants of Northampton Countie," a phrase that may have reflected a high attendance at what must have been viewed as a very important meeting of the county court, the first following the surrender to the parliamentary commissioners.

When the Assembly met the next month, the Eastern Shore was represented by five burgesses (more than any county except James City County).⁴⁸ No account survives of the Assembly's reaction to what has come to be called the Northampton Protest. But a review of some of the laws passed at this session reveals significant concessions to the spirit of the grievances. Although the Eastern Shore was not granted the degree of autonomy that it sought, the Assembly did extend the powers of the commissioners of all the counties, both in and out of court. Meeting as a county court, the commissioners received a broader criminal jurisdiction in order to reduce the burden of bringing such cases to James City. They were also given, for the first time, admiralty jurisdiction. As individual commissioners, they were granted increased authority to act in small causes.⁴⁹ The trend toward dispersing more authority from James City to

47. CCR-4, fol. 67–p. 68.
48. One of the six burgesses chosen did not attend (CCR-4, fol. 63; Hening, ed., *Statutes at Large*, I, 369–371). Elizabeth Haight gives great significance to the fact that three of the six chosen as burgesses were not commissioners ("The Northampton Protest of 1652," *Am. Jour. Leg. Hist.*, XXVIII [1984], 366–367). In fact, from 1633, when the county record begins, through 1647, the last year when Northampton County had regularly sent a burgess, there was an invariable pattern, whereby noncommissioners attending the Assembly as burgesses became commissioners within a few months. Thus, John Wilkins attended the Assembly of February 1633 and was sitting with the commission at its next meeting (Hening, ed., *Statutes at Large*, I, 203; CCR-1, pp. 7–8). Edmund Scarburgh sat as a burgess in March 1643 and received his commission that year (Hening, ed., *Statutes at Large*, I, 239; CCR-2, p. 307). Thomas Johnson was a burgess in November 1645 and a commissioner within eight months (Hening, ed., *Statutes at Large*, I, 299; CCR-3, p. 40). This sequence may have been intended to give the governor a personal look at a candidate for the county bench before appointing him. The same motive may have been operative in 1652. Two of the three noncommissioners attending the Assembly that year, William Jones and Anthony Hodgskins, became members of the county commission immediately on their return to the Eastern Shore (CCR-4, p. 81). It is probable that the third, Ralph Barlow, would have been appointed to the commission too; but he had not been able to attend the Assembly and was dead within months (CCR-4, fol. 131–p. 132).
49. Warren M. Billings, ed., "Some Acts Not in Hening's *Statutes*: The Acts of Assembly, April 1652, November 1652, and July 1653," *VMHB*, LXXXIII (1975), 33, 70–71.

the county and from the local court to individual commissioners reflected a recognition that the burden of time and expense imposed by travel to distant courts could be reduced by settling certain cases closer to the people involved. Although all counties benefited from the stipulations of this redistribution of power, Northampton County was one of the few beneficiaries of an act granting to local officials greater authority to deal with natives in their jurisdiction. According to the preamble of this statute, it was passed "Uppon the Desyre of the Inhabitants of . . . Northampton." A change in the prevailing situation negated the complaint of Eastern Shore residents about excessive taxation without representation. In the first place, the tax level dropped from forty-six pounds of tobacco per poll to fifteen per poll. Second, the inhabitants of Northampton County, disabused of their delusion of total autonomy, were represented in this and subsequent assemblies.[50] It is interesting to note that the choice for governor was Richard Bennett, the candidate supported by the residents of Northampton County.

Having augmented the power of local officials and defused the potentially explosive tax revolt on the Eastern Shore, the Assembly enlisted their aid in defense of the new status quo. To prevent the spread of seditious rumors, the legislature passed the following act:

> If any person, or persons, shall fforge, or Divulge any false newes tendinge to the disturbance of the peace of this Collony under the government now Established, Shall (unlesse he produce his Author forthwith) by the Next Commission for the peace bee Committed to prison.

The act stipulated further steps for any refusal of the culprit to name the source of the statement.[51]

An action related to the Assembly's desire for increased oversight was the addition of commissioners to the local court. The Northampton County commission had included thirteen men in January. Three new members sat for the first time in May 1652.[52] Through fluctuations in personnel, the total increased by one a year until there were nineteen commissioners in 1655. This increase in the number of local officials

---

50. *Ibid.*, 71, 76; CCR-4, fol. 67–p. 68; Hening, ed., *Statutes at Large*, I, 379, 387.
51. Billings, ed., "Some Acts Not in Hening's *Statutes*," *VMHB*, LXXXIII (1975), 33.
52. CCR-4, p. 83. The new commissioners were William Jones, Anthony Hodgskins, and William Whittington.

responsible for oversight may help to explain the continued acceptance of authority on the Eastern Shore. Although people still drank in court, insulted commissioners on occasion, or spoke disrespectfully of the local authorities, these occurrences were no more numerous or serious than before the change in allegiance.

The only serious threat to the authority of the court after Virginia declared for Parliament happened in 1653. It is important to emphasize that the disturbance in this year was fundamentally different from the complaints in early 1652. The Northampton Protest of 1652 appears to have been an expression of the will of all the inhabitants, who had voiced their feelings in open court. The challenge to authority in 1653 resulted from the actions of individuals who definitely did not represent all inhabitants of the peninsula. The first had been a movement to wrest additional power from James City; the second was an internally disruptive challenge by a dissident minority to the local exercise of power. The distinction is crucial to an understanding of the harsh response of the colony's officials to the second outbreak.[53]

The events of 1653 grew out of England's increasing hostility to the trade between its colonies and the Dutch. That trade was particularly important to Virginia in the 1640s, when the English Civil War had disrupted exchange with England. Parliament struck at the Dutch trade with its colonies by passing navigation acts in 1650 and 1651. In 1652, the same year that Virginia surrendered to parliamentary control, war broke out between England and Holland.[54]

53. Until Warren Billings edited the acts of 1652 for publication, historians had missed the importance of the events of 1652 and 1653 on the Eastern Shore because they had misinterpreted the sequence of cause and effect. The standard interpretation was that the Assembly's harsh response of 1653 was prompted by the complaints of early 1652. See Jennings Cropper Wise, *Ye Kingdome of Accawmacke; or, The Eastern Shore of Virginia in the Seventeenth Century* (Richmond, Va., 1911), 124–152, which is also marred by innumerable errors in chronology; Ralph T. Whitelaw, *Virginia's Eastern Shore: A History of Northampton and Accomack Counties,* 2 vols. (Richmond, Va., 1951), I, 29–31; Nora Miller Turman, *The Eastern Shore of Virginia, 1603–1964* (Onancock, Va., 1964), 53–56. Although Susie M. Ames separates the incidents of 1652 and 1653, she is not explicit in her explanation of the Assembly's response, in *Studies of the Virginia Eastern Shore in the Seventeenth Century* (Richmond, Va., 1940), 8–9.

54. Craven, *Southern Colonies,* 239–243, 249, 250, 253–254n; J. E. Farnell, "The Navigation Act of 1651, the First Dutch War, and the London Merchant Community," *Economic History Review,* 2d Ser., XVI (1964), 439–440; John R. Pagan, "Dutch Maritime and Commercial Activity in Mid-Seventeenth-Century Virginia," *VMHB,* XC (1982), 493–495. For a contemporary statement of the importance of

Almost immediately the Eastern Shore became involved in the imperial cause. In June 1652 Captain Robert Henfield, acting in the name of Parliament, stopped the ship *Fame*, which was owned by Walter Chiles, a citizen of Virginia. A crew under the command of Captain Richard Husbands then occupied the ship as a prize, claiming the ship and its crew to be Dutch and not properly licensed. The commissioners on the Eastern Shore did not agree and, exercising their newly granted admiralty jurisdiction, ordered the ship returned to Walter Chiles. Henfield agreed to surrender the ship. Husbands, a prisoner of the commission and subject to its coercion, commanded his crew to comply. They at first refused but then surrendered the prize. Allowed to return to his ship, Husbands complained that the prize had in fact been lawful and announced his intention to sue for its recovery. Meanwhile, Chiles claimed that some of his goods had not been returned with his ship. The case was sent to England for resolution.[55] This was the only such incident in 1652, but the continuing conflict between England and Holland threatened trade relations.

In early 1653, two ship seizures occurred that upset the status quo. One involved the seizure of the ship of Captain Daniel Howe by Edmund Scarburgh, who acted by authority of a commission granted to him by Captain Peter Wraxall, who in turn had received his commission from the Admiralty office in England.[56] Scarburgh was the highest-ranking commissioner in the northern part of the Eastern Shore. Around the same time, February 1653, a crew of men hired by Scarburgh also seized the ship of Captain John Jacob. The latter objected strenuously to the seizure. A German, he had taken the oath in support of Parliament and

---

the Dutch trade to Virginia, see "By the Governor, Counsell, and Burgesses of the Grand Assembly in Virginia, April the 5th 1647," in H. R. McIlwaine, ed., *Journals of the House of Burgesses of Virginia, 1619–1658/1659* (Richmond, Va., 1915).

55. CCR-4, fol. 126–fol. 129; Peter Wilson Coldham, ed., *English Adventurers and Emigrants, 1609–1660: Abstracts of Examinations in the High Court of Admiralty with Reference to Colonial America* (Baltimore, 1984), 138.

56. CCR-4, fol. 144. For the depositions filed in this case, see CCR-4, p. 130, fol. 144. Several months before this seizure, Scarburgh had arrested Howe to force the latter's appearance at court. Scarburgh, however, failed to attend himself and therefore defaulted (CCR-4, p. 105). Although no final decision appears on record in the case of *Howe v. Scarburgh*, the latter seems to have won. One deposition suggested that Howe supported the Dutch cause. More definitively, two years later, Scarburgh deposed that the ship had been taken "upon the warrant of our Nationall warr, And the wrightings surprised in her Togither with the maysters oath (viva voce) proved the said shipp Lawfull prise" (CCR-4, p. 130, CCR-5, p. 133).

was employed in a New England ship on New England trade. Scarburgh's men physically beat Jacobs and took his goods to the ship of Peter Wraxall, who refused to return them as ordered by Lieutenant Colonel Obedience Robins, the highest-ranking commissioner in the southern part of the peninsula. Robins protested as he had in the earlier incident.

However, this second seizure had even more ominous overtones. The dignity and authority of the commissioners had been assailed. One deponent reported that the surgeon on the ship had told the commissioners

> that they had English faces, but Dutch harts, But they would never bee quiett (untill they had swingeinge cabins made for them) And further . . . the Mate said that hee had a Horse att home which hee thought to have brought with him, But that hee was affrayd hee should have bine made one Officer or another They would have made him either a Collonel, a Major, or a Justice of Peace And that made him leave him behind him, And further . . . that the Chirurgion said The most (or all that were here) were Rouges, or whores, or Vagabones, or Theeives, or Beggers, and many other scandalous names . . . And they bringe them in, and when they are free, They were put into office presently.

If these insults were not enough to enrage the members of the commission, a report that Scarburgh, one of their own, had called them "overgrown puppyes" probably was.[57] Tensions increased.

The most serious immediate danger was to the peaceful Dutch immigrants residing on the Eastern Shore. The people of Northampton County had previously enjoyed an extensive trade with the Dutch, and their representatives continued to live on the peninsula. Several witnesses testified to the threats hurled against these residents by Scarburgh and his men. The Dutch inhabitants complained about them to the commissioners and, proclaiming their obedience to England and the colony, requested a clarification of their status. The commissioners supported their cause. Arguing that the Dutch residents had subscribed the engagement, "behaved themselves like honest men and loyall subjects (to the Government they live under)," and therefore merited protection, the local officials sought the support of Deputy Governor William Claiborne. They pointed out that, if the Dutch residents were not protected, then the

57. CCR-4, fol. 162–p. 164.

whole county was in danger. Claiborne agreed and issued orders for their security.[58]

But this decision did not defuse the situation. In June 1653 a group of inhabitants met in the northern part of the county. The commissioners had recently ordered the return of a prize ship. The vessel seized had been that of Daniel Gyles, who had been trading in New England and New Netherlands. Apparently neither the ship nor crew was Dutch. It is probably not inconsequential that the ship was in the hire of William Payne and William Stranguidge, with whom Edmund Scarburgh had unsettled, disputed accounts.[59] Thomas Johnson, a commissioner in that part of the county, was a neighbor of Scarburgh and had been Scarburgh's accomplice in the 1651 assault on the Eastern Shore Indians. Johnson harangued the assembled crowd and asked whether the commission was competent to return a prize ship. Stephen Horsey voiced his opinion that there was "no man in that court able to judge her a prise." But he didn't stop with this; he continued in a seditious vein as reported in the commissioners' petition to the governor and Council for redress. They complained that Horsey had

> Calumniated and scandalized your petitioners (By callinge them Asses and villanes) Thereby incenseinge the people of this County against them (As they were magistrates placed by the Grand Assemblye under the power of the Commonwealth of England) Endevoringe (as much as in him laye) to cause an Insurrection and Mutiney Against the Magistrates Established by the Authorytye aforesaid.[60]

It was probably at this meeting in the northern part of the county that some of the inhabitants, under the influence of Scarburgh and Johnson, signed a complaint to the governor, Council, and burgesses. Although no copies of this document have survived, some of its contents can be reconstructed from the events that followed. It seems that it reflected all too transparently Stephen Horsey's view of the commission. It must also have complained of the commissioners' recent decisions returning reputed prize ships to their owners. In particular, there seems to have been some concern that the county would be held liable for having taken the *Fame* from Richard Husbands and restoring it to Walter Chiles the year

58. CCR-4, fol. 162–p. 164, p. 171.
59. CCR-4, fol. 183, p. 199–fol. 199, fol. 217–p. 218, CCR-5, fol. 33, fol. 36–p. 37, p. 56, CCR-7, p. 70.
60. CCR-4, fol. 183.

before. Finally, the signers of the complaint requested a division of the county.[61] This last clause may have reflected a division between the northern part of the county, under the sway of Scarburgh and Johnson, and the southern part, in agreement with the rest of the commission. Or it may have represented a pragmatic effort to divide into two manageable counties the single governmental unit, rapidly becoming unwieldy because of the spread of an ever-increasing population over a larger area. Possibly both of these explanations, personal and practical, played a part in the request.

The commissioners from Nuswattocks Creek to the tip of the peninsula reacted quickly. Along with their petition concerning the seditious speeches of Stephen Horsey, they requested that the governor and Council act against those who had signed the complaint. Their petitions came before the Assembly that met in early July. They had to rely on presenting their concerns in this form, because the three burgesses representing the Eastern Shore all supported Scarburgh. William Melling was Scarburgh's cousin and longtime associate, and the other two burgesses were the culprits Thomas Johnson and Stephen Horsey.[62] Whether they were elected at a meeting in the northern part of the county where Scarburgh was influential or whether the majority of inhabitants on the peninsula supported his views (an unlikely possibility), the three burgesses must have entered strong opinions about the petitions from the rest of the commission.

But Scarburgh's partisans lost the argument. The Assembly described the complaint as "scandalous and seditious" and forbade anyone who had signed it from holding county office. It also ordered Scarburgh removed from office until he accounted for his actions. Finally, several members of the Council were appointed to attend the governor and secretary of the colony to the Eastern Shore, where they were to see to

> the settlement of the peace of that county, and the punishment of delinquents there according to their demerrits, the appointment of all officers both for peace and warr, the division of that county, and the hearing and determineing of the businesse of damages between Capt. Daniel How and Left. Coll. Edm'd. Scarbrough, As also between Capt. John Jacob and the said Edmund Scarbrough.[63]

61. CCR-4, fol. 179–p. 180, p. 183; Hening, ed., *Statutes at Large*, I, 380, 384.
62. CCR-1, p. 8, CCR-4, fol. 179–p. 180, CCR-5, p. 125; Hening, ed., *Statutes at Large*, I, 379, 380.
63. Hening, ed., *Statutes at Large*, I, 380, 384.

One additional action of this Assembly is worth mentioning, because it related directly to a point of conflict on the Eastern Shore. Authorized by letters of January 27, 1653, from the Council of State in England, the Assembly ordered the colony to prepare for defense against the Dutch and to seize all Dutch ships that appeared in Virginia waters. Mentioning reports of a "shipp belongeinge unto Amsterdam" off the Eastern Shore, the Assembly placed the peninsula on defensive alert and authorized the inhabitants there to seize the vessel.[64] The residents on the Eastern Shore obeyed these instructions.

In late July 1653 the governor and his entourage arrived on the peninsula to reestablish order. Their first action, in a session on July 25 with eminent members of the local commission as witnesses, involved the condemnation of two Dutch ships seized there as prizes. For the next three days the governor and councillors sat with the local commissioners to carry out the mandate of the Assembly to settle the peace of the county.[65] The remarkable attendance at this meeting suggests the importance of the occasion. Of sixteen men holding commissions as of June, three were disqualified because of their involvement in the recent protest. Of the thirteen remaining, ten sat. Three newly appointed commissioners joined them.[66] Thus thirteen of a possible fifteen nontraveling officials attended: 86.7 percent, compared to an overall 64 percent for the period 1651–1655.

Having appointed new officials in conformity with the instructions of the Assembly, the board next turned its attention to those responsible for the recent protest. Although Edmund Scarburgh had fled the peninsula, the governor, councillors, and commissioners attempted to settle some of his outstanding accounts with William Stranguidge and the colony's customs collectors.[67] "Part of the inhabitants of Northampton County"— those who had signed the complaint—filed a petition that they had not intended "(in the least measure) by the said paper, nor otherwise, To scandalise any Gentleman whomsoever or to contemne Government nor

64. CCR-4, p. 144–fol. 144.

65. CCR-4, p. 179–p. 180, p. 181, p. 182–fol. 182, p. 184.

66. The three were Edmund Scarburgh, who had fled the Eastern Shore, Thomas Johnson, and Anthony Hodgskins. CCR-4, p. 199–fol. 199, p. 222, CCR-5, p. 73. The three missing: Peter Walker was traveling off the Eastern Shore (CCR-4, fol. 2); Richard Vaughan had not sat from January 1652 through June 1653; Thomas Sprigg had not yet signed the engagement and was therefore not qualified to sit. The three new commissioners: CCR-4, p. 180, fols. 198, 201, p. 217.

67. CCR-4, fol. 180, p. 181, p. 199–fol. 199.

to cause any sedition, or discord in the County." Despite this effort, the board ruled that "the demeanor of many of the persons complayned of had bine very mutinous and repugnant to the Government of the Commissioners settled over them, by the Assembly, And scandalous to the places and persons." Those who had signed the complaint were forbidden to hold any office in the county until the governor and Council ruled otherwise, and they also had to acknowledge their errors at court and pay a fine.[68] The authority of the commission was restored.

The aftermath of the turmoil of 1653 reveals a gradual healing of the body politic. In November William Melling was restored to his former office as surveyor. That same month the governor and Council allowed Anthony Hodgskins to reassume his position as a commissioner, which he did at the meeting of the county court in March 1654. As merited by Thomas Johnson's more active role in the protest, a longer time passed before he received his pardon. In November 1654 the inhabitants elected him one of three burgesses to the Assembly that met that month. While in James City, Johnson was restored to his former offices in the county commission and militia. Edmund Scarburgh's return to an active public life took a more circuitous route. He had left the Eastern Shore before Governor Bennett arrived in July 1653. He came back some time the next spring but quickly departed again and became involved in political events in Maryland that summer. In August 1654 he sat as a commissioner, but he did not attend regularly until the next year.[69]

One of the proposals contained in the 1653 protest ultimately became reality: the division of the Eastern Shore into two counties. Although the request did not receive the approval of Governor Bennett and the Council when they sat with the local commission in July 1653, they must have been aware of the inadequacy of the court's sitting in a single location as ordered by the Eastern Shore commissioners in March 1652. Those present at the July 1653 meeting issued an order for the commissioners to rotate their sittings from Cherrystone to Hungars to Occohannock creeks. But at the county court meeting on March 29, 1654, the commis-

68. CCR-4, fol. 179–p. 180, p. 183.
69. On Melling and Hodgskins: CCR-4, fol. 204, p. 213–fol. 213, p. 222. On Johnson: CCR-5, pp. 60, 73; Hening, ed., *Statutes at Large*, I, 386. On Scarburgh: CCR-4, fol. 192–p. 193, CCR-5, fol. 26; *Virginia and Maryland; or, The Lord Baltamore's Printed Case, Uncased and Answered*, 38–39, in Peter Force, ed., *Tracts and Other Papers, Relating Principally to the Origin, Settlement, and Progress of the Colonies in North America, from the Discovery of the Country to the Year 1776*, 4 vols. (Washington, D.C., 1836–1847), II.

224 The Societal Network and the Role of Authority

sioners voted for a return to a single location for the court to meet. Surely it was not coincidental that this action was taken by those commissioners who lived in the southern part of the county and who had opposed the efforts of those signing the 1653 complaint. Possibly they hoped to retain control of the proceedings of the court by holding sessions only at Walter Williams's ordinary between Hungars and Nuswattocks creeks. This maneuver would prevent Scarburgh, Johnson, and their associates from the area around Occohannock Creek and to the north from dominating those sessions held there. But this plan failed. The Assembly overruled it the next year when it enacted legislation requiring two locations for the court sessions: one south and one north of Hungars Creek. The Assembly may have hoped to reduce internecine tensions by stipulating as part of this act "that the comissioners of the respective divisions shall attend the courts held therein."[70] This provision would have lessened friction between commissioners in the two jurisdictions by having them hold sessions in different locations. The Assembly's action served another purpose as well. It reflected the demands for convenient government needed by a population growing numerically and spreading geographically. Both of these motives, political as well as pragmatic, influenced the decision eight years later to divide the Eastern Shore into two counties. As with the Assembly's act of 1655, the original line of division ran west from the head of Hungars Creek to the seaboard side of the peninsula.[71]

The resolution of the tense situation in 1653 ended a particularly serious threat to the exercise of a unified governmental authority on the Eastern Shore. The actions of Edmund Scarburgh and Thomas Johnson divided the local commission into two factions. Because of the nature of the conflict, the only power capable of acting as arbiter was that at the colony's center. The governor, councillors, and burgesses acted quickly and responsibly. Significantly, they joined the majority faction of commissioners on the peninsula in viewing the actions of Scarburgh, Johnson, and their followers as a perilous breach of unity, a threat to authority and therefore stability. The role of the county court in mediating disputes generated within the societal network depended on a county-

70. Hening, ed., *Statutes at Large*, I, 409. For the March 1652, July 1653, and March 1654 orders, see CCR-4, fol. 66–p. 67, p. 180, CCR-5, p. 4.
71. For the history of the division of the Eastern Shore into two counties, see Whitelaw, *Virginia's Eastern Shore*, I, 32–34; Susie M. Ames, "The Reunion of Two Virginia Counties," *Journal of Southern History*, VIII (1942), 536–548.

wide consensus of local officials.[72] Any threat to this consensus jeopardized the effective exercise of the commission's authority and therefore, by extension, endangered the peace of the county.

But the crisis in 1653 reveals something else. In the absence of any evidence of a breakdown in social relations, it must be concluded that the societal network was sufficiently well integrated and self-supporting to sustain at least a temporary loss of controlling power. The confluence of kin and affectional ties, neighborhood contacts, economic links, and an effective exercise of authority had created a society that could survive political conflict.

72. On very rare occasions, individual commissioners did register their dissent to particular decisions of the county court, but the issues involved were minor and the dissension not cumulative as it was in 1653. CCR-3, fol. 179, CCR-4, fol. 57.

9 Beyond Local Networks

THE EASTERN SHORE of Virginia was just one place in the larger English-speaking world of the seventeenth century. Yet the formation of a society there provides an important perspective on that larger world. The Eastern Shore shared many characteristics with other settlements in the Chesapeake. A river-laced geography and tobacco-based staple economy defined the Chesapeake as a region, clearly distinguishing it from England and New England. Demographically, the Chesapeake more resembled England than it did New England, but was still different from either. Yet these features can disguise significant similarities that reveal much about the social culture of seventeenth-century Englishmen.[1]

A basic element of that social culture was its spatial restriction. Whether in England, New England, or the Chesapeake, individuals were embedded within networks of contacts that rarely extended more than a few miles from their homes. Although residential patterns might be nuclear or nonnuclear and although population density might vary, the distance that people traveled for neighborly contact was surprisingly constant. Individuals sought sociability, favors, support, and marriage alliances with friends living nearby. Whereas the network of kinship might be limited or attenuated by death or mobility, neighbors were always there.[2] Economic networks generally extended no farther than

1. For a demographic comparison of the Chesapeake and England, see Daniel Blake Smith, "Mortality and Family in the Colonial Chesapeake," *Journal of Interdisciplinary History*, VIII (1977–1978), 426–427; for a comparison of the Chesapeake and New England, see Russell R. Menard, "Immigrants and Their Increase: The Process of Population Growth in Early Colonial Maryland," in Aubrey C. Land *et al.*, eds., *Law, Society, and Politics in Early Maryland* (Baltimore, 1977), 102–104; Lorena S. Walsh, " 'Till Death Do Us Part': Marriage and Family in Seventeenth-Century Maryland," in Thad W. Tate and David L. Ammerman, eds., *The Chesapeake in the Seventeenth Century: Essays on Anglo-American Society* (Chapel Hill, N.C., 1979), 126–128; Daniel Blake Smith, "The Study of the Family in Early America: Trends, Problems, and Prospects," *WMQ*, 3d Ser., XXXIX (1982), 5–10. See Darrett B. Rutman, "Assessing the Little Communities of Early America," *WMQ*, 3d Ser., XLIII (1986), 163–178, for an analysis of a multiplicity of local studies and an effort to find commonalities as well as processes of change that characterize the localities studied.

2. For New England, see Linda Auwers Bissell, "Family, Friends, and Neighbors: Social Interaction in Seventeenth-Century Windsor, Connecticut" (Ph.D. diss., Brandeis University, 1973), 139–144; for England, see James P. P. Horn, "Social and

neighborly networks, although certain occupations—for example, merchant, tradesman, and ordinarykeeper—and certain political offices encouraged contacts at greater distances. The seamless web of the debt structure bound together the society, as did the web of neighborly contacts.[3]

The restricted extent of individual ties reinforced a second cultural constant: a deeply ingrained and fiercely defended localism. Provincial life in seventeenth-century England was characterized by a marked insularity, which shielded locals from events in the larger world, at least until those events intruded themselves unavoidably. Thus, as in Virginia, the mass of provincial Englanders probably supported neither Charles I nor the Commonwealth. They became involved only when a decision was thrust on them. New England towns exhibited a heightened form of localism and insularity, even opposing their own central government when local concerns were in question.[4] In Virginia, localism reinforced efforts to expand the counties' jurisdiction at the expense of the governor, Council, and Assembly. On the Eastern Shore, the Northampton Protest of 1652 demonstrates a specific instance of a Virginia locality's attempting to assert an extraordinary claim of autonomy.

Economic Aspects of Local Society in England and the Chesapeake: A Comparative Study of the Vale of Berkeley, Gloucestershire, and the Lower Western Shore of Maryland, 1660–1700" (Ph.D. diss., University of Sussex, 1982), 291–294, 307; Horn, "Adapting to a New World: A Comparative Study of Local Society in England and Maryland, 1650–1700," 164–172, and Lorena S. Walsh, "Community Networks in the Early Chesapeake," 218–219, in Lois Green Carr, Philip D. Morgan, and Jean B. Russo, eds., *Colonial Chesapeake Society* (Chapel Hill, N.C., 1988). Darrett B. Rutman and Anita H. Rutman argue that these spatially restricted networks of kin and friends were particularly important to women, who lacked men's opportunities for economic and political contact, in *A Place in Time: Middlesex County, Virginia, 1650–1750* (New York, 1984), 104–113. The impact on emigration of neighborly ties in England has been examined by Anthony Salerno, "The Character of Emigration from Wiltshire to the American Colonies, 1630–1660" (Ph.D. diss., University of Virginia, 1977), 15, 18–19, 39–40.
3. James A. Henretta, "Families and Farms: Mentalité in Pre-Industrial America," *WMQ*, 3d Ser., XXXV (1978), 16; David Thomas Konig, *Law and Society in Puritan Massachusetts: Essex County, 1629–1692* (Chapel Hill, N.C., 1979), 84; Horn, "Social and Economic Aspects of Local Society in England and the Chesapeake," 326, 332–334; Walsh, "Community Networks in the Early Chesapeake," in Carr, Morgan, and Russo, eds., *Colonial Chesapeake Society*, 226–227.
4. Alan Everitt, "Change in the Provinces: The Seventeenth Century," Leicester University Department of English Local History, *Occasional Papers*, 2d Ser., no. 1 (Leicester, 1969), 35, 46–52; Steven D. Crow, " 'Your Majesty's Good Subjects': A Reconsideration of Royalism in Virginia, 1642–1652," *VMHB*, LXXXVII (1979), 158–173. For New England, see T. H. Breen, "Persistent Localism: English Social

But the more successful a locality was in insulating itself, the more important was the effective exercise of local authority. In England, the most important source of local authority was the commission of the peace issued to justices. As with commissioners in Virginia, justices of the peace in England were scattered throughout the population and given authority to act out of court sittings. This brought convenient redress of minor offenses directly to the people and spared them the inconvenience of attending court sessions. The judges also held court in different parts of the county in order to make justice more accessible, a practice that was followed in Massachusetts counties as well.[5]

The effectiveness of commissioners or justices of the peace rested on acceptance of their authority by their fellow countymen. For Virginia, it has been argued that a population of brutal, grasping, selfish individuals was governed by the most brutal, grasping, and selfish and that the result was political instability. This view received succinct formulation in Bernard Bailyn's enormously influential essay "Politics and Social Structure in Virginia" of the 1950s. Although Bailyn's primary concern was the shape of provincial politics, his brief comments about the people and local government of early seventeenth-century Virginia quickly became the framework within which others interpreted their research. Subsequent historians, looking for a quick sketch of early seventeenth-century Virginia society and politics or searching for a larger meaning for their own research, have found Bailyn's essay a convenient reference point. In 1975 Edmund S. Morgan, in his immensely important *American Society, American Freedom: The Ordeal of Colonial Virginia*, did much to revise Bailyn's depiction, but Morgan continued to see those who governed Virginia before the Restoration as "ruthless."[6] Bailyn's view, now modi-

---

Change and the Shaping of New England Institutions," *WMQ*, 3d Ser., XXXII (1975), 3–28.

5. J. H. Gleason, *The Justices of the Peace in England, 1558–1640* (Oxford, 1969), 52–53, 59; Konig, *Law and Society in Puritan Massachusetts*, 13, 32–33.

6. Bernard Bailyn, "Politics and Social Structure in Virginia," in James Morton Smith, ed., *Seventeenth-Century America: Essays in Colonial History* (Chapel Hill, N.C., 1959), 90–115, but esp. 94–98. Bailyn's argument was provocative but thinly documented. For example, see his comments about poor attendance at court on the Eastern Shore during the 1630s (96) and compare them with the attendance rate cited in table 20, above. Bailyn was not the first to describe Virginia society in unflattering terms. Charles M. Andrews, although noting that his view was biased because based entirely on court records, wrote anyway that Virginia society was characterized by quarreling, abusive language, fistfighting, slander, heavy drinking, and fornication. Charles M. Andrews, *The Colonial Period of American History*, I, *The Settlements* (1934; reprint ed., New Haven, Conn., 1964), 212–213. The most recent challenge to

fied and balanced by Morgan's, has been the prevailing orthodoxy even through the 1980s. The most persistent advocate of this view of Virginia society and politics has been T. H. Breen. In "Looking out for Number One: Conflicting Cultural Values in Early Seventeenth-Century Virginia," Breen limned in harsh tones a violent society of selfish individualists, the more successful of whom exploited their dependents and undermined trust in political authority. As a result, Breen viewed Virginia society as extremely fragile and prone to unrest.[7]

Bailyn's argument is Jon Kukla, "Order and Chaos in Early America: Political and Social Stability in Pre-Restoration Virginia," *American Historical Review*, XC (1985), 275–298, where he presents evidence for the development of "a stable indigenous political order" (297) in pre-Restoration Virginia.

The accommodation to Bailyn's view began immediately with William H. Seiler, "The Anglican Parish in Virginia," which appeared with Bailyn's essay in Morton, ed., *Seventeenth-Century America*, 129. Warren M. Billings, in his valuable analysis of the accretion of power to the county courts, interpreted his results in light of Bailyn's thesis, in "The Growth of Political Institutions in Virginia, 1634 to 1676," *WMQ*, 3d Ser., XXXI (1974), 225–226.

Edmund S. Morgan, *American Slavery, American Freedom: The Ordeal of Colonial Virginia* (New York, 1975); see esp. chap. 7, "Settling Down." It seems strange that 17th-century Virginians should be branded as "ruthless" in part because they de- manded "deference from their inferiors" (148); deference was the underpinning of authority in the English-speaking world of the 17th century.

7. For examples of the prevailing view, see Nicholas Canny, "The Permissive Fron- tier: The Problem of Social Control in English Settlements in Ireland and Virginia, 1550–1650," and Warren M. Billings, "The Transfer of English Law to Virginia, 1606–1650," both in K. R. Andrews *et al.*, eds., *The Westward Enterprise: English Activities in Ireland, the Atlantic, and Americas, 1480–1650* (Detroit, 1979), 40– 42, 244. For another summary and refutation of this orthodoxy, see Lois Green Carr, "Sources of Political Stability and Upheaval in Seventeenth-Century Maryland," *MHM*, LXXIX (1984), 44–70.

T. H. Breen, "Looking out for Number One," *South Atlantic Quarterly*, LXXVIII (1979), 342–360. This same view permeated and helped shape the reading of evi- dence by Breen and Stephen Innes in *"Myne Owne Ground": Race and Freedom on Virginia's Eastern Shore, 1640–1676* (New York, 1980). Chap. 3 depicts a white society led by "fiercely independent people, competitive, materialistic, frequently tru- culent" (48). Some of these adjectives are pejorative versions of those used to praise the "ambition, energy, [and] perseverence" (78) of blacks as described in chap. 4. This latter chapter, based on the full range of county court records through Bacon's Rebel- lion, traces the development of African-American society and culture. Chap. 3, on the other hand, clearly is based on a cursory reading of the county record, with almost all citations to the two volumes of court records that have been published. Perhaps a closer reading of the entire court record would have resulted in a less negative view of white society on the Eastern Shore. William L. Shea, at the same time that he notes evidence refuting Breen's depiction, cites *"Myne Owne Ground"* as the "currently accepted view of early Chesapeake society," in *The Virginia Militia in the Seventeenth Century* (Baton Rouge, La., 1983), 71. For a thorough and balanced view of black society on the Eastern Shore, see Joseph Douglas Deal III, "Race and Class in Colo-

Clearly the society described thus far on the Eastern Shore does not resemble that projected by Bailyn and Breen. Far from being an anarchy of selfish individualists, society on the Eastern Shore was characterized by a complex network linking kin, friends, and neighbors in a web of sociability, favors, and economic exchange. In addition, the institutions of church and court served to draw people beyond the more narrow confines of their personal networks. Most important for local stability, colonists on the Eastern Shore accepted the authority of the local governing establishment.

The point needs to be stressed that Englishmen of the seventeenth century believed that, without recognized authority, there would be no public peace. And public peace and order—the prerequisites for a well-ordered society—were the prime concerns of the county court. The establishment in the Chesapeake of county courts that successfully maintained peace and order provided the framework within which society could function.[8] Even in New England, county courts began to serve the same purpose when adherence to original communal goals weakened, towns grew and became more diversified, and disputes required a forum for resolution. More and more during the seventeenth century, courts there played a role in defining and maintaining standards of behavior. Thus, by the end of the century, New England was coming to rely on the authority of courts and the law as guarantors of peace and order. Virginia had done so from the beginning.[9]

----

nial Virginia: Indians, Englishmen, and Africans on the Eastern Shore during the Seventeenth Century" (Ph.D. diss., University of Rochester, 1981), chap. 3.

8. John C. Rainbolt, "The Absence of Towns in Seventeenth-Century Virginia," *Journal of Southern History*, XXXV (1969), 346; Clara Ann Bowler, "Carted Whores and White-Shrouded Apologies: Slander in the County Courts of Seventeenth-Century Virginia," *VMHB*, LXXXV (1977), 421, 425; Lois Green Carr, "The Foundations of Social Order: Local Government in Colonial Maryland," in Bruce C. Daniels, ed., *Town and County: Essays on the Structure of Local Government in the American Colonies* (Middletown, Conn., 1978), 91; Warren M. Billings, "English Legal Literature as a Source of Law and Legal Practice for Seventeenth-Century Virginia," *VMHB*, LXXXVII (1979), 406; Konig, *Law and Society in Puritan Massachusetts*, 13–14. See also Virginia Bernhard, "Poverty and the Social Order in Seventeenth-Century Virginia," *VMHB*, LXXXV (1977), 141–155.

9. David Thomas Konig, "Community Custom and the Common Law: Social Change and the Development of Land Law in Seventeenth-Century Massachusetts," *American Journal of Legal History*, XVIII (1974), 137–177; Konig, *Law and Society in Puritan Massachusetts*, xii–xiii, 29, 65, 188–191; David Grayson Allen, *In English Ways: The Movement of Societies and the Transferal of English Local Law and Custom to Massachusetts Bay in the Seventeenth Century* (Chapel Hill, N.C., 1981),

But courts were not the only source of order in the Chesapeake. Although lacking a communal goal, colonists there shared with New Englanders a common English reliance on informal mechanisms to maintain a locally defined peace and order. The goal was to foster a climate where personal relationships could thrive and to avoid conflict or contain it when it occurred. This goal was frequently achieved at the expense of a more formal sense of order as expressed in statutes. Thus locals overlooked minor breaches of the law—for example, drunkenness unless it disrupted court sessions or Sabbath observance. Or they sought local solutions to minor infractions by referring them to arbitration out of court, thus saving themselves the expense of a court hearing and the heightened disruption of local peace. Conformity to an impersonal law was far less important than the maintenance of local order and peace.[10] The operation of this informal process in conjunction with the success of neighborly oversight in bringing breaches of local order to court served to maintain local peace on the Eastern Shore and elsewhere in the Chesapeake and New England.[11] It is worth noting in this context that the open country Chesapeake settlement pattern, rather than undermining local peace and order by giving free rein to individual will, may actually have promoted peace and order by keeping some distance between set-

---

221–222, 242. For a perceptive account of the transition from this conception of the county court as keeper of the peace to a bureaucratic model of county government, see Hendrik Hartog, "The Public Law of a County Court: Judicial Government in Eighteenth-Century Massachusetts," *Am. Jour. Leg. Hist.*, XX (1976), 282–329. In some areas of New England, a communal goal did not exist from the beginning; see Christine Leigh Heyrman, *Commerce and Culture: The Maritime Communities of Colonial Massachusetts, 1690–1750* (New York, 1984), 15–20, 27–51, 207–230.

10. See esp. Keith Wrightson, "Two Concepts of Order: Justices, Constables, and Jurymen in Seventeenth-Century England," in John Brewer and John Styles, eds., *An Ungovernable People: The English and Their Law in the Seventeenth and Eighteenth Centuries* (New Brunswick, N.J., 1980), 24–25, 29–31, 45–46. See also G. R. Quaife, *Wanton Wenches and Wayward Wives: Peasants and Illicit Sex in Early Seventeenth-Century England* (New Brunswick, N.J., 1979), 16; J. A. Sharpe, "Enforcing the Law in the Seventeenth-Century English Village," in V.A.C. Gatrell *et al.*, eds., *Crime and the Law: The Social History of Crime in Western Europe since 1500* (London, 1980), 99, 117–118.

11. See Chapter 4, above. See also George B. Curtis, "The Colonial County Court, Social Forum and Legislative Precedent: Accomack, Virginia, 1633–1639," *VMHB*, LXXXV (1977), 248; David H. Flaherty, "Law and the Enforcement of Morals in Early America," *Perspectives in American History*, V (1971), 241–242, 244–245; Carr, "Sources of Political Stability and Upheaval," *MHM*, LXXIX (1984), 52; Walsh, "Community Networks in the Early Chesapeake," in Carr, Morgan, and Russo, eds., *Colonial Chesapeake Society*, 231–232, 236–241.

tlers who lacked the communal goals of their New England brethren. There is some evidence of this phenomenon on the Eastern Shore, where more slanders and land disputes seem to have occurred in the earliest and densest area of settlement around Cherrystone, King's, and Old Plantation creeks. The dispersed settlement pattern did not prevent contact and the development of local standards of behavior, but it did allow a salutary privacy compared to the situation in New England towns.

It is relevant at this point to refocus on the question that began this study of the Eastern Shore. What formed the basis of social cohesion at the local level in Virginia during the first generation following the dissolution of the Virginia Company? Clearly, the societal web formed by the interweaving of individual kinship, friendship, neighborhood, and economic networks was crucial. Claiming land in a contiguous pattern created the precondition for these networks. Blood relationships, sociability, support structures, and exchange contacts bound the landholders together. As people patented land more and more distant from the original area of settlement, institutional development—especially of the county court and church—accommodated this growth and provided a focus for individuals outside the normal network of personal contacts. These institutions were accepted and supported because many inhabitants were involved in their operation and because they performed their functions responsibly. In turn, these institutions provided a stable setting within which personal networks could flourish, an arena for the resolution of conflicts that could not be settled otherwise.

Did a growing sense of "community"—an attachment to a local collective—accompany the development of the societal web and authoritative local institutions? Unlike many New England towns, primary sources for the Eastern Shore in the early seventeenth century are too limited to attempt a definitive answer. But evidence is not altogether lacking. One such indicator is the contiguous spread of settlement. In view of the absence of restrictions on where acreage could be claimed, it is not insignificant that the settlers claimed land next to one another. Although the settlement pattern was not nuclear as in New England, it did not preclude contact and the development of a societal web and communal ties.[12]

12. Other historians have overemphasized the isolation of settlers in Virginia. Some have assumed that a nonnuclear settlement hindered the development of a sense of community: Breen and Innes, *"Myne Owne Ground,"* 40; Breen, "Looking out for Number One," *SAQ,* LXXVIII (1979), 347, 358–359; Morgan, *American Slavery, American Freedom,* 150. Darrett Rutman and Anita Rutman provide a valuable cor-

Another indicator of the development of a sense of community is the use of the word "stranger" in different contexts, all suggesting an effort to distinguish "outsiders" from "insiders." The word appears in the court record to describe the relationship between inhabitants on the Eastern Shore and other Englishmen not resident. Thus, Robert Warder, described in 1642 as a stranger, requested Andrew Jacob to act as a witness to a conversation with a third party. More explicit is an order of the court in 1653 that noted "Jno. Edwards . . . is a stranger in this County his residence beinge over the Baye."[13] Having identified their position vis-à-vis nonresident Englishmen, inhabitants went one step further and defined all foreigners, whether resident or nonresident, as strangers.[14] Locally resident Englishmen, having set up a boundary separating nonresidents and foreigners, could more easily shape the local culture of acceptable behavior.

Inhabitants on the peninsula molded their local culture within the framework of noninstitutional networks as well as institutional controls. Those who persistently violated these norms or perpetrated some heinous offense were ostracized or even banished. Consider the history of John Little. Arriving on the Eastern Shore in 1629 when he was twenty years old, Little does not seem to have acquired land of his own until 1639. By that time he had already appeared before the court on a charge of fornication with another man's servant, although the evidence had not been sufficient to convict him. During the 1640s, Little compiled a rich record of antisocial behavior, including slander, profanity, and brawling. His inability to get along with his fellows may have suggested his move to the peninsula's seaside. But he could not escape the effects of his own temper. In 1652 he was fined for slandering Commissioner John Stringer, with whom he had earlier been involved in litigation. By 1655 Little, unable to conform to the required behavior, left the county and moved to Maryland.[15]

---

rective to this view in *A Place in Time: Middlesex County,* 59–60; so too does Walsh, in "Community Networks in the Early Chesapeake," in Carr, Morgan, and Russo, eds., *Colonial Chesapeake Society,* 200–241.

13. CCR-4, fol. 166–p. 167. See also CCR-2, pp. 69–70, 221, CCR-3, fol. 235–p. 236, CCR-4, fol. 164, CCR-5, page preceding fol. 1.

14. CCR-4, fol. 146, CCR-5, fol. 120–fol. 121, fol. 122.

15. CCR-1, pp. 19, 20, 33, 35, CCR-2, pp. 15, 189–190, 317, 396–397, 414, CCR-3, fol. 173, p. 177, p. 178–fol. 178, CCR-4, pp. 99, 141, fol. 141–p. 142, CCR-5, fol. 145, CCR-7, fol. 43; Nell Marion Nugent, ed., *Cavaliers and Pioneers: Abstracts of Virginia Land Patents and Grants,* I, 1623–1666, II, 1666–1695 (Richmond, Va., 1934, 1977), I, 170. Little's contentiousness continued following his move

The history of Thomas Parks was even more stormy and far briefer. First mentioned in 1643, Parks appeared before the commissioners for an incredible string of offenses during the next four years: slandering Commissioner Argoll Yardley on two separate occasions, killing hogs belonging to Andrew Jacob as well as insulting him, slandering Commissioner Obedience Robins, encouraging servants to disobey and run away from their masters, "entertaining" a female servant of Phillip Taylor, abusing a jury, and slandering the court. It can be surmised that most of his fellow residents were glad to see him move off the Eastern Shore.[16]

Whether Little and Parks left voluntarily or under duress, it is known that on other occasions individuals in violation of local patterns of behavior were banished. All known banishments were for immoral behavior. In 1647 and 1648 Richard Buckland was punished, following the complaints of his wife, Mary, for his sexual misconduct with Mary Russell. But Buckland seems to have returned on occasion and made demands on his wife's small savings. Finally, in 1655, following the deaths of Mary Russell and the bastard son she had borne, Buckland returned to his legal wife, who petitioned the court for a divorce. The commissioners granted her request and ordered that Richard be whipped and banished. His actions were definitely beyond the bounds of acceptable behavior. So too were Mary Powell's "scandalous, abusive speeches" against the minister and Ann Gardner's "Actions lyfe and Conversation," which marked her as "a most infamous incorrigible woman." Both Powell and Gardner were banished.[17]

Because local cultural norms were defined in the mutual give-and-take between individuals within the societal network, it was crucial that settlers on the Eastern Shore be a part of the web of contacts. To exist outside or on the fringes of that network increased the danger of an individual's committing some unacceptable act. When John Culpepper was convicted and punished for hog stealing, he was asked to name any accomplices. He thereupn implicated John Greene, "a lone man," who had encouraged Culpepper to kill hogs and steal pumpkins. It may have been the threat posed by such free agents as Greene that made John

---

to Maryland; see Mary Beth Norton, "Gender and Defamation in Seventeenth-Century Maryland," *WMQ*, 3d Ser., XLIV (1987), 16–17.

16. CCR-2, pp. 313–314, 315, 351, 383, 392–393, 395, CCR-3, fol. 2, pp. 5, 16, fol. 37. References to Parks stop abruptly, and there are no indications that he died.

17. Buckland: CCR-3, p. 121, fol. 160, CCR-4, p. 156–fol. 156, CCR-7, p. 9, fol. 16. Mary Buckland remarried almost immediately following the divorce (CCR-7, fol. 8). Powell and Gardner: CCR-5, p. 23, CCR-6, p. 3.

Johnson free Robert Watson only on the condition that Watson live with his brother or "any other man (whereby hee might injoye the benefitt of a freeman)."[18] The equation and its implication were clear. To "injoye the benefitt of a freeman" was to play a role in the decision making that shaped the local society. But to exercise this benefit meant that one had to be an integral part of that society, not alone, and subject to the effective oversight of others. With participation came privileges as well as rules and supervision.

This is not to deny that conflicts occurred. Conflict between servants and masters, arguments over economic transactions, land disputes, theft, and slander are all amply recorded in the court record. But it is important to note that they occurred within an institutional structure designed to contain the potential for their escalation into a socially destabilizing situation.

The most severe test for these institutions came during the early 1650s, when the Eastern Shore underwent several potentially disruptive changes. During those years, a land boom, fueled by an increase in immigration and a favorable tobacco market, rapidly pushed the edge of settlement north of Occohannock Creek. From 1651 through 1655, the amount of land patented increased 339 percent over the figure from 1646 through 1650. The median size of these patents increased to 500 acres from 450 acres in the five preceding years. Some of the land patented was not contiguous with land patented earlier.[19] New landholders totaled 113, compared to 82 from 1646 to 1650. The surge of development upset the status quo with the Eastern Shore Indians, and the commissioners disagreed about how to manage the resulting conflict. With help from James City, the commission settled on a policy and healed its division.

But this was not the end of the commission's problems. In early 1652 it had to face the governmental crisis precipitated by Virginia's surrender to parliamentary control. The terms of surrender were quite favorable to Virginia, and the residents on the Eastern Shore seized this time of transition in James City to try to gain an extraordinary degree of autonomy by filing the Northampton Protest. Although they did not win everything

18. CCR-1, pp. 47–48, CCR-4, fol. 47.
19. Balancing the disruptive impact of this growth, some of it undoubtedly speculative, was the fact that the amount of first landholding remained steady and that the overwhelming majority of new landholders still chose acreage contiguous to that held earlier. Furthermore, the median number of years in the record before first landholding ranged from seven to nine years.

they wanted, they gained significant concessions that probably strengthened the position of the local commission. At the same time as the signing of the Northampton Protest, the commission decided to meet in a single location, possibly in an effort to unify the county by forcing attendance at a single place. But concurrently, two vestries were appointed to serve the two parishes on the peninsula, a significant division of the church establishment and one that recognized the impossibility of a single parish's serving the rapidly growing and expanding population.

Within a year, the war against the Dutch and the seizure of ships in the waters off the Eastern Shore split the commission. A few commissioners around Occohannock Creek and to the north supported Edmund Scarburgh and his efforts to seize vessels in local waters. Most of the commissioners south of there were opposed to these actions, not only because of the doubtful legality of the seizures but also because the perpetrators threatened the large Dutch-born population on the Eastern Shore. This feud between northern and southern commissioners became entangled in demands for a division of the county, reflecting the increasing size of the settled part of the peninsula and the difficulty of accommodating the institutions of church and court to the increased demands. Those in the northern part of the county filed a complaint in James City in 1653, but it was quickly denounced as treasonous by the colony's leaders. A special board was dispatched to the Eastern Shore to resolve outstanding disputes. The board, led by the governor in July 1653, did resolve the disagreement concerning ship seizures, but it decided that the court, instead of meeting in one place, should meet in three, including a sitting at Occohannock Creek. Some of the commissioners tried to return to a single place of sitting in early 1654, but the Assembly the next year formally divided sittings again, this time specifying a division at Hungars Creek with the court to alternate sittings north and south of that waterway.

To divide the commission in this way was to some extent a de facto division of the county. It would not be too many years before a de jure division occurred.[20] Disagreements between the southern and northern commissioners, the latter led by the indomitable Edmund Scarburgh, undoubtedly played some part in the ultimate split of the county.[21] In

20. For an account of the division, reunion, and redivision of the Eastern Shore, see Susie M. Ames, "The Reunion of Two Virginia Counties," *Journal of Southern History*, VIII (1942), 536–548.

21. Breen and Innes choose Edmund Scarburgh—an altogether unique figure on the Eastern Shore—as their exemplar of the ruling elite. The conclusions they base

fact, Scarburgh may have taken advantage of the death of many of the old commissioners to impose his will on the remaining. Between 1654 and 1657, Nathaniel Littleton, Stephen Charlton, Argoll Yardley, William Andrews, and Edward Douglas, all of whom had been appointed before or during 1642, died. So too did Peter Walker, Richard Vaughan, and Thomas Hunt. Of these men, only Richard Vaughan lived north of Occohannock Creek. One lived on Nuswattocks Creek, two on Hungars, and the remaining four even further south on the peninsula. But it was the death in 1662 of Obedience Robins, the only commissioner who had seniority over Scarburgh, that gave the latter the opportunity to make his move the following year. Yet such infighting should not be overemphasized. An informal division within the commission had existed as early as the 1640s, when the attendance rate among commissioners had dropped and the tendency for commissioners to attend meetings only near their homes was already evident. These developments were to a large extent the result of the same sort of population increase and geographic spread of settlement that prompted divisions within other Chesapeake counties.[22]

It is easy to see the sort of conflict that occurred on the Eastern Shore as destabilizing. But such a conclusion is too facile. Disagreements within the commission were not incompatible with social stability. The important point is that, even when the court was most divided, it continued to function and continued to command the respect and obedience of those governed. Virginia's county governments were not characterized by "chaotic factionalism," nor were they socially destabilizing. Factions there were, but not chaos, either political or social. Elsewhere in the Chesapeake, it has been observed that local institutions continued to function adequately to maintain social order even when political disorder seemed most acute.[23]

---

on their analysis of his unusually unruly and unrepresentative career are therefore flawed. *"Myne Owne Ground,"* 49–52.

22. Wesley Frank Craven, *The Southern Colonies in the Seventeenth Century, 1607–1689* (1949; reprint ed., Baton Rouge, La., 1970), 270. After the Eastern Shore was divided into two counties in 1663, it was reunited briefly. It is worth noting that, during the period of reunion, there was difficulty in forming courts because of the distances to be traveled. Ames, "Reunion of Two Virginia Counties," *Jour. So. Hist.,* VIII (1942), 543.

23. In 1974 Warren Billings published "The Growth of Political Institutions in Virginia, 1634 to 1676," *WMQ,* 3d Ser., XXXI (1974), a valuable study of the rise of local government in Virginia. But his effort to document "chaotic factionalism" within the counties led to some poorly substantiated assertions and strained readings of evidence. "Chaotic factionalism" rests on the assertion that, as time passed, there

In sum, the settlers who came to the Chesapeake brought with them certain cultural attributes that were common to the English-speaking world of the seventeenth century and that helped to shape their local societies. First, the individual networks of those within the societal web were spatially restricted, a feature shared by the societies of the Chesapeake, England, and New England. This feature served to magnify a marked localism within English culture. At the local level, peace and order were fostered by the development of effective institutions, which earned the respect that their exercise of authority required. And, finally, informal mechanisms of social control and conflict resolution supplemented the official institutions. Together these features laid the groundwork for social stability and a sense of community. Even in the Chesapeake, where individualism was accepted more than in New England, a counterbalancing sense of belonging to a larger social whole was evident.[24] Despite the potential for political conflict and infighting, social stability was assured as long as recognized authority was exercised by someone. This resilience can be seen in developments on the Eastern Shore, where an effective exercise of authority allowed for, and in turn depended on, a continuing, ever-elaborating local societal web. For an area with no initial communal purpose, settled primarily by individuals rather than by families, and lacking the advantage of religious and political institutions overlapping in a small territory, this was a considerable achievement.

---

were not enough positions on the county courts to absorb the number of individuals seeking appointment (225–226, 240–242). The problem with this assertion is that Billings never establishes convincingly that there was such a competition for seats. The economic advantages cited (236) were available as well to those not commissioners. Furthermore, any advantage of sitting on the commission could be gained also by those with ties to those on the bench, a point that Billings himself makes (241). Billings assumes that "Virginia society was extremely fragile" (242) by positing that Virginia's institutions did not provide the settlers "a sense that change was occurring within an orderly and gradually evolving framework." Billings's own research, as well as that presented here, refutes this assertion.

For elsewhere in the Chesapeake, see Carr, "The Foundations of Social Order," in Daniels, ed., *Town and County*, 90–91; Carr, "Sources of Political Stability and Upheaval," *MHM*, LXXIX (1984), 62–63.

24. Breen overemphasizes the extent to which individualism ruled the lives of Virginians; "Looking out for Number One," *SAQ*, LXXVIII (1979), 342–360. Here, Breen focuses on the period before 1630, but argues for the persistence of "extreme individualism" and a consequent fragility of the social system even after that period (358–360). For an intriguing analysis of the concepts of individualism and community in 17th-century English culture, see Michael Zuckerman, "The Fabrication of Identity in Early America," *WMQ*, 3d Ser., XXXIV (1977), 183–214.

Index

courtroom behavior, 203–204; and English Civil War, 208, 214, 219–220; and Charles II, 209n; and Eastern Shore Indians, 211–212, 235; selection of, 214; and ship seizures, 218–219, 220–221, 236; complaint against, 220–223, 224, 236. *See also* County court

County court records: as sources, 6, 8, 9, 41, 53, 133; conflicts in, 76, 235; contacts between relatives in, 76, 77; economic contacts in, 76, 124, 126; responses to death in, 77, 83; personal contacts in, 90, 194; establishment of, 127n; tobacco warehouses in, 140; mercantile activity in, 145–147; nonlandholding resident merchants in, 153; contacts outside Eastern Shore in, 160

Cowdery, Benjamin, 109

Craddock Creek, 37

Cradock, Lieutenant, 15

Crime. *See* Accusations of wrongdoing; Assault; Banishment; Brawling; Contempt of court; Disturbing the peace; Drunkenness; Illegitimacy; Immoral behavior; Slander; Social control; Swearing

Crowdie, Thomas, 150, 158n

Cudgley, Pattricke, 104

Cugley, Daniel, 93, 99, 100, 126–127, 203

Cugley, Hannah Savage, 23, 93n, 99, 100n, 126

Cugley, Margery, 86, 99–100

Culpepper, John, 234

Cursonstam, Aaron, 138

Custis, Ann. *See* Yardley, Ann (Custis)

Custis, John, 55, 71, 74, 152, 155

Dale, David, 53, 95

Dale, Mrs. David. *See* Dale, Elizabeth Neale

Dale, Lady Elizabeth, 24, 36n, 98

Dale, Elizabeth Neale, 53, 95, 156n

Dale, Sir Thomas, 13, 24, 36n

Deacon, Thomas, 154

Death. *See* Mortality

De Boll, John Clawse, 151

Debt, 173, 227

Defense, 22, 28, 174, 189–191

Delaware Bay, 144, 147

Denham, William, 81

Denham, Mrs. William, 81

Denwood, Levin, 92, 172

Derrickson, Jacob, 151n

Derrickson, Syvert, 151n

De Vries, David Pietersz., 144, 145, 146

Disturbing the peace, 216

Diversification. *See* Economic development

Dixon, Ambrose, 45n

Dixon, John, 93n, 136, 141, 177

Doctors, 54

Dodsworth, Philip, 153

Dolby, John, 103

Dorman, John, 75

Doughty, Ann (Graves) Cotton Eaton, 71, 184, 185n, 187n

Doughty, Francis, 185n, 187

Douglas, Edward (father), 98, 237

Douglas, Edward (son), 98

Douglas, Elizabeth, 98

Douglas, Sarah, 98

Dowdridge, Susanna, 107–108

Drake, Robert, 49

Drew, Edward, 92, 93–94, 102–103, 116n, 154

Drew, Mary. *See* Stranguidge, Mary Drew

Drunkenness, 203

Eastern Shore: definition of, 6n, 8; and network analysis, 8; geography of, 8; historiography of, 8; sources for study of, 8, 232; establishment of counties on, 9, 40, 223–224, 236, 237n; representativeness of, 9; exploration of, 12, 13, 15; demography of, 41, 226; mortality on, 77–79, 83, 146. *See also* Landholding;

Population; Settlement
Eaton, Ann. *See* Doughty, Ann
(Graves) Cotton Eaton
Eaton, Nathaniel, 55, 184–185
Economic contacts: geographic dispersion of, 116–127, 139–140; effect
of occupation on, 117–120, 127,
143, 193, 226–227; of county court
commissioners, 117–125, 143, 196;
of merchants, 117–125, 143, 226–
227; effect of mobility on, 124–
125; effect of kinship ties on, 126;
role of stores in, 139–140; role of
ordinaries in, 141, 143; extent of,
143, 193, 226–227; outside Eastern
Shore, 144, 147, 149, 154, 158; importance of, to social cohesion, 230,
232. *See also* Trade
Economic development, 15–17, 19
Economy, 48, 226. *See also* Trade
Edwards, John, 233
Ellis, John, 103, 174–175
Emigration from Eastern Shore, 161–
162
England: Persistence rates of landholders in, 64; trade with, 144, 147,
148, 149, 217; contacts with, 149,
160; justices of the peace in, 199–
200, 228; reaction to slander in,
201–202; relations with, 205, 206,
210, 212–214, 235; war of, with
Holland, 217, 236; social culture in,
226–228, 230, 238
English Civil War, 148, 206–210,
212–214, 217, 235–236
English Commonwealth, 174, 206,
227. *See also* English Civil War
Epes, William, 25, 26, 27, 162, 164
Estates, administration of, 79–80, 82–
83, 92, 93–95, 102–103
Evans, Kathryne, 94n
Evans, Thomas, 94n
Evans, Welthiana, 94n
Eveling, Dorothy (Robins), 72, 73,
108
Eveling, Mountjoy, 73

Executors, 102–103
Executrices, 79–80

Fame (ship), 218, 220–221
Farewell (ship), 151
Favors, 74–75, 92–93, 95, 194. *See
also* Gifts
Fences, 110
Feoffees-in-trust, 102
Ferries, 44, 46
Fish, 12, 13, 15
Fisher, John, 85
Fisher, Philip, 85
Fisher, Stephen, 85
Fishing. *See* Fish
Fleet, Henry, 145, 146
Flood, Mrs. Frances, 72
Foscutt, Simon, 106, 136
Foster, Armstrong, 75, 106, 108, 109
Foster, Bridgett. *See* Billiott, Bridgett
Foster
Foster, John, 75
Frethorne, Richard, 22n

Games, Ann, 75
Games, Mary, 75
Gardner, Ann, 234
Gascoyne, Thomas, 111
Gayny, William, 36n
General Assembly, Virginia: election
of burgesses to, 182; representation
of Eastern Shore in, 215, 223; and
complaint against county court
commissioners, 221, 224; in relation to local government, 227
—legislation of: on orphans, 87, 88;
on land records, 112n; on tobacco
warehouses, 140; on town development, 141; on county court, 165–
166, 176, 178, 224, 236; on county
court commissioners, 173, 176,
178, 179–180, 195, 215–216; on
election of burgesses, 182; on
churches, 183, 185, 186, 194–195,
209; on location of public facilities,
188n; on militias, 189; on local

government, 194–195; on English
Civil War, 209; on government au-
thority, 209; in support of Virginia
Company, 209n; on disturbing the
peace, 216; defense, 222; on ship
seizures, 222
General Court, Virginia, 164, 165
Gibbons, Edward, 158, 159
Gibbons, Oliver, 208–209, 210
Gifts, 74–75, 93–94. *See also* Favors
Godparents, 97–99, 196
Goldsmith, Samuel, 180–181, 191
Government, local: importance of, to
social cohesion, 5, 7, 228, 237; under Virginia Company, 18, 20, 27;
effect of dissolution of Virginia
Company on, 164–165; effect of
immigration on, 164–165; effect of
population growth on, 165, 166–
172, 175, 176, 181, 194–195, 236,
237; establishment of county court
for, 165–166; effect of geographic
expansion on, 175, 176, 181, 194–
195, 236, 237; legislation of Virginia General Assembly on, 194–
195; and slander, 201–202; importance of authority to, 201; relations
of, with James City, 206–207; effect
of English Civil War on, 212–214,
235–236; challenge to, 217, 219,
220–223, 224. *See also* County
court; County court commissioners
Gowers, William, 92
Granger, Nicholas, 74, 108
Graves, Ann. *See* Doughty, Ann
(Graves) Cotton Eaton
Graves, Thomas, 71, 165n
Graves, Verlinda. *See* Stone, Verlinda
(Graves)
Greene, John, 234
Greening, William, 44
Gyles, Daniel, 220

Hammon, Mark, 106
Hammond, John, 92, 114–115, 173
Hamor, Ralph, 13–15

Hanser, Richard. *See* Hensfield, Roger
Harlow, Elizabeth, 94
Harlow, John, 94, 106, 116n
Harmanson, Thomas, 77
Harmar, Ann. *See* Littleton, Ann
Harmar
Harmar, Charles, 36n, 98
Hartry, Elias, 96–97
Harvey, Gov. John, 205–206
Harwood, Nicholas, 102
Hatton, Thomas, 202
Hawis, Reginald, 87, 88
Headright system, 18
Henfield, Robert, 218
Hensfield, Roger, 45n
Hensley, William, 134–135
Herle, Randall, 51n
Higby, Ann Wilkins, 187n
Higby, Thomas, 187, 205
Hill, Richard, 42, 92, 138
Hinman, John, 51n, 74, 86, 136
Hinman, Sarah Smith, 70, 74, 96, 136
*History and Present State of Virginia,
The* (Beverley), 3
Hodgskins, Anthony, 140, 141, 215n,
216n, 222n, 223
Holland, John, 158
Holland: trade with, 144, 147, 148,
149, 150, 217, 219; war of, with
England, 217, 236
Holloway, John, 91, 95–96, 136
Hookings, Ann, 94
Horses, 42–43, 46, 125, 148. *See also*
Livestock
Horsey, Stephen, 87n, 174–175, 186n,
220, 221
Howe, Daniel, 218, 221
Howe, John, 161
Hudson, Jonathan, 92
Hudson, Richard, 115, 203
Hungars Creek: settlement along, 36–
37; bridges over, 43; ferries on, 44;
as location of county court meet-
ings, 176, 177, 223, 236; as bound-
ary of Eastern Shore jurisdictions,
179; as polling place, 182n; loca-
tion of church on, 184n

Rosier, John, 183–186
Russell, Charles, 94n
Russell, John, 94n
Russell, Mary, 94n, 234
Rutman, Darrett B., 6–7
Rutter, John, 85n

Salt, 12, 13, 15. *See also* Saltworks
Saltworks, 15, 17, 19–20. *See also* Salt
Sancta Maria (ship), 157
Sanders, Frances. *See* Burdett, Frances Blower Sanders
Sanders, Roger, 82
Sandys, George, 22
Savage, Hannah. *See* Cugley, Hannah Savage
Savage, John: disputes of, with Thomas Savage, 76, 105; as guardian of Margaret Cugley, 86, 100; relatives of, 76, 86, 99, 105; personal contacts of, 91, 93; and John Webster, 86n, 99; economic contacts of, 116n
Savage, Jonathan, 134
Savage, Thomas (cousin of John Savage): disputes of, with John Savage, 76, 105
Savage, Thomas (father of John Savage): landholding of, 23, 24, 36n, 47, 49, 186; wife of, 23
Savery, Rowland, 151
Scarburgh, Charles, 51
Scarburgh, Edmund: landholding of, 36, 55; travel by, 42, 159, 161, 222, 223; daughter of, 55; relatives of, 55, 75, 221; as surveyor, 75, 112; economic contacts of, 93, 138, 159, 220, 222; as attorney for nonresident merchants, 150n; and dispute with Thomas Teackle, 187; and attacks on Eastern Shore Indians, 211; and other county court commissioners, 211, 219, 220–222, 224, 236–237; as burgess, 215n; as county court commissioner, 215n, 218, 221, 223, 224, 236–237; and

ship seizures, 218–219, 220, 236; flight of, from Eastern Shore, 222, 223; return of, 223
Scarburgh, Tabitha. *See* Smart, Tabitha (Scarburgh)
Scott, Nicholas, 142n
Scott, Walter, 102
Seaside, 36
Selby, Elizabeth, 210n
Selby, Tobias, 210n
Servants: presence of, in county court records, 9, 41; study of, 9; background of, 46; motivations of, 46; acquisition of land by, 53; length of residence of, 53; relatives as, 75; support of, 81; abuse of, 106–108; access of, to county court commissioners, 173
Settlement: geographic expansion of, 8, 36–37, 39, 46, 165, 166, 194; under Virginia Company, 8, 15, 20–21, 22–25; effect of Eastern Shore Indians on, 9, 21, 38–40; effect of 1622 uprising on, 22, 28; effect of tobacco cultivation on, 23, 48, 68, 235; location of, 28, 29–30, 36–38, 39, 68, 165, 166, 193, 194, 232; effect of dissolution of Virginia Company on, 29–30; importance of waterways to, 37–38, 68, 193; and length of residency, 52–53, 69; effect of kinship ties on, 71, 73–74
Severne, Bridgett. *See* Charlton, Bridgett (Pott) Severne
Severne, Elizabeth (Chapman), 88, 96–97, 102
Severne, John, Jr., 86, 96–97, 102
Severne, John, Sr., 55n, 74, 76, 84, 86, 92, 96
Severne, Peter, 84
Sharecropping, 138–139
Sheriffs, 179–180, 199, 200
Shipbuilders, 45, 46. *See also* Carpenters; Tradesmen
Ship seizures, 218–219, 220–221, 222, 236

Vaughan, Grace Waltham, 84–85
Vaughan, John, 94n
Vaughan, Richard, 84–85, 103, 188n,
    222n, 237
Vestries, 183, 186–187, 195–196, 236
Vestrymen, 199, 200
Virginia: historiography of, 3–6;
    sources for study of, 6; trade with,
    144, 147, 149; contacts with, 160;
    and emigration from Eastern Shore,
    162; effect of dissolution of Virginia
    Company on, 206; relations of,
    with Parliament, 210. *See also* Gen-
    eral Assembly, Virginia; General
    Court, Virginia; James City; Vir-
    ginia Company
Virginia Assembly. *See* General Assem-
    bly, Virginia
Virginia Company: settlement under,
    8, 15, 20–21, 22–25; dissolution of,
    11, 29–30, 164–165, 206, 232;
    plans of, for Virginia, 11, 12; re-
    forms of, 12, 17–19, 22–23, 26;
    and economic development, 15–17,
    19; and tobacco cultivation, 17; and
    1622 uprising, 22, 28; legislation of
    Virginia General Assembly in sup-
    port of, 209n
Virginia General Assembly. *See* Gen-
    eral Assembly, Virginia
Virginia General Court. *See* General
    Court, Virginia
*Virginia's Eastern Shore: A History of
    Northampton and Accomack Coun-
    ties* (Whitelaw), 8
Voting, 182, 201

Walker, Alice Traveller Burdett, 82,
    92, 101
Walker, Peter, 82, 101n, 202–203,
    209–210, 222n, 237
Walking, 42, 46
Waltham, Grace. *See* Vaughan, Grace
    Waltham
Waltham, John, 83, 84, 102
Waltham, John, Jr., 83, 84, 85

War, Anglo-Dutch. *See* Anglo-Dutch
    war
Ward, Anne. *See* Smith, Anne Ward
Ward, Ann Stockdell, 91, 155
Ward, William, 91, 154
Ward, Mrs. William. *See* Ward, Ann
    Stockdell
Warder, Robert, 232, 233
Warehouses, tobacco. *See* Tobacco:
    warehouses for
Warwick (ship), 145
Waters, Edward, 72, 155–156
Waters, Grace. *See* Robins, Grace
    (O'Neill) Waters
Waters, Katherine, 157n
Waters, Margaret (daughter of Ed-
    ward and Grace Waters), 72, 156
Waters, Margaret Clark, 157
Waters, William, 37, 72, 73, 76, 85,
    155–159, 161
Waterways, 21, 37–38, 44–45, 46,
    193
Watson, Robert, 235
Webster, John, 86n, 99, 100n
Weed, Elizabeth. *See* Baily, Elizabeth
    Weed
Weed, Henry, 136
West, Ann. *See* Charlton, Ann West
West, Anthony, 71, 77
West, John, 51n, 71, 77
West, Kathryne. *See* Barlow, Kathryne
    (West)
West Indies, 144, 147, 162
White, Kathryne, 100
White, Lewis, 100
Whitehead, John, 75
Whitelaw, Ralph T., 8
Whittington, William, 44, 108–109,
    136, 216n
Widows, 79–83, 95
Wilkins, Ann. *See* Higby, Ann Wilkins
Wilkins, John, 55, 76, 111, 157, 187n,
    215n
Wilkins, Mary. *See* Baldwin, Mary
    (Wilkins)
Williams, Ann, 91